THE COMPLETE
BOOK OF THE
GUITAR

THIS IS A CARLTON BOOK

Text and Design copyright © 1998 Carlton Books Limited

This edition published by Carlton Books Limited in 1998

A CIP catalogue for this book is available from the British Library.

ISBN 1 85868 529X

Project Editor: Lucian Randall
Senior Art Editor: Zoë Maggs
Design: Alyson Kyles
Picture Research: Jane Lambert
Production: Sarah Schuman

1 2 3 4 5 6 7 8 9 10

Printed and bound in Dubai

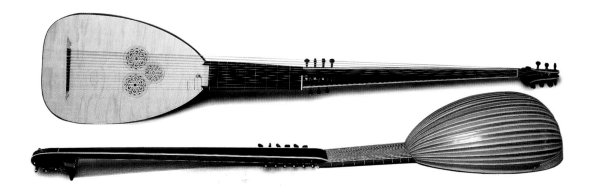

THE COMPLETE
BOOK OF THE
GUITAR

GENERAL EDITOR TERRY BURROWS

THE DEFINITIVE GUIDE TO THE WORLD'S
MOST POPULAR INSTRUMENT

CARLTON

CONTENTS

INTRODUCTION

although the guitar has existed in a recognizable form for the past 400 years, it is only during the past century that it has established its significance, both as a musical and cultural entity. Indeed, there can be little doubt that its impact on popular music makes it a serious candidate for THE instrument of the 20th century.

There are a good many reasons why the guitar has won over so many fans. One major factor is undoubtedly its durability. At one extreme, just as with any other musical instrument, the most demanding pieces may require years of study and practice before they can even be attempted. And yet it's fair to say that most complete novices would probably be capable of learning to play five or six simple chords within a few weeks – enough, in fact, to be able to accompany themselves on some of the most popular songs ever written.

This duality largely describes the dilemma that the status of the guitar has had to endure throughout its life. In the first few hundred years of its true existence the guitar was largely viewed as a poor relative of "nobler" court instruments, such as the more popular lute and vihuela. It was during this period that the instrument became rooted in the more populist folk tradition. So much so, in fact, that in spite of the efforts of the first generation of great guitar composer/virtuosi of the late 19th century – names such as

Carulli and Sor – the guitar never found itself afforded the same status as the established orchestral instruments.

Similarly, during the 20th century, even as the guitar gradually came to dominate popular music, it was only the drive and motivation of the self-taught maestro Andres Segovia – the instrument's greatest classical exponent – that brought the guitar respectability throughout the concert halls of the world. Nonetheless it seems strange to imagine that London's Royal College of Music – one of the most prestigious music schools in the world – did not create a faculty for the teaching of the instrument until as late as 1960.

In fact, the relatively recent acceptance of the guitar is still evident. Although Segovia's emergence helped to attract some of the finest composers of the 20th century – masters such as Rodrigo, Villa-Lobos and Castelnuevo-Tadesco – unlike comparable instruments, the vast majority of the classical guitar repertoire is contemporary.

It is in other areas that the guitar has undoubtedly made its mark as an instrument of the people, finding itself at the very heart of the most popular contemporary musical forms. This was a process that began to gather momentum early in the 20th century, as the guitar established a popular base with the the fledgling jazz, blues and country stars. However, it was the electrification of the guitar that truly revolutionised the modern world of

music. From the moment when the amplified guitar first found its way onto a recording into 1935 – allegedly when Eddie Durham let rip on Jimmie Lunceford's "Hitting The Bottle" – the die was cast. It was Durham who provided the inspiration for the first electric virtuoso, Charlie Christian. From that point onwards, the popularity of the electric guitar went unchecked. During the 1940s, T-Bone Walker provided a blueprint for the electric R&B sound of the following decade, influencing the likes of B.B. King and Muddy Waters. In turn, these blues giants provided the impetus for the first generation young rock players of the 1960s.

During this period, the guitar once again managed to elicit extreme attitudes, as the now respectable classical guitar fraternity looked sternly down its nose at the world of pop and rock: Segovia himself even expressed his own horror at the sounds and music of the electric guitar. So it came to pass that along with the birth of rock and roll and the cult of youth in the 1950s, the electric guitar became another of the many new inter-generational division markers.

Inevitably, things that once may have seemed revolutionary or shocking gradually integrate with the mainstream. Now, as we approach the millenium, the guitar, in all its varied forms, is accepted without question in every imaginable walk of musical life. Indeed, the guitar can now surely claim to be the most popular musical instrument in the world.

6

CONTRIBUTORS

TERRY BURROWS General Editor
AUTHOR OF CHAPTERS 3, 4, 5, 7 AND 8

One of Europe's top-selling guitar authors, Terry Burrows' tutorials *Play Rock Guitar* and *Play Country Guitar* (Dorling Kindersley) have been published in 11 different countries and translated into six languages. He has also just completed *Total Guitar Tutor* for Carlton and was responsible for the revision of Ralph Denyer's benchmark *The Guitar Handbook*.

He has also been published on subjects as diverse as popular culture, history, business and management, the Internet, cinema, computer software and psychology, including six volumes of Time-Life's *Mindpower* series. He has also written for a number of music magazines in Britain and Germany.

As a musician, for the past decade he has plied his own eclectic brand of music, having been responsible for over forty commercial releases in a bewildering variety of styles and guises. A recent publication on the British underground music scene described his alter ego, Yukio Yung, as a "lo-fi legend".

MIKE FLYNN
AUTHOR OF CHAPTERS 1 AND 2

A widely published freelance writer, editor and musican, Mike Flynn has a degree in music and has taught guitar at the Performing Arts Centre (PAS) in London. He is also a session guitarist and, most recently, acted as music consultant on a joint Oxford University Press/Dorling Kindersley illustrated encylopedia of music. A devoted fan of country music and an accomplished player, Mike's regular band perform many country classics including a mean version of 'Stand By Your Man'.

NICK KAÇAL
AUTHOR OF CHAPTER 6

After graduating in electro-acoustics from Salford University in 1990, Nick Kaçal embarked on a career as a jazz musician and freelance producer/engineer/arranger. He has since worked with many notable names on the European jazz scene.

In the world of publishing he has acted as musical and technical consultant on a number of well-known guitar tutors, including Dorling Kindersley's *Play Rock Guitar* and *Play Country Guitar* titles.

7

THE BIRTH AND EVOLUTION OF THE GUITAR

8

the origins of the world's most popular musical instrument are shrouded in mystery, a mystery made all the deeper by scholarly disagreement over what actually constitutes a guitar. Further confusion is added to this by the fact that, until relatively recently, the guitar and many of its predecessors were instruments on which folk music was played. As such, they were considered of little interest or consequence by those strata of polite society from whom we learned the lessons of history.

No one can be certain just when the guitar, or guitar-like instruments, arrived in Europe, although it is fairly safe to assume that the instrument did not originate there. That said, investigations of its origins are often muddied by the almost random way in which some historians have given the name "guitar" to almost any instrument from the Middle East or Far East which bears even a passing resemblance to this instrument. This was often done without any knowledge of how the instruments were constructed, tuned or played. While it is true that some of them possessed strings, a neck and frets, they may well have been played with a bow, or may even have been made solely for use as artefacts in religious or cultural ceremonies.

While we know for certain the history of the guitar in the period following the Renaissance, it has become a rather tired cliché to claim that the guitar is merely a development of the European lute. To do so ignores its rich history and its non-European origins.

THE LUTE AS DEPICTED IN ASIAN ART

THE KITHARA RESEMBLES THE GUITAR IN NAME ONLY

GUITAR-LIKE INSTRUMENTS CAN BE FOUND IN EGYPTIAN ART

ANCIENT ANCESTORS

Some people point to an ancient Greek instrument called the *kithara* as a possible ancestor of the guitar, although any similarity to the modern instrument appears to be in name only. It is also true that certain long-necked lutes found in what used to be Mesopotamia bear a passing resemblance to the guitar, as do a number of lutes found in Egypt from a slightly later period. These instruments possess flat backs and sides and in this respect resemble the modern guitar more so than the lute. That said, not all guitar-shaped instruments had flat backs. In order to narrow down the number that might be considered as precursors to the modern guitar, this chapter concentrates on those stringed and fretted instruments which, from the front, most resemble the modern guitar: those which are said to have a waisted look. (It was not until the twentieth century that the fashion for wasted guitarists began.)

The earliest recorded instrument with the classic pinched-waist look also dates from ancient Egypt. This instrument bore a closer resemblance to a long-necked lute, but it did possess a guitar-shaped resonating body. The shape did not persist in later designs, however, so it cannot really be counted as a true ancestor of the guitar.

The next earliest example of a guitar-shaped instrument was found in Central Asia. It dates from the earliest days of the Christian era and, although it was probably a form of lute, its shape resembles most closely that of the guitar. This design persisted in the region for around four hundred years but then disappeared, not to be seen again until the eleventh century. By then there were already a variety of guitar-shaped instruments in use in Europe, and a number of these had names suggesting they were among the first true ancestors of the guitar.

THE GITTERN

The gittern was a plucked instrument constructed with parallel sides, a flat back, a fretted neck and gut strings – a description that could almost describe the modern classical guitar. The back, sides and neck of the only known surviving example of the instrument are carved from a single piece of wood. Paintings and carvings from this period show, however, that there were several variations on the basic design. Early gitterns normally had at least two sound holes, rather like a violin, but these had been replaced by the thirteenth century with a single rounded hole decorated with a "rose", a piece of wood carved ornately to resemble a rose. The tuning pegs were placed at the end of the fretted neck on the peg box, which was usually carved ornately and set back at an angle to the neck. The gittern had three or four pairs of strings, called courses, which were attached at the base of the instrument – near the bridge – and again at the peg box. The space beneath the fretboard was hollowed out, making it easier for the musician to reach the strings. The earliest known example of the gittern appears in a carving which dates from the first century AD and it continued to be depicted for at least the next thousand years. There is an example in a carving (of a musical angel) in London's Westminster Abbey, which dates from around the year 1250.

A brief check of the accounts of court from this period can also be very enlightening as to the extent of the popularity of the gittern, which by now was known by a variety of similar names, such as *gitar*, *quitarra* and *guiterre*. A *gitarer* was employed to play at the Feast of Westminster in 1306. In France, the Duke of Normandy had a musician on his staff called Jean Hautemar, who played the *guitare latine*, an instrument which scholars have since identified as the gittern. The name was used deliberately to signify that the instrument's origins were European (Spanish, to be precise), rather than the *guitare morisca* – the name given to the guitar-like instruments believed to have originated in the Middle and Far East.

The original medieval gittern had slipped out of fashion in Northern Europe by the beginning of the fifteenth century – to be replaced by the lute – but the name persisted and was used to describe all manner of guitar-shaped instruments. The fact that the gittern was believed to have originated in Spain along-side the lute may partly explain the belief that the guitar was merely a development of it. In Southern Europe, the gittern continued to be popular and the instrument eventually evolved into the *viola da mano*, or *vihuela*.

Even the English king Henry VIII found time to play the gittern. In the inventory of his instruments, drawn up after his death, was found "Foure Gitterons with iiii cases to them:

they are caulled Spanish Vialles [vihuelas]." It is not beyond the bounds of possibility that 'Greensleeves', a top Tudor tune normally credited to the king, may actually have been composed on this instrument.

The gittern also warrants a mention in Chaucer's *The Canterbury Tales*. In *The Pardoner's Tale* there is mention of the instrument being played at something resembling a raucous pub gig:

> In Flandres whilom was a compaignye
> Of yonge folk that haunteden folye
> As riot, hasard, stywes, and tavernes
> Wher as with harpes, lutes and
> *gyternes* [gitterns]
> They daunce and pleyen at dees bothe day
> and nyght.

It is a tragedy that no living person has ever heard music that was composed originally for the gittern. None survives and we can only guess at what the instrument might have been

used for. Although it was possible to pick out melodies on the instrument, and occasionally strum a few chords, it was most likely used to provide a rhythmical drone to accompany dances. We are given just a hint of how the instrument might have sounded by a character in *Ralph Roister Doister*, a play from the early 1500s, who says: "Anon to our gitterne, thrumpledum, thrumpledum, thrumpledum thrum."

While it is true to say that the gittern was essentially a box and a neck carved from a single piece of wood, with another piece laid over the resulting hole to create a sound box, instruments of the lute family were beginning to show signs of the more sophisticated building techniques that were eventually to be applied to the classical guitar.

THE LUTE

As early as the tenth century, the body of the Arabic *al ud* (from which we get "lute") was being delicately fashioned from thin strips of wood, which were carefully steamed to bend them into a shape that even now we would recognize as the back of a lute. It was to be several hundred years, however, before European craftsmen mastered the techniques needed to perform this operation and began to apply them to the lute, using strips of maple or sycamore cut into shape. These were moulded to form the characteristic shell-like back. The strips were held together on the reverse of the shell by a similar strip of wood and attached at the front of the shell to a wooden block, to which the neck was joined. Until around the middle of the eighteenth century, the neck was simply held in place with a large nail.

The neck of the lute was rounded at the back to accommodate the player's hand and shaved until the optimum point between

KING HENRY VIII OWNED FOUR GITTERNS AND SEVERAL LUTES

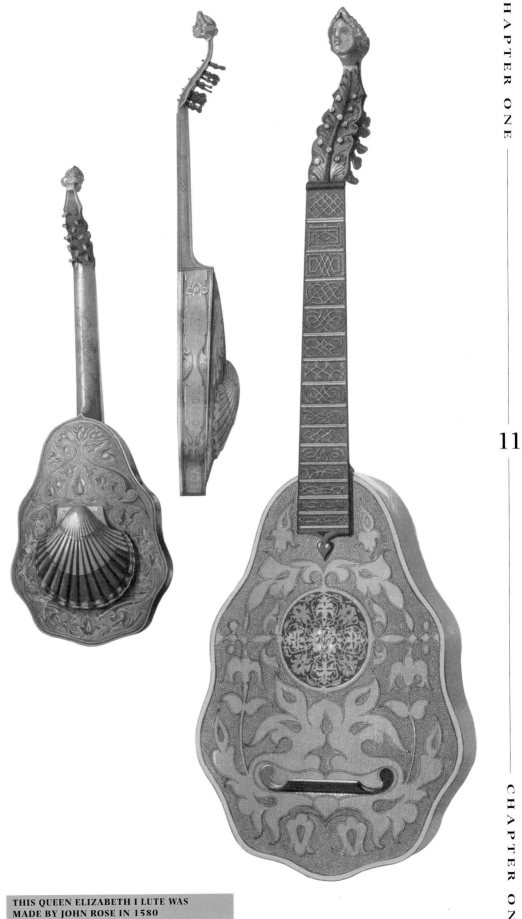

**THE DELICATE EARLY LUTES
SURVIVED ONLY IN PAINTINGS**

strength and playability was reached. A fret-board made from a separate piece of wood was then added. The peg box was set back from the neck at quite a sharp angle, and tuning pegs made of hard wood were inserted into holes drilled in the side of the box.

The soundboard, which fits over the front of the instrument, was usually made from a single flat piece of pine, into which was carved the rose-patterned sound hole. The soundboard was very thin – around 2 mm (0.08 in) – which is all the more remarkable considering the relatively crude tools with which these instruments were made. (Such was the delicacy that no lutes from before about 1500 have survived intact to the present day.) The bridge – to which the strings were attached – was glued to the surface of the soundboard. Tension from the strings tended to cause the thin wood of the soundboard to warp in the direction of the neck. This was combated by fitting the underside of the soundboard with supporting struts.

Fitting supporting struts to the underside of the soundboard had the double benefit of strengthening the lute and improving the quality of its sound. The struts effectively divide the soundboard into separate, smaller areas. This raises the natural resonant

**THIS QUEEN ELIZABETH I LUTE WAS
MADE BY JOHN ROSE IN 1580**

frequency of the instrument, causing the soundboard to produce more of the supporting harmonic frequencies of the fundamental notes played. In non-technical terms, this use of struts made the lute stronger and yet sweeter sounding. It also had the added benefit of introducing an "edge" to the sound, which enabled it to be heard above other larger and louder instruments when played as part of an ensemble.

THE VIHUELA

As lute-building techniques developed, the range of the instrument was increased by fitting it with extra pairs of strings, or "courses", as they were known. By the end of the fifteenth century, some were being built so that six courses could be fitted. But the lute was not the only instrument to benefit from these improvements. In fifteenth-century Spain, it had been passed in popularity by the *vihuela*.

The earliest accounts of the vihuela date from the thirteenth century and describe a Spanish instrument that was smaller than a lute and fitted with a flat back. But things had changed somewhat by the fifteenth century, when the vihuela would be instantly recognizable to any guitarist, who might be forgiven for thinking that it was simply an old guitar. In shape and structure it resembled the guitar in many ways. A glance at even the oldest surviving examples reveal a distinctive guitar-like body (much larger than the

AN EARLY FIVE-COURSE VIHUELA

lute's) and a long, guitar-like neck. The body is not as deep as that of the modern guitar and the narrower waist, a common feature of the guitar family, is only slightly pinched in. The vihuela's long neck extends far beyond the body to the peg box, which was set back from the fretboard at a much flatter angle than that of the lute.

The fretboard was fitted with 10 frets, which at this stage were made of gut. They could be moved around to suit the mode or key in which a piece of music was being played. The instrument was fitted with six pairs (or courses) of strings, with each pair tuned in unison. These were attached to a fixed bridge and heard via the guitar-like sound hole.

THE FOUR-COURSE GUITAR

The vihuela achieved its peak of popularity in the middle of the sixteenth century, when it was considered to be the instrument of choice among the musical élite. However, its days were numbered. By the end of the century, it had been all but replaced by the guitar. This did not please everybody, as can be seen from the work of one Sebastian Orosco, who wrote shortly after the turn of the century:

"...since the invention of the guitar there are very few who study the vihuela. This is a great loss because...the guitar is nothing but a cow-bell, so easy to play, especially when strummed, that there is not a stable-boy who is not a musician of the guitar."

And so it was that during this period the very first guitars – in name and design – appeared. There can be no doubt that the design of the early guitar was based heavily on

ROVING MINSTRELS WERE A COMMON SIGHT IN EUROPE

that of the lute and the vihuela, and although some have argued that these first guitars were merely simplified versions of these instruments, it is clear that a new instrument was beginning to emerge.

It was known as the four-course guitar, so called because it was fitted with four pairs of strings. It had a waisted front, flat back and sides, and a fretted neck. The first mention of its "invention" appeared in a work by Johannes Tinctoris in which he claims, in 1487, that it was "invented by the Catalans", the inhabitants of a region that is now in north-east Spain. This appears to indicate that this instrument – which many argue was the first true guitar – originated in Europe, but one cannot ignore the influence of the lute and vihuela, which provided the inspiration that led to the design in the first place.

The typical sixteenth-century four-course

guitar resembled the modern classical guitar in many respects, although anyone acquainted with today's instrument would be struck immediately by the small size of its ancestor. There were also other, more subtle differences. In common with lutes of this period, the four-course, and later five-course, guitar was fitted with a rose over the sound hole. The frets were made of gut, which would be tied around the neck. The number of frets the guitar possessed would vary depending on the type of music played. Simple strumming required no more than a handful of frets, whereas more complex music called for a greater number.

The four-course guitar was tuned in such a way that the intervals between the courses were laid out as a perfect fourth, a major third and another perfect fourth. This arrangement corresponds to the top four strings of the modern classical guitar, although during this period the guitar was tuned a tone lower, to C-F-A-D rather than D-G-B-E.

The five-course guitar appeared in the sixteenth century, and was essentially the same instrument with an extra course. Although this usually meant adding strings in the bass register, there were a number of guitars constructed with additional strings in the treble register, above what is now the top E string on the modern instrument. Like the four-course guitar, the five-course version was small by today's standards (about 80 cm in length – 31.5 in) and had the variable fret arrangement. It seems that it originated in Spain and was probably produced to satisfy the demands of slightly more ambitious pieces composed for the guitar at this time.

One of the most noticeable and striking features of the guitars made after 1600 is the incredibly ornate manner in which they tended to be decorated. Although the guitar was still overshadowed by the lute, which continued to be the most popular plucked instrument throughout the Baroque period

13

(*circa* 1600–1750), the sheer effort and care involved in creating the beautiful designs with which guitars of this period were decorated suggests a great love for the instrument among those who possessed them. These designs were achieved by staining the woods that were used in the guitar's construction. Sometimes the maker might dispense with wood altogether and create extraordinarily intricate inlaid designs from tortoise-shell or ivory. Among the most outstanding examples of guitar makers' art of this period are those by the Voboam family, based in France, Joachim Tielke in Germany and the Sellas brothers in Italy. Then as now, some makers went way beyond the bounds of good taste in their choice of adornments for the instruments, in contrast to the subtle beauty of guitars created by Antonio Stradivari, better known for his work as a violin maker.

By this time the techniques that one would normally associate with playing the classical guitar were beginning to appear. Up to this stage, the guitar had been played with

techniques developed for the lute and the vihuela. This usually involved the little finger of the right hand resting on either the bridge or the soundboard of the guitar, while the player plucked at the strings using a pinching motion with the thumb and the first two fingers of the right hand. As the instrument grew in size, the right arm rested on the top of the guitar body and the right hand floated free over the strings. This meant that the player could achieve different qualities of sound by plucking the strings at different locations. If the strings were plucked near to the bridge, the guitar produced a bright, almost metallic sound; if played over the sound hole, it was much warmer and softer.

Most of the music played on the guitar at this time was, however, still strummed, so the guitar was still not considered a fit instrument for a serious soloist. This did not in any way affect its popularity. The fact that the guitar could be "mastered" in a relatively short period of time made it all the more appealing to people who wished to create music without the

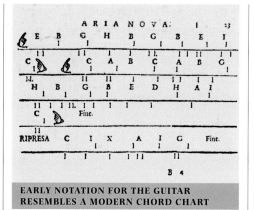

EARLY NOTATION FOR THE GUITAR RESEMBLES A MODERN CHORD CHART

bother of having first to undergo a long period of training. This perhaps explains why it was so popular in royal circles, where the affairs of state and otherwise left a busy monarch with little time for the complexities of the lute.

Francesco Corbetta was one of the first guitarist to achieve an international reputation, which he used to gain a position as guitar teacher to King Louis XIV of France. His first book of music, *La Guitare Royalle* (1674), was dedicated to the king and was filled with simple pieces that could, for the most part, be easily strummed by monarchs with short attention

spans. Corbetta very sensibly failed to mention to the king that he had already dedicated the book to King Charles II of England three years earlier. Charles was an enthusiastic player whose lack of any real talent was more than made up for by his royal status, which contributed to the guitar becoming extremely fashionable in England at this time – even though diarist Samuel Pepys loathed and despised the sound of the thing.

Several tutor books began to appear during this period, testifying to the fact that the instrument was becoming established in its own right and was not merely some freakish variant of the lute family. One of the first known tutor books for the guitar had been written by the Frenchman Adrian Le Roy in around 1550, and translated into English by James Rowbotham. Corbetta himself is believed to be the author of a book called *Easie Lessons On The Guittar For Young Practioners* (a sort of seventeenth-century *Play In A Day*), which appeared in 1677. Other tutor books published around this time include *The False Consonances Of Musik* by Nicola Matteis and *Instrucción* by Gaspar Sanz.

As the general level of musicianship rose among guitar players, so too did the quality of the repertoire for the guitar, until it eventually came to rival the lute in terms of the complexity and beauty of the compositions written for it. And so it was that, with the nineteenth century peeking out over the distant horizon, guitarists could begin to look forward to the first golden age of the classical guitar. Improvements in the design and construction of the instrument were to have a profound effect on the way the guitar was perceived by composers, performers and the world at large. From its humble origins as an instrument of peasants, the guitar was to grow until it would eventually dominate the world's stages. Truly, a star was about to be born.

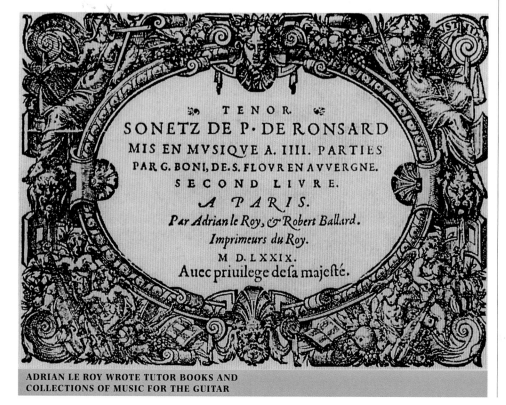

ADRIAN LE ROY WROTE TUTOR BOOKS AND COLLECTIONS OF MUSIC FOR THE GUITAR

14

Early Music for the Guitar

Early guitar music was nearly always written down as tablature, although in a variety of different styles dependent largely on the country in which the music was produced. Tablature, still used today by some guitarists, is a method of notating music by means of numbers (representing frets) and horizontal lines (representing guitar strings). Because the earliest guitars had only four courses, with each pair of strings tuned in unison, early guitar tablature displayed only four horizontal lines, which can be thought of as corresponding to the modern five-line stave or staff.

The Spanish placed any notes that were to be played on the top (highest-sounding) string on the lowest line of the stave, reasoning that, in physical terms, the highest-sounding string was the one nearest the ground. The French and the Italians, however, placed the highest-sounding string at the top of the stave on the grounds that the top notes should go on the top line. Anyone fearing that the French and the Italians might have been forming some sort of unholy musical alliance against the Spanish will be heartened to hear that while the Italians and the Spanish used numbers to indicate which frets were to be fingered, the French used a visually appealing but slightly confusing system of letters: the letter A indicated that the string was to be played open (unfingered), while the letter B indicated that the note at the first fret was to be fingered, and so on. The rhythm to be played was indicated above the stave but

applied only to the fastest-moving parts. It was left to the discretion and good taste of the individual musician to decide just how long the other notes should be held.

The first printed music for the four-course guitar appeared in 1546. It was a collection of six pieces written by Alonso Mudarra and titled *Tres Libros*. Three years later four short dances, arranged for guitar, were included in a collection of pieces for the lute written by Melchiore de Barberis. To include pieces for the guitar in collections of other works for fretted string instruments was a fairly common practice at the time, as seen in the inclusion of nine compositions for guitar in a collection of pieces for the vihuela by Miguel de Fuenllana, called *Orphénca Lyra* and published in 1554. The fact that these pieces were included almost as an afterthought is indicative of the degree of interest in the guitar in the countries where these works were produced (Spain and Italy). Over in France, however, it was an entirely different story.

The guitar exceeded the lute in popularity in sixteenth-century France and so guitar music was deemed worthy of publication in its own right. Between 1551 and 1555, nine books of tablature for the instrument were pub-

lished in Paris alone. These included four books by Adrian Le Roy.

On the whole, the guitar music published at this time did not make too many demands on the player – after all, the instrument really had only four strings. The lack of strings limited the amount of harmonic variation that was available to the composer and, as a result of this, chords tended to be implied by the music rather than stated. Only rarely did guitar music published during this period approach that composed for the lute or the vihuela. Generally it seems that the guitar was a popular instrument because it was perceived as being easy to play and could be mastered in a short space of time. This meant that there was an enormous demand among players for the kind of dull, simplistic material that so often clogs up compilations of guitar music of this era.

At an even simpler level were those books of guitar music that were created for the strummers. These provided easy-to-play chord sequences for those whom talent had neglected. This style of playing was named *rasguedo* (meaning chordal strumming) while the more demanding finger-picking style was called *punteado*. Surprisingly, at this time the *rasguedo* style tended to be favoured by players of the five-course guitar, while the *punteado* style was the preserve of the four-course guitarist.

15

THE TORRES REVOLUTION AND THE
CLASSICAL GUITAR

16

the eighteenth century reached its end with America electing its first president, Britain in the throes of the world's first industrial revolution and Napoleon Bonaparte seizing power in France. But of far greater importance was the fact that, while all this was going on, the five-course guitar had evolved into the six-string guitar.

THE SIX-STRING GUITAR

History is remarkably vague on the details at this point – it's almost as if it happened while no one was looking – so investigations into the origins of the modern classical guitar are temporarily reduced to the level of hearsay, conjecture and supposition. We know that the six-string guitar appeared first in France or Italy, although the Germans may have some claim to having added the sixth string in the bass – our modern E string. There had been guitars built before with six courses, and others built with five single strings, but none of these was tuned like the modern instrument and so cannot truly be considered the first "real" six-string classical guitar.

Over the next 30 or 40 years, the guitar ceased to have much in common with the lute, and instead began to take on the form that we now recognize as the modern guitar. The changes that this transition required – to the way the instrument was constructed – were many and varied. Starting at the head, the peg box as we know it was dispensed with, and usually replaced by an ornately carved design which served the double purpose of making the guitar even more beautiful, and allowing

the maker to leave his distinctive mark upon the instrument. This also led to a degree of restraint in other areas of decoration, and the guitar gradually became less garish until the simple beauty of the wood, and the art of the maker, were allowed to shine through.

The wooden pegs that had been used to tune the instrument were replaced with machine heads, a simple metal screw-type worm and gear mechanism that is still in use to this day. A separate fingerboard was added

**A DAZZLING ARRAY OF INSTRUMENTS
IN A MASTER CRAFTSMAN'S WORKSHOP**

THE GUITAR CAN EVOKE A VARIETY OF SUBTLE MOODS

The new guitar design led to changes in the way the instrument was played. Guitar tutor books from this time reveal that the practice of resting the little finger of the right hand on the soundboard (a remnant of the lute players' technique that had been handed down to guitarists) was largely abandoned. It was replaced with the "floating arm" technique, which allowed the guitarist's right arm to pivot from the elbow, but the strings were still plucked using only the thumb, index and middle finger of the right hand. It was not until later – in the nineteenth century – that the practice of using the ring finger along with the other fingers was introduced. (It was not until the '80s that plucking the strings with the little finger of the right hand

and though this initially lay flush with the soundboard, it was later raised so as to allow the inclusion of extra frets. The fretboard itself was no longer fitted with adjustable gut frets. Guitars from the very early eighteenth century were fitted with frets made of hard woods such as ebony – or even hard bits of elephant, such as ivory. These were both later replaced with much more hard-wearing frets made of metal. The relationship between the neck and the body of the guitar changed, allowing the neck to be fixed to the body at the twelfth fret. The soundboard, on the surface at least, changed little, but the rose design over the sound hole was swept away and the hole left open. It became standard for guitars to be built with flat backs, taking the instrument even further away from the lute both in terms of its design and the way in which it was constructed. The raised fretboard meant that the strings had to be raised also. To this end, the bridge was

made higher and a proper bridge saddle was introduced.

Striking as these changes were, they were nothing compared to the mysteries unfolding under the surface of the instrument, for it was at this stage that the guitar makers began their truly ground-breaking work.

Fan struts, literally struts fixed under the soundboard and arranged in a fan-like pattern, were first used on six-course guitars built by José Pagés and Josef Benedid in the late eighteenth century. These builders, based in Cádiz, introduced fan struts to the lower half of the soundboard (below the sound hole), and added cross struts that ran perpendicular to the neck on either side of the sound hole. This greatly improved the quality of the sound and was taken up by other makers during this period, the most notable of whom were René François Lacôte, who was based in Paris, and Louis Panormo, who was based in London.

THIS GUITAR, BY JOSÉ PAGÉS, DATES FROM 1809

became a common sight – although not among classical guitar players, whose technique was by then frozen in time and dictated by the music colleges.)

The strings were usually struck using the *tirando* technique, whereby the fingers of the right hand return to a raised position above the strings after they have been plucked. The *apoyando* stroke, bringing the fingers to rest on the string next to the one just plucked (rather as a modern electric bass player might strike a string) was known but seldom applied at this time. Some players, such as Dionysio Aguado, plucked at the strings with their fingernails, whereas others, including the great Fernando Sor, used the tips of their fingers.

Even the great players of this period were known to use the thumb of the left hand to fret notes on the bottom E string. This was made possible by the fact that the neck of the classical guitar was getting thinner all the time. Nowadays, fingering classical guitar music with the thumb of the left hand is an offence punishable by two weeks in banjo class, but at this time playing techniques had yet to be formalized.

There were also many variations in the positions guitarists adopted while playing their instruments. Some played standing up, wearing the guitar on a strap around their necks. Dionysio Aguado even had a special stand made called a triodion, on which he would balance his instrument.

THE GOLDEN AGE

This was the first golden age of the guitar. Here was an exciting new instrument that had the potential for enormous popular appeal. It enabled you to play music that could challenge the world's greatest virtuosi and yet at the same time the most cloth-eared sections of society could experience the joy and pride of being able to provide a simple, strummed accompaniment to a popular song.

As the reputations of the great players of this period spread, so too did the popularity of the instrument. For several years, Fernando Sor pursued a career as a touring soloist, thrilling audiences with the brilliance of his playing and no doubt inspiring many others to take up the instrument. Among those who took their inspiration from Sor was the great violinist Niccolo Paganini, who briefly abandoned the violin in favour of the guitar before finally returning to his original choice.

Even England was not immune to the charms of this new instrument. After Sor's visit in 1815, the popularity of the instrument rose enormously, as was evident from the outpouring of tutor books that accompanied his departure from England. As is often the case when a new instrument appears, the quality and scope of the tutor books varied wildly. Players willing to spend a little more time learning the guitar found that they could take

Fernando Sor

It is somehow fitting that Fernando Sor was born on St Valentine's Day, for here was a man whose life story and career appeared to have been conceived as part of a romantic novel. He was an unusual man; he combined the qualities of supreme musician with the fighting spirit (and experience) of a warrior and the diplomatic, some might say pragmatic, nature of a career civil servant.

The Spanish composer and guitarist attended the choir school of the Monastery of Monserrat, where he received a solid musical education before going on to learn the art of war at Barcelona's famous military academy. His first major musical work – an opera called *Telemaco en la Isla de Calipso* – was performed in 1797, while Sor was still a teenager. After moving to Madrid in 1799, he went on to compose symphonies, string quartets and his first pieces for guitar, although at this stage in his career these were mostly popular songs with guitar accompaniment. Sor might well have carried on mining this rich musical seam were it not for the invasion of Spain by the French in 1808.

Like many a young man raised at the Barcelona Military Academy, Sor set off to fight the French, even taking time out from the daily battles to compose a few popular patriotic songs. But stirring as the songs may have been, they did not help to win the day for Spain and so Sor, like many young men of his background and education, went to work for the French in an administrative role – a position viewed by some of his countrymen as collaboration. Such was the ill-feeling directed at Sor and men of his ilk that the guitarist was forced to flee to Paris when the French retreated from Spain in 1813.

Sor's stay in Paris was relatively brief and by 1815 he was resident in London, where he began to produce serious compositions for solo classical guitar. In 1826 he returned to Paris, where he very quickly established the reputation of being the world's finest guitarist.

In 1830 he produced what was to be his most influential work for the guitar, his famous *Méthode Pour la Guitare*. Although Sor's reputation among his contemporaries was earned for the quality of his guitar-playing, it is this work, which has been called "easily the most remarkable book on guitar technique ever written", plus over 60 compositions for the instrument, on which his current reputation rests. Sor plucked his last breath from the air in Paris on July 10, 1839.

Dionysio Aguado

Dionysio Aguado may have been a superb guitarist, but he was not an ambitious man. A fellow countryman and contemporary of Fernando Sor's (see previous page), in 1803 he chose to take refuge in the small village of Fuenlabrada after the French invaded Spain. He lived there with his mother, perfecting his technique, giving the odd guitar lesson and even publishing a set of compositions for the guitar entitled *Colección de Estudios Para La Guitarra*. He seemed quite happy with this simple existence and no doubt would have stayed there for many years longer had his mother not died in 1824. By now, the French invasion was all but forgotten and so Aguado came down from the hills and headed for the bright(ish) lights of nineteenth-century Paris.

It was perhaps fortunate for Aguado that 1825 was the year that Sor was away on tour in Russia. In his absence, Aguado quickly acquired a reputation as one of the finest guitarists and teachers in the whole of Paris. When Sor returned in 1826, he befriended the young pretender and the two of them would regularly be seen performing together at a number of venues in the city. Sor even dedicated a duet, *Les Deux Amis*, to Aguado, although the two would often argue about the merits of fingernails over fingers as the best way to pluck strings. It seems Sor was prepared to forgive Aguado's use of the fingernails on account of his remarkable technique and the sheer majesty of his musicianship.

Aguado published his *Méthode Complète Pour la Guitare* some time around 1830. This was without doubt the most popular guitar tutor book of the nineteenth century, and was reprinted many times. After Sor's death in 1839, Aguado moved to Madrid, where he spent the last 10 years of his life revising his technique and doing a little teaching. He died on December 29, 1849.

Carcassi

Of all the nineteenth-century guitarists, Matteo Carcassi was second only to Fernando Sor (see opposite) in his influence on the music and technique of the twentieth-century guitar. Born in Florence in 1792, he began as a pianist but soon changed to the guitar, achieving a mastery that made him a concert performer at 18. He first found success in Germany before moving to Paris, where he took over from the ageing Ferdinando Carulli (see page 20) to become the city's most important guitarist for a while.

In the 1820s Carcassi played all over Europe. His technique enabled him to produce a greater variety of sounds than many other Italians guitarists of the day, even though he did not use his fingernails to play. His own compositions owed more to French than Italian or Spanish traditions and are marked out by their melodic content and interesting use of harmony.

Carcassi stopped performing in 1840, devoting the rest of his life to composition and tuition. When he died, in 1853, he left behind almost 100 guitar works, and is best remembered for *Studies (Opus 60)* and *Method (Opus 59)*.

19

on the simple, cliché-ridden pieces that were all but spewing forth from the hands and minds of journeymen composers – the equivalent of today's "hack" songwriters. Not that guitar composition was restricted to men alone. In England the leading guitar composer and performer by the end of the century was one Catharina Josepha Pelzer, who had a reputation for churning out the kind of music that allowed the guitar to be used in what Grove's Dictionary Of Music calls "a facile way".

It was left to the great guitarists of the day to produce the serious tutor books. Fernando Sor's book of studies still sends shivers down the spine of any player who has been compelled to learn it from cover to cover. Contained within its pages are a series of pieces, each progressively more difficult than the last, and each devoted to an aspect of the techniques required to play like one of the greats. Nor was Sor alone in producing such a work. Today it is still possible to walk into a quality music shop and leave with a copy of Matteo Carcassi's tutor book, which contains some excellent technique-building exercises as well as any number of pieces with which one can demonstrate the newly acquired techniques.

HEITOR VILLA-LOBOS, ONE OF THE GIANTS OF TWENTIETH-CENTURY GUITAR

Ferdinando Carulli

Originally a student of the cello, Carulli must have rued the day he abandoned the instrument in favour of the guitar. In any other period in history he would have been hailed as an innovator and a virtuoso. Alas, Carulli had the misfortune to be born as a contemporary of the great Fernando Sor (see page 18).

Carulli first saw the light of day in Naples, Italy, in February 1770. After abandoning his cello studies, he taught himself to play the guitar. His early compositions displayed much of the conventions of notation associated with the cello and this was not to change until he moved to Paris in 1808 where, for a time, he rivalled Matteo Carcassi for the rep-

utation as the city's leading guitarist. Like Clapton and Page in '60s London, these two men slugged it out regularly to establish supremacy, with Carulli little realizing that Fernando Sor was about to take the scene by storm and make the battle an irrelevance, as Hendrix's appearance would do to Clapton and Page over a hundred years later.

Carulli is now remembered mostly for his tutor book, *Méthode Complète de Guitare ou Lyre*, and a couple of concertos (*Opus 140* and *Opus 207*), although he did compose over 300 sonatas, studies, variations and duets for the guitar before his death in Paris on February 17, 1841.

Likewise, it was left to the great players to produce the truly challenging music for the guitar. Guitar greats Fernando Sor and Mauro Giuliani were responsible for establishing much of the guitar repertoire in the nineteenth century, and their music is still played today (*see* pages 18 and 21). Although their works do not stand up well in comparison with the works of the truly great composers, of this or any other period, they have much to recommend them – and Beethoven, a contemporary of both Sor and Giuliani, though never much of a guitarist, was reputed to have stolen the theme for the *Moonlight Sonata* from Sor.

Ultimately, however, composition for the guitar in this period often suffered because of the limitations imposed upon it by the instrument itself, and the imaginations of the composers. One has to wait until the twentieth century, and the work of the great Latin-American composers such as Villa-Lobos, for the guitar's true potential to be realized – and this was helped in no small part by improvements in the design and construction of the classical guitar that occurred in Spain in the latter half of the nineteenth century.

THE FATHER OF MODERN GUITARS

The name of Antonio de Torres Jurado is well known to any serious student of the classical guitar. More than any other maker before or since, he modernized the instrument, vastly improving its tone and at the same time increasing the sheer amount of sound that could be produced on it. This enabled guitarists to be heard as part of larger ensembles and also to play in larger concert halls. The richness of tone inspired ever more composers to write for the instrument and thus helped to increase its repertoire.

Torres was responsible for increasing the overall size of the guitar, and determined that the scale length – the distance from the nut, at the top of the neck, to the bridge, near the back of the soundboard – should be 65 cm (25.6 in). He took the fan-struts idea of Pagés and Benedid and improved on it, placing seven struts, laid out in the shape of a fan, behind the sound hole – to distribute the vibrations from the bridge better – and a further two struts at a tangent to the fan. Torres also introduced a bridge saddle to which the strings were tied after passing over the bridge, an arrange-

ment that is still the norm for guitars built today.

As the lute makers of old had discovered, by using struts it was possible to "break up" the surface area of the soundboard. This had the double benefit of introducing extra rigidity to the thinnest part of the guitar (allowing the delicate soundboard to be made even thinner) while also raising the resonant frequency of the instrument. This meant that far more of the supporting harmonics of the fundamental note were produced when the strings were plucked, producing a noticeably richer tone on the instrument. The increase in size of the guitar also made it a lot louder. Put simply, the extra space inside the body increased the amount of air being shifted as the soundboard vibrated, causing a louder sound to be emitted.

Antonio de Torres

No other individual has contributed more to the design of the modern classical guitar than Antonio de Torres Jurado. Born in 1817, at La Canada, near Almería, southern Spain, he was apprenticed as a carpenter at the age of 12. In 1833, he managed to avoid military service with the combination of a mysterious stomach complaint (which never troubled him again) and a hasty marriage to a 13-year-old girl, who bore him the first of three daughters a year later.

Between 1836 and 1842, Torres learned to make guitars in Granada, becoming a guitar maker in the 1850s. In a shop in Seville, he produced a series of outstanding instruments – several were used by leading players. His status as the world's leading maker of guitars was assured with a bronze medal at the Seville Exhibition for one of his instruments. Despite this, he ran into financial difficulties and eventually abandoned guitar-making in 1870, although, after opening a china shop, he made some simple guitars for local players. Torres died, in deep debt, in 1892.

Mauro Giuliani

Mauro (Giuseppe Sergio Pantaleo) Giuliani, was born near Bari, in Italy, on July 27, 1781. He was not an especially exciting man, nor did he lead an unusually exciting life. He did, however, write several hundred pieces of music for the guitar and, perhaps more importantly, established a notation style for the instrument which persists to this day.

Giuliani concentrated on the six-string guitar from very early on in life. Like many young Italian musicians of his day, he was forced to head north in order to make a living playing his chosen instrument – then as now, the Italians were almost aggressively indifferent to any music that did not sound like opera. He settled in Vienna in 1806, and soon established a reputation as Europe's greatest living guitarist. April 1808 saw the première of his first guitar concerto with full orchestral accompaniment. The success of this made Giuliani the leading figure in the classical guitar movement in Vienna. He went on to establish a career for himself as a guitar teacher, performer and composer of over 200 works for the instrument.

Giuliani wrote in the treble clef, distinguishing the separate parts of the music (melody, bass and inner chord-voices) by means of clever use of the stems of the notes themselves. As his fame grew, so too did his reputation and in 1814 he was appointed to the court of the Empress Marie-Louise. This favourable position was not to last, however, and he returned to Italy, in considerable debt, in 1819. He eventually settled in Naples, patronized by the nobility at court, until his death on May 8, 1829.

Antonio de Torres was the father of the modern classical guitar. Many very fine instruments have been built since his death, but they all owe a debt to Torres' pioneering work. He was succeeded in Spain by a generation or two of very fine guitar makers: men such as Manuel and José Ramirez. The Ramirez company survives to this day, and continues to make some of the most sought-after instruments in the world.

MAKING THE TWENTIETH-CENTURY GUITAR

The renewed interest in the classical guitar in the twentieth century has seen the arrival of new, non-Spanish guitar makers on the scene. The quality of their work is such that it can now be said with some degree of certainty that the best classical guitars are no longer made in Spain. Chief among these new makers are Hermann Hauser in Germany, Robert Bouchet in France, David Rubio and Paul Fisher in England and father-and-son partnership John and William Gilbert in America.

These makers are able to take advantage of a range of woods that would have been undreamed of in Torres' day. A typical modern quality classical guitar maker might choose to use Brazilian or Indian rosewood for the back and sides of the instrument and Brazilian rosewood for the neck. The sides and the soundboard would be anchored to a piece of South American mahogany or cedar wood and the fingerboard would be made of ebony from Ceylon. The head might well be decorated with a veneer of South American snakewood and the all-important soundboard made from Alpine spruce, which is specially grown at high altitude.

Once all of this wood has been seasoned – a process which involves storing it under controlled conditions while it dries out and ceases to move around – the maker can begin construction of the instrument, a process which usually takes well over one hundred hours of intensive, hands-on work. The first stage in

this process involves creating the characteristic shape of the neck. Slots are cut into the sides of the base of the neck, at the point where the twelfth fret will be once the fretboard has been added. The sides of the instrument, which are around 2 mm (0.08 in) thick, will have been given their waisted shape by steam-bending them and clamping them to a mould. Once this process has been completed, one end of each side will be placed in one of the slots on the neck and the other end fixed to a solid block of a hard wood such as mahogany or cedar. This piece of wood, called the end block, provides a vital anchor point for the various components that go to make up the body of the guitar. The back of the instrument is then attached. It usually consists of two pieces of matched hardwood,

THE MODERN CLASSICAL GUITAR STILL RESEMBLES THOSE PRODUCED BY TORRES

21

**FLAMENCO MASTER PACO PENA COMBINES
TECHNICAL SKILL WITH PASSION**

which are cut into shape and joined down the middle. At one end the pieces connect to the end block and at the other they are fixed to what is known as the "toe" of the neck. A thin strip of wood called a cleat is then fixed along the join on the inside of the instrument. This runs for the entire length of the back of the body and serves to seal the join between the two pieces of wood that make up the back of the instrument. The back is then fixed to the sides by means of a strip of wood which has been "kerfed" (slit or scored) to make it more pliable and therefore easy to fit inside the contours of the instrument.

The soundboard, with its various struts already attached, is then fitted to the rest of the body of the guitar, once again being joined at the neck and to the end block, as well as to

the sides of the instrument. Then the fingerboard is fitted to the neck and body, the bridge is glued on to the soundboard and the ornate "purfling" around the perimeter of the body is fixed on. (The rosette around the sound hole is normally attached when the soundboard is being constructed.) At this point the instrument receives its finish – layers of varnish or French polishing of the wood.

An astonishing degree of variation in tonal colour and general sound characteristics such as volume and response can be achieved through the use of different woods

or by changing key elements of the instrument's construction. Virtually every component part of the guitar will have some bearing on the volume, tone and sustain of the finished instrument. The flamenco guitar, for instance, bears a superficial resemblance to the classical guitar, but is made using different woods, has a thinner sound-

**A MODERN FLAMENCO GUITAR BUILT
BY RAMIREZ IN MADRID**

board, a shallower body and is generally of a much lighter construction. This is for creating the particular tonal characteristics that one associates with the flamenco guitar – warmer tone, greater attack and a stronger but shorter sustain. The guitar maker's art is in achieving a balance between these properties in order to produce a fine instrument. Learning how to combine and control all of these elements constitutes a life's work, and so even those guitarists who can afford a instrument made by an established and respected guitar maker may have to wait quite some time before getting their hands on one.

In terms of outward appearance, the guitar has changed little in the last hundred years. However, beneath the surface of the soundboard all kinds of changes have been taking place. Torres' struts are still there, but they now run in parallel along the grain of the soundboard. By strengthening the internal bracing, it has been possible to cut down the amount of vibration occurring within the body of the instrument, allowing more of the guitar's sound to be heard as it is projected more efficiently than ever before.

MODERN PLAYING TECHNIQUES

The changes in the way the guitar has been constructed, and therefore the way it sounds and responds, has led to a number of changes in the way the instrument is played. These can roughly be dated as beginning around the time when Torres launched his guitars at the world, although the actual changes in technique can be credited, in the first instance, to Francisco Tárrega, one of the world's leading guitarists toward the end of the nineteenth century (see page 120). Tárrega, by means of the floating-arm technique mentioned earlier, established the *apoyando* stroke. This had the double benefit to the player of being louder than the conventional *tirando* stroke (which was used almost exclusively at this time) and also of helping to bring out more of the richer qualities of these new instruments. The Torres guitar was bigger than had been the norm up to this point and as such fitted more comfortably across the left thigh – before, guitarists would just as often sit with the instrument placed over the right thigh. It became standard practice to sit with the classical guitar over the left thigh and remains so.

Although Tárrega did not play the guitar using the finger nails of his right hand, several of his students did and so this technique was passed down to succeeding generations of guitarists. At this time, however, the right hand position had not been formalized and it was not until the twentieth century that Andrés Segovia (see page 118) established the practice of playing with a relaxed right hand and striking the strings with the left-hand side of the fingernails. Interestingly, a very small number of concert players favour the right-hand side of the finger nail and so adapt their techniques accordingly.

ANDRÉS SEGOVIA – GREATEST CLASSICAL GUITAR PLAYER OF THE CENTURY

FRENCH COMPOSER PIERRE BOULEZ IN HIS
HOME STUDIO IN PARIS

JULIAN BREAM, CONSIDERED THE NATURAL
SUCCESSOR TO SEGOVIA

TRANSCRIPTION AND COMPOSITION

In real terms, it is only in the last hundred years or so that the modern classical guitar, and the techniques required to achieve a level of virtuosity comparable with other concert instruments, such as the violin or piano, has been in existence. At the start of this period there was little music available to put the new instrument and its players through their paces, but this situation changed enormously in the twentieth century. Following on from a practice initiated by Francisco Tárrega, more and more players began making transcriptions of music written for instruments other than

the guitar. Initially these were of music originally written for the guitar's close relatives – the lute and the vihuela – but as confidence and technique grew, works originally written for the keyboard, violin, cello and flute began to be transcribed. The difficulties encountered in transcribing music written for an essentially alien instrument on to the guitar did much to stretch the playing abilities of all those who attempted such feats. It also made many more composers aware of the myriad possibilities presented by the instrument.

Until the twentieth century, much of the serious music written for the guitar had been composed by the leading guitarists of the day.

While some of it can be quite beautiful, one is almost left with a feeling that much of it was written more to educate than to enthral. Also, the music was very much at the mercy of the guitarist-composer's ego. After all, what better way to show off an astounding technique than to write a piece of music that requires endlessly displaying it? Interestingly enough, it was one of the greatest guitarists of the twentieth century, Andrés Segovia, who led the movement away from the guitarist-composers and in so doing raised the profile of the instrument to a level where it is now taken seriously as a concert instrument. (As recently as the '50s, world-renowned classic guitarist Julian

Heitor Villa-Lobos

Considered by many to have been Brazil's finest export, Heitor Villa-Lobos was a musician who was as much at home playing in bar room bands as he was composing some of the most enduring serious music to have emerged from Latin America. Villa-Lobos' father, himself a fine musician, decided that his son should have an early start to his musical career. To this end he converted a violin into a pint-sized cello for the boy and began to instruct him in how to play the instrument as soon as Heitor was old enough to understand which end to hold. As soon as he was able, the young Villa-Lobos took up the guitar seriously, achieving a mastery of the instrument that was considered extraordinary by all who heard him play.

At the age of 18, Villa-Lobos hit the road. For the next seven years he travelled around Brazil with his guitar, playing in small bands, improvising music based on themes he heard along the way and soaking up the Latin sounds of his native land. (He later told the rather fanciful story of how he had been captured by cannibals while trekking in the rainforest, but managed to avoid ending up on the menu by virtue of the sheer quality of his playing, which so impressed the would-be diners that they let him go.)

Moving back to the city, Villa-Lobos attempted to study music at the National Music Institute, but quickly discovered that he was simply not suited to such a staid environment. Despite this, he so deeply impressed a couple of his tutors that they continued to offer him guidance and help throughout his career. For the next few years, he survived by playing the cello in an assortment of cinema orchestras and playing the guitar in small cafés.

In 1923, Villa-Lobos moved to Paris, and over the next seven years found tremendous financial and critical success as a composer. On his return to Brazil in 1930, he began work on establishing methods for teaching music in Brazilian schools and colleges, methods that would see Brazilian folk music elevated to the same level as that handed down by European classical composers. His work in this area, in particular the way he safeguarded Brazil's popular music traditions, led to him being awarded the Brazilian Order of Merit, one of many awards, including the French Légion d'Honneur, that he received towards the end of his life.

Villa-Lobos died in Rio de Janeiro on November 17, 1959. After his death, a museum was established in his honour by his widow.

Bream (see page 98) was threatened with expulsion from music college for practising his guitar on the premises, where it was seen as little more than an accessory favoured by Teddy boys and the other "louts" who played skiffle music.)

In many ways, Segovia can be credited with kick-starting the second golden age of the classical guitar. His pioneering work, combined with the almost evangelical way in which he campaigned to raise the profile of the instrument, has been, and continues to be, an inspiration to players and composers alike. Several of the leading Spanish composers of the twentieth century wrote music especially for Segovia after he made approaches to them and made them aware of the tremendous potential of the instrument. Turina, Torroba and Rodrigo all produced works for Segovia and, in the case of Rodrigo, went on to write for other guitarists. Joaquín Rodrigo's *Concierto de Aranjuez* (see page 23) was written as a tribute to Spanish guitarist Regino Sainz de la Maza. Although this is the most famous piece of music written in the concerto form for guitar, it is by no means the only one to have been written this century. Many composers have used this form, in which the guitar acts as the featured solo instrument, playing around a theme that is repeated in various keys by the orchestra. Before the improvements in the output of the guitar – attributable to the design changes instigated by Torres – it would have been difficult to imagine how the guitar could have been heard in such a setting. But the

Spanish were by no means alone in their appreciation of the instrument.

Latin America, which has often featured the guitar in its native folk music, embraced the modern classical guitar with a passion that all but bordered on hysteria and the first half of the twentieth century saw the production of some of the finest music written for any instrument. Chief among these Latin-American composers was Brazilian guitarist and cellist Heitor Villa-Lobos (*see* previous page), who managed to capture the essence of European classical guitar music and wrap it in the passionate beauty of the music of his homeland. His *Douze Etudes* and *Cinq Etudes* combine the conventions of the classical tradition with the heady folk music traditions of Brazil to create a music that is at once alien and yet familiar. The Mexican composer Manuel Ponce (*see* overleaf) wrote many pieces for the instrument, including five sonatas, 24 preludes and a concerto, the *Concierto del Sur*, although he will probably be best remembered by guitarists for his challenging but beautiful *Sonatina Meridional*, which was adapted for the guitar by Andrés Segovia. Other South Americans who have written important music for the guitar include the Venezuelan composer Antonio Lauro and the Paraguayan composer Augustin Barrios. Also noteworthy, and still very popular with guitarists the world over, is the work of Cuban composer Leo Brouwer.

By the second half of the twentieth century Europe was beginning to catch up once more with the South Americans. Despite the fact that the classical guitar was not accepted as an instrument for serious study by the English music colleges until the '60s – and even then only really as little more than a six-string lute – there are some quite surprising names among the list of British composers who took up their guitars and played. Malcolm Arnold (who was to collaborate with Deep Purple on

JOHN WILLIAMS, WHO DID MUCH TO POPULARIZE THE CLASSICAL GUITAR, WITH COMPOSER ANDRE PREVIN

the first concerto for group and orchestra), Stephen Dodgson and André Previn have all expanded the available repertoire for the guitar with their concertos, and Benjamin Britten and William Walton both wrote solo pieces for the instrument. Meanwhile, the rest of Europe was also busy making work for idle hands, with compositions emerging from the pens of such major-league maestros as Francis Poulenc and Pierre Boulez.

As the century progressed, guitar music, in common with most serious music, began to acquire elements of other styles. Most prominent among these is flamenco, although some

26

Manuel Ponce

Manuel Ponce (pronounced "Pon-thay", by the way) was born in Zacatecas, in Mexico, on December 8, 1882. At a very early stage he showed enormous promise as a musician. He received piano lessons from his big sister from the age of six, before studying with the renowned Mexican pianist Cipriano Ávila from the age of 10. By then he had already composed his first significant piece of music, *La Marcha del Sarampión*.

In 1895 Ponce was made assistant organist at the local cathedral, becoming chief organist in 1897. He moved to Mexico City in 1900, where he taught, gave recitals, composed and even found time to write a regular column of music criticism for *El Observador (The Observer)*. 1904 saw Ponce on his way to Europe via the US, where he gave a few concerts before going on to study in Bologna and Berlin. in 1917, after spending a couple of years in Mexico and then working as a music critic in Cuba, he moved back to Mexico and married an opera singer called Clema Maurel.

Had Ponce stayed in Mexico, his life and work would have been of no interest to guitarists. Fortunately, however, he went to live in Paris in 1925, ostensibly to edit the *Gaceta Musical*. While he was there he sought out the French composer Paul Dukas, who introduced him to French impressionism and neo-classical counterpoint. His "consultations" with Dukas changed Ponce's approach to composition and led, indirectly, to him being invited to tour Uruguay with Andrés Segovia in 1942. It was during this tour that Segovia gave the debut performance of Ponce's *Concierto del Sur*, and it was Segovia who enabled Ponce to bring his music, via the guitar, to a much wider audience.

It is unfortunate for guitarists that Manuel Ponce died (of uremic poisoning) in Mexico City on April 24, 1948, for here was a composer who would surely have rivalled the great Villa-Lobos had he lived to write more music for the guitar.

27

jazz and avant-garde influences can be spotted in music written after 1950. The classical guitar continues to play a valid part in the world of serious music and now, more than ever, can be said to be established as a credible instrument, one which has earned its place on the world's concert platforms.

Improvements in our understanding of the science of acoustics, combined with a renewal of interest in classical guitar making and the vast repertoire available for the instrument, means that guitarists can be confident in the knowledge that the classical guitar is about to enter its third golden age.

THE ACOUSTIC TRADITION

28

all acoustic stringed instruments follow a similar principle to create and project sound. Each time the finger or plectrum touches the string the vibrations disturb the surrounding airwaves. However, this in itself cannot project sufficient volume or produce a pleasant tone. The strings are passed from the nut to the bridge, which is fixed to the top of the guitar body – the soundboard. The energy created by the vibrating string is passed from the nut or frets into the soundbox via the bridge saddle – this is the point at which each string comes into direct contact with the body. The soundbox acts as an acoustic chamber, vibrating in sympathy with the strings. This projects the sound, most of which emerges through the sound hole.

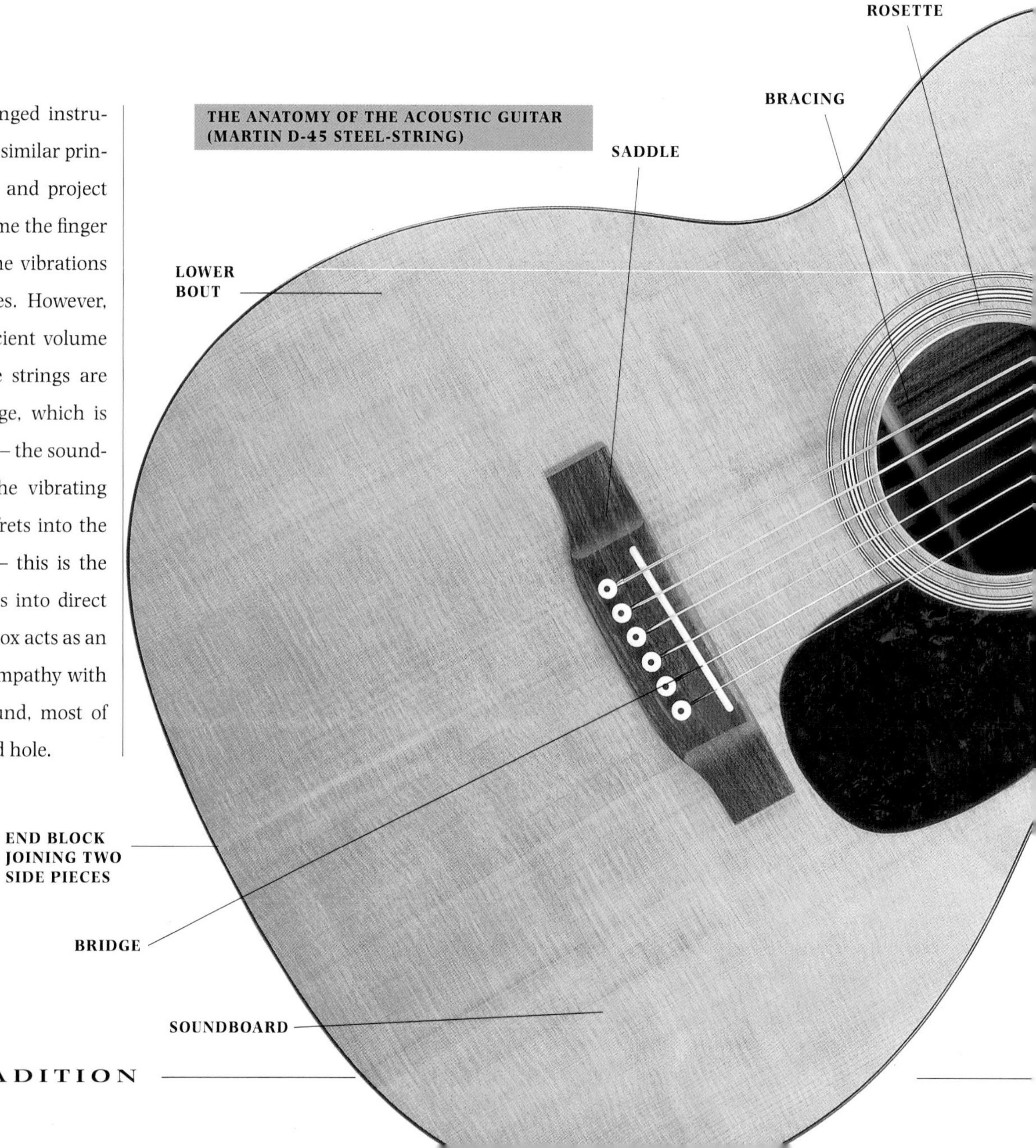

THE ANATOMY OF THE ACOUSTIC GUITAR (MARTIN D-45 STEEL-STRING)

ROSETTE

BRACING

SADDLE

LOWER BOUT

END BLOCK JOINING TWO SIDE PIECES

BRIDGE

SOUNDBOARD

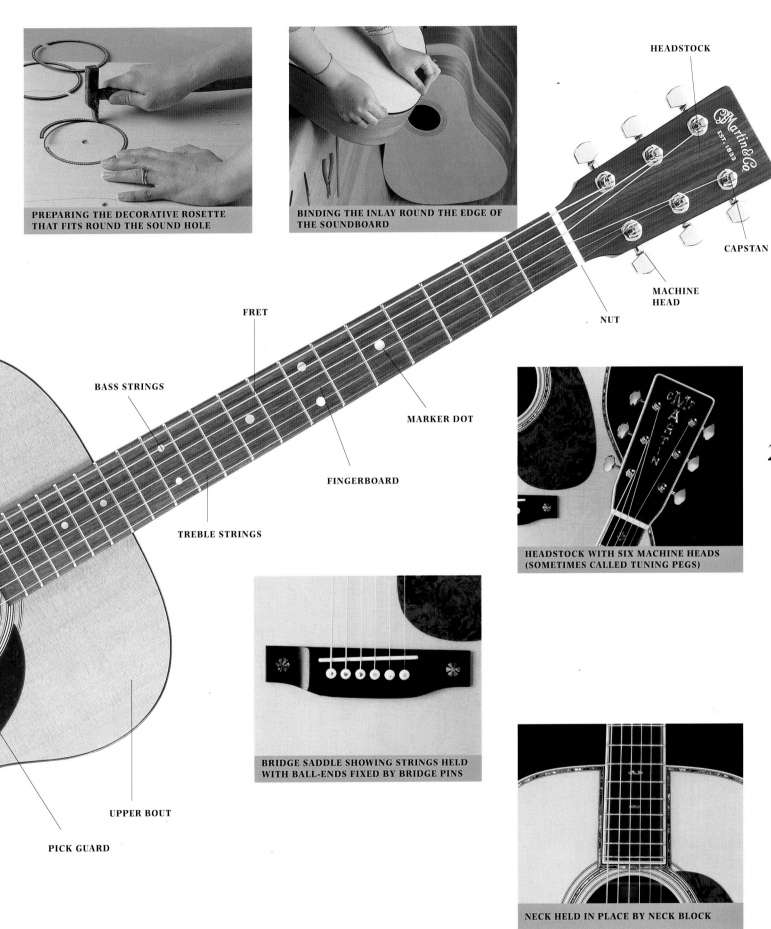

PREPARING THE DECORATIVE ROSETTE
THAT FITS ROUND THE SOUND HOLE

BINDING THE INLAY ROUND THE EDGE OF
THE SOUNDBOARD

HEADSTOCK

CAPSTAN

MACHINE
HEAD

NUT

FRET

BASS STRINGS

MARKER DOT

FINGERBOARD

TREBLE STRINGS

HEADSTOCK WITH SIX MACHINE HEADS
(SOMETIMES CALLED TUNING PEGS)

29

BRIDGE SADDLE SHOWING STRINGS HELD
WITH BALL-ENDS FIXED BY BRIDGE PINS

UPPER BOUT

PICK GUARD

NECK HELD IN PLACE BY NECK BLOCK

Bridge Design

As the point at which the strings come into contact with the soundboard, the bridge plays a vital part in transferring to the soundbox the energy that creates the amplified sound. The actual contact point is between the string and the bridge saddle: a small, narrow piece traditionally made from ivory which sits on the bridge unit. Nowadays, saddles are often made from plastic, although most makers agree that this considerably affects the tone of the instrument.

There are two distinct types of bridge unit used on acoustic guitars: flat-top instruments generally have fixed bridges, while archtops usually incorporate a floating bridge design (*see* picture).

The fixed bridge is glued firmly to the surface of the soundboard and cannot be moved back and forth – if the intonation of the guitar is poor, it can only be remedied by the removal and reapplication of the whole unit. Because of its high density, ebony is the most effective material for the fixed bridge,

as for the fingerboard, transferring the string vibration without "soaking" or dampening the sound, which would result from using softer woods. Walnut, rosewood and mahogany are also commonly used alternatives. Strings are secured to the bridge unit using bridge pins which slot vertically behind the saddle trapping the strings in place.

The floating bridge design makes use of a tailpiece which is secured with a screw or bolt to the bottom side of the guitar. This secures the strings in place at the ball-end. The bridge unit is not actually fixed to the soundboard but is clamped in place by the tension of the strings when they are tightened. As the bridge floats freely, it is possible to move the unit back and forth to alter the intonation.

Some floating bridge units (and, rather less commonly, some fixed bridges) also include a height adjustment screw, which allows the overall action of the strings to be raised or lowered.

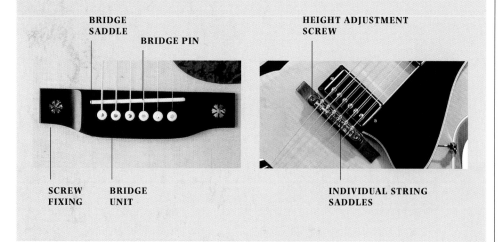

BRIDGE SADDLE
BRIDGE PIN
SCREW FIXING
BRIDGE UNIT

HEIGHT ADJUSTMENT SCREW
INDIVIDUAL STRING SADDLES

FACTORS AFFECTING SOUND

There are two main factors that govern the way a guitar sounds: the materials used and design of the instrument. These elements play a crucial role in both the volume projected and quality of tone. Nevertheless, there remains no definitive formula for the perfect guitar design. For one thing, not all players like the same kind of sound; equally, some acoustics are better suited to different styles of music.

A more complex factor is the nature of wood. No matter what practical steps a luthier takes to standardize production, no two pieces of wood – even if they have come from the same tree – have identical characteristics. Therefore no two guitars are exactly the same.

DESIGN FACTORS

Makers like Gibson (*see* page 38), Martin (*see* page 33) and National (*see* page 62) expended
great energy in the '20s producing instruments which could produce a higher volume. This they largely achieved by increasing the body shape and size. However, the tone of the instrument can be affected by numerous factors, not least the bracing used on the underside of the soundboard and on the back. Bracing fulfils two functions: it is a necessity for giving strength to the body, and for preventing the wood from distorting. However, by their very existence, the bracing struts exert an impact on soundwaves moving around within the body, which alters the tonal characteristics.

A number of different bracing systems have been used by different makers. Most classical designs use a fan-bracing system, the type that was pioneered in Spain at the start of the nineteenth century by the respected luthier Pagés .

The stronger cross-bracing system was developed by the manufacturer Martin in the '20s when the dominant use of steel strings forced guitar makers to produce instruments capable of withstanding greater degrees of stress.

MATERIALS

A variety of materials have been used in the construction of acoustic guitars through the ages, but manufacturers have generally settled on a fairly restricted range of woods.

The main consideration for a luthier is that whatever wood is used must have been allowed to "settle", which means that it has to lose most of its natural moisture. This can be achieved naturally using a process known as "seasoning", whereby the wood is stored and allowed to dry out over a long period of time – sometimes a number of years. The top-quality luthiers generally insist on using woods treated in this way. The increasingly common alternative, however, is to use kiln-dried timbers. In this process the wood is placed in enormous kilns which can dry it out within a matter of weeks. If timber was used straight from the tree, it would lose its shape as it dried out naturally – not ideal for a precision musical instrument.

Different types of wood have different properties capable of creating a wide variation in tonal characteristics. Therefore all acoustic instruments are built from a combination of different timbers. The soundboard of most reasonable quality instruments are crafted from European or Canadian spruce, but on expensive instruments the slightly thicker cedar is sometimes used. Cheap acoustic models are generally made from laminated timbers or plywood, which often results in lack of tonal definition. For the back and sides (the ribs), rosewood, maple or mahogany are most commonly used, although some makers have successfully introduced African walnut and sycamore. The struts and bracing are usually made from spruce.

A wider variety of material has been applied in the construction of the guitar neck. Brazilian mahogany is rated by many luthiers as the best, although as a protected wood it is increasingly difficult to obtain. A cheaper alternative is maple. Fingerboards are commonly carved from rosewood, although on the more expensive models ebony is prized as a more attractive, dense and hard-wearing wood.

A notable exception to acoustic manufacturers' preference for wood has been the Ovation company, the most significant makers of acoustic guitars to emerge since the war. Their guitars are revolutionary not only because of their bowl-shaped bodies, but because they are made from materials such as fibreglass, carbon fibre and plastics (*see* page 82).

SKILFUL FIXING OF THE NECK TO THE BODY IS CRUCIAL FOR STRENGTH AND TONE

MACHINE HEADS

On the earliest instruments, the string tension which defines the tuning of the guitar was controlled by friction pegs. One peg per string was fitted to the headstock. The string was wound around the peg until in tune and then the peg was pushed firmly into the headstock to hold it in place. Indeed, on early guitars the headstock was known as the "pegbox".

At the beginning of the nineteenth century guitar makers began using mechanical machine heads (or tuning heads, as they are sometimes known). These systems replaced the tuning peg with a capstan fitted to a gear wheel. The tuning head is linked to a "worm" gear which causes the capstan to rotate but stay firmly in position after adjustment.

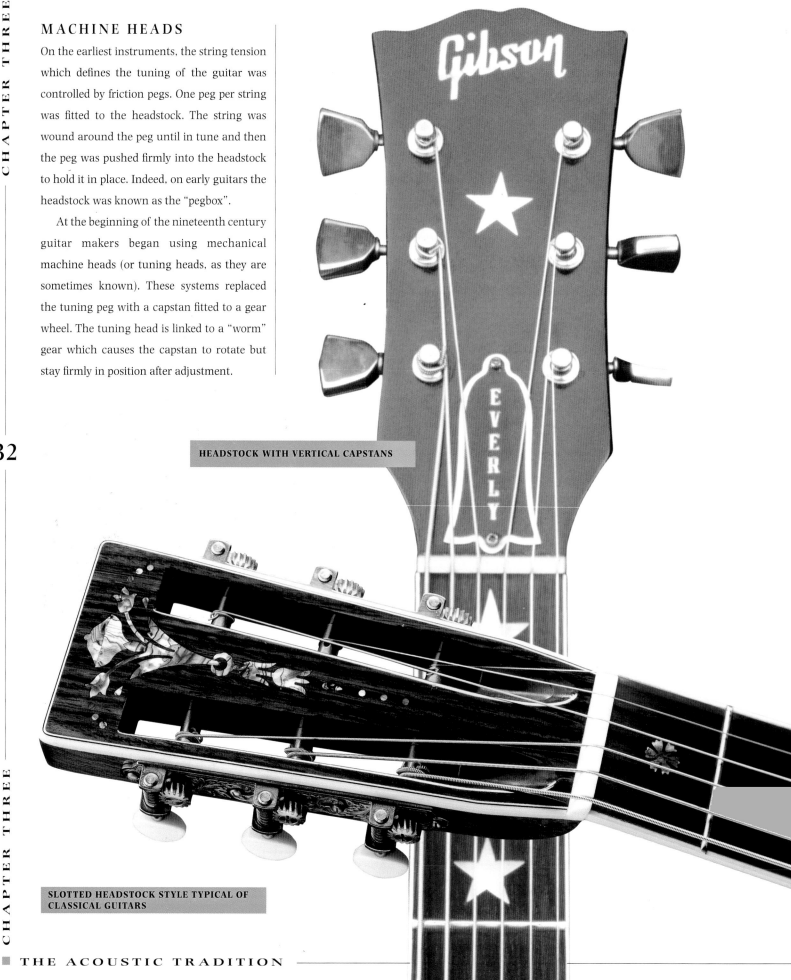

HEADSTOCK WITH VERTICAL CAPSTANS

SLOTTED HEADSTOCK STYLE TYPICAL OF CLASSICAL GUITARS

32

AMERICAN INNOVATIONS

The evolution of the modern classical guitar tradition can be traced back to European folk and other "low-brow" musical forms, all of which created a view among the upper classes that the guitar was a "common" instrument not worthy of serious attention. Although it now has broad parity with other traditional classical instruments, its greatest asset has been its enduring significance as an unashamedly populist instrument – indeed, the guitar has been at the very heart of much of the non-classical music of the twentieth century, from folk, country and western, and jazz to rock and pop. This line of popular heritage stems mainly from developments by European immigrants in the United States. For while a classical revolution was taking place in Spain during the nineteenth century, history was also being forged in America, where two distinct styles were being developed by two of the most significant figures in guitar history: C.F. Martin, maker of guitars with traditional, flat soundboards, and Orville Gibson, who developed archtop guitars with curved fronts in the tradition of violin-making.

THE MARTIN FLAT-TOP TRADITION

Hailing from a long line of musical instrument makers, Christian Frederick Martin was born in 1796 in Germany. At the age of 15 he left home for Vienna where he became an apprentice to the noted luthier Johann Stauffer. By all accounts Martin was an eager, motivated worker who within a few years had become a master craftsman and factory foreman. In about 1820, after marrying, he returned to his home town to open up his own guitar-manufacturing business. However, shortly after his return, Martin quickly became embroiled in a bitter dispute between rival guilds. The Martin family had been long-

CHRISTIAN FREDERICK MARTIN – FATHER OF THE AMERICAN GUITAR

33

standing members of the cabinet makers' guild, whose craftsmen had traditionally built lutes and guitars. In an effort to restrict competition, the violin makers' guild argued that, as supposedly inferior craftsmen, the cabinet makers ought not to be allowed to make any musical instruments.

The cabinet makers cited the importance of the work of Georg Martin and his son Christian in the development of the guitar. It was testimony from a noted wholesaler, who declared that Martin "produced guitars which

in point of quality and appearance leave nothing to be desired and which mark him as a distinguished craftsman", that finally won the battle for the cabinet makers. Martin was allowed to stay in business, but was disillusioned by the experience and decided to start again from scratch in America.

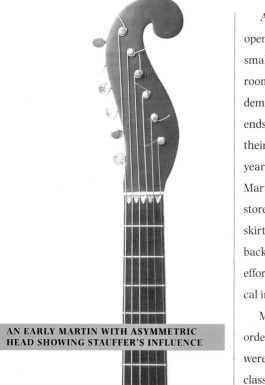

AN EARLY MARTIN WITH ASYMMETRIC
HEAD SHOWING STAUFFER'S INFLUENCE

Arriving in New York City in 1833, Martin opened a modest music store which housed a small guitar production workshop in the back room. At this time there was little widespread demand for guitars in America and to make ends meet early makers sometimes bartered their instruments for food and wine. After six years of life in New York City – a place that Martin had never much liked – he sold his store to buy eight acres of land on the outskirts of Nazareth, Pennsylvania. Turning his back on retailing, Martin concentrated his efforts solely on the production of his musical instruments.

Martin's first guitars were hand-crafted to order, and showed little standardization. They were, however, strongly reminiscent of the classical instruments he built for Stauffer back in Vienna, most notably in the headstock design which positioned all the tuning pegs on one side. Although this approach was abandoned after C.F. Martin's death in 1873, the idea influenced later solid-body designers such as Paul Bigsby and Leo Fender (*see* page 53). An unusual feature of the early Martin guitars was the adjustable neck, the tilt of which could be altered by means of a clock key fitted into the heel – the joint between the neck and the body. During the 1890s, when steel strings began gradually replacing those made from gut, this system was dropped, steel strings exerting greater stress on the neck fixture (*see* page 43).

During the 1850s C.F. Martin made one of his most important design innovations – the development of the cross-bracing system fitted to the underside of the soundboard. This was a pattern of struts which gave the instruments a distinctive treble tone. By the turn of the turn of the century the majority of steel-string guitar makers used variations on this system.

THE NEXT GENERATION

After the death of C.F. Martin in 1873, the company continued successfully under the guidance of successive generations of the family. It was under the presidency of Martin's grandson, Frank Henry, that some of the company's most innovative products were developed, perhaps the most significant being the Dreadnought guitar style.

In 1916, Frank Henry Martin developed a

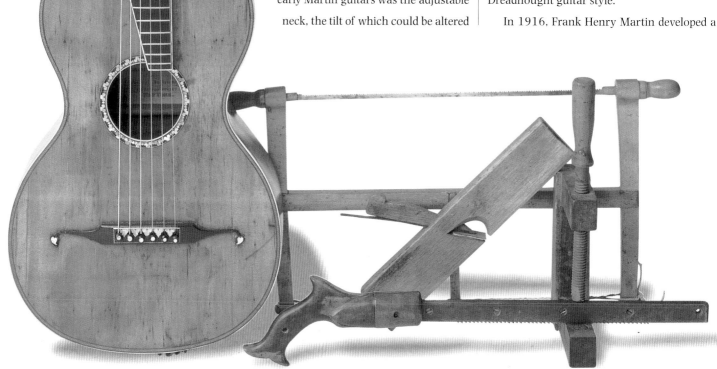

large-bodied instrument with a man named Harry Hunt, who worked for the Ditson music store in New York. Named after the British First World War battleship, the Ditson Dreadnought was built with a wide waist and narrow sloped shoulders. The new instrument was capable of producing a vastly greater volume and bass response, making it an ideal accompaniment for vocalists. In spite of Martin's role in its development, the first Dreadnoughts were available exclusively from the Ditson store. In 1928 Ditsons went out of business and Martin designers began to experiment with their own Dreadnought models. Strengthening the neck and replacing the traditional classical fan-bracing system with Martin's own "X-brace", they built the prototype D-1 and D-2 models. The first genuine Martin Dreadnoughts – the classic D-18 and D-28 styles – went into general production in 1935.

Perhaps the most famous Dreadnought model is the legendary Martin D-45, the first of which was made as a one-off for "singing cowboy" Gene Autry in 1933. Although production of the D-45 was discontinued in 1942, this instrument carved out a reputation among folk and country artists alike, and in 1968, after a renaissance of the acoustic guitar, production of the D-45 resumed. Since this important innovation virtually every significant guitar manufacturer has produced its own alternative to the Dreadnought, such as the Gibson "Jumbo" models of the late '30s.

F.H. Martin made a further influential innovation in 1929 with the introduction of the Orchestral Model. This line of instruments (prefixed with OM) featured a neck that joined the body at the fourteenth fret, rather than the traditional twelfth fret, which, by increasing the guitar's range, was

SINGING COWBOY GENE AUTRY PLAYED A MAJOR ROLE IN POPULARIZING THE GUITAR

THE MARTIN D-45 WITH ITS "DREAD-NOUGHT" BODY

35

Martin Model Coding

Martin guitars can be identified by the simple coding system in letter–hyphen–number format. The letter indicates the size of the body; the number indicates the "style" of the instrument, which generally means the particular features and quality of finish. For example, a Martin D-45 is a Dreadnought body with spruce soundboards, rosewood backs and sides, ebony fingerboards and abalone pearl inlays. The principal codes are shown below:

SIZE		STYLE	
O	Concert size	16	Spruce top, quarter-sawn
OO	Grand concert size		mahogany back and sides, slotted
OOO	Auditorium size		headstock, wide rosewood finger-
D	Dreadnought size		board, no fret markers or fingerplate.
DS	Dreadnought with 12 frets	18	14 frets to the body, solid headstock,
	to the body		white dot position markers, "belly"
M	Grand auditorium size		bridge, dark edgings and fingerplate.
MC	Grand auditorium with cutaway body	28	Rosewood back and sides, spruce
OM	Orchestral model		top, and white edging
C	Classical	45	Spruce soundboard, rosewood back
N	Classical (European)		and side, ebony fingerboard, and
F	F-hole model		abalone pearl inlays

rival companies such as Guild and Epiphone who were able to thrive during the '60s steel-string boom period.

OTHER FLAT-TOP GUITAR MAKERS

Martin designs defined the US flat-top steel-string tradition, and although there were other successful manufacturers producing flat-top instruments before the Second World War, such as Washburn, they were largely overshadowed by Martin. However, one significant design innovation came about in Europe, the Selmer Maccaferri. The Paris-based Selmer company had a long history of instrument-

intended to make it a more versatile instrument. This quickly became a standard design feature of American-built guitars.

From the '30s onwards, Martin enjoyed continued prosperity establishing a world-wide reputation for its flat-top acoustic instruments. Part of the company's success was due to limiting production to the highest quality instruments, creating an aura of exclusivity which remains to this day. Indeed, by the early '60s demand for Martin guitars was so great that there was a waiting list of three years for new models. This inevitably opened up the market to

THE SELMER MACCAFERRI, AS IMMORTALIZED BY DJANGO REINHARDT

making, and in 1931 they joined forces with Italian designer Mario Maccaferri. The resulting instrument was unique in that it featured an internal sound chamber suspended from from four fixed points inside the top of the large-bodied instrument. The chamber enabled the guitar to produce greater volume and a warmer tone.

Selmer Maccaferris are instantly recognizable from the Art Nouveau styling of the body and the unique "D"-shaped sound hole. Although only around 280 of the instruments were made at the time, they have

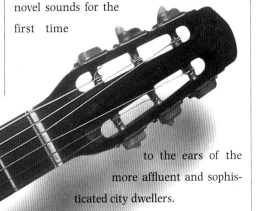

become well known as a result of their use by the guitarists in the Quintet du Hot Club de France, whose soloist was the legendary Django Reinhardt (*see* page 116). A number of custom guitar makers produce replicas of this classic instrument.

Since the war, although every major guitar manufacturer has produced flat-top steel-string guitars, the most significant rival to Martin has been Guild. Formed in 1952 from former Epiphone craftsmen, Guild guitars have been widely played in the fields of folk, pop and rock music.

THE AMERICAN FOLK AND COUNTRY TRADITIONS

From the late nineteenth century onwards the guitar was at the heart of most new American folk music forms. The oral storytelling folk traditions had been brought over to the continent by European settlers during the previous century and were often Celtic in origin. By the end of the nineteenth century, especially in the Southern states, some of these forms had blended and evolved to create a unique new voice. During the '20s, the first record companies began to take an interest in this new "country" music, bringing novel sounds for the first time to the ears of the more affluent and sophisticated city dwellers.

The first country guitar player to reach a large audience was Jimmie Rodgers. As a youth, he had been taught to play the guitar by black railroad workers. Although he died young in 1933, in his short lifetime he left a legacy that would be carried on by a new generation of popular guitarists. Also important in both the development of country music and the popularity of the guitar were the Carter Family, who introduced many traditional gospel-country songs that are now known as standards. At this time, country music was often tagged as "hillbilly" after the derogatory term applied by city dwellers to rural Southern whites.

The popularity of the guitar spread widely during the '30s as the "singing cowboy" stars like Gene Autry and the other "singing cowboy" Roy Rogers glamorized the instrument among young movie-goers. This period also saw the birth of a number of sub-genres, such as western swing, which combined the rhythms of jazz dance music with the hillbilly sound. At the same time in the South-West, the honky-tonk tradition evolved, making stars out of fine singer-songwriters such as Hank Williams. In other parts of the US, unique localized traditions integrated the new country sounds into their own cultural heritage: bluegrass picking styles emerged from the Appalachian mountain regions; Cajun music came about from the self-contained communities of the French-speaking settlers in Louisiana.

During the '50s country music became more mainstream with the widespread availability of television and the phonograph. During this decade Nashville, Tennessee, became the indisputable home of country music, broadcasting the Grand Ole Opry television shows. The Opry tradition had slowly expanded from regional radio in 1926 to become a nationwide television spectacular, introducing the American public to singing stars like Jim Reeves as well as pioneering pickers such as Merle Travis and Chet Atkins (*see* page 94), who was central to the next phase of development in country music – the Nashville Sound.

Since the '60s, country and western music, as it is widely known, has spread its popularity throughout the world, recent stars like Garth Brooks and Dwight Yoakam being among the most successful performers in any musical genre.

Although the showbiz excesses of the Grand Ole Opry are one leg of a heritage that began with Jimmie Rodgers and the Carter Family, a stark alternative was provided by Woody Guthrie who introduced politics and social commentary, and gave birth to a new American folk tradition. A left-wing activist, between 1936 and 1954 he is reputed to have written over 1,000 songs. When the protest movement erupted in the early '60s, prime movers like Pete Seeger, Bob Dylan and Phil Ochs found fame with music rooted in the Guthrie tradition. Dylan, in particular, has gone on to exert a major influence on much of the popular music of the '60s and '70s.

38

GIBSON AND THE ARCH-TOP TRADITION

Although it was Christian Frederick Martin and his ancestors who established the US as the source of most important innovations to the non-classical guitar, it was Orville Gibson who founded the company that would not only provide an alternative tradition to the flat-top acoustic guitar, but would also play a crucial role in the transition to the electric era.

Born in 1856, the son of a British immigrant, Orville Gibson was not only a skilled woodcarver but an accomplished mandolin player. During the 1880s he began to produce a new range of intricately carved mandolins using methods of construction more usually applied to violins. The principal difference between Gibson's mandolins and others was the curved tops with the bridge and saddles positioned across the highest point of the curve. During the decade that followed, Gibson applied the same ideas to his guitars, which became known as "archtops". In 1902, backed by a group of businessmen in Kalamazoo, Michigan, the Gibson Mandolin-Guitar Manufacturing Company was founded.

The first widespread success was the Style O guitar, launched in 1908. Its body shape was similar to that of Gibson's famed mandolins, and the bass side of the upper bout (*see* picture page 29) was carved into an ornate scroll. This model is noteworthy in the history of the American guitar because it features a perpendicular cutaway near the fifteenth fret – probably the first production instrument to feature such a device. The greater access this provided to the upper register made the Style O a great success.

Gibson continued to innovate during this period, one of his more fascinating experiments being the harp-guitar – a Style O-type guitar with 12 additional bass strings, each tuned to a different note. Although this partic-

Early Jazz Guitar

While the flat-top instruments dominated the country and folk fields, it was the archtop models that dominated the jazz world during the pre-electric era. With the development of louder guitars like the Gibson L-5, the banjo found itself with a greatly reduced role. Nonetheless, because it was unable to compete with the volume of brass and reed instruments – such as the trumpet, clarinet or saxophone – the guitar was still heavily restricted to vamping chordal rhythms. It was in chamber settings that the potential for the guitar as a solo instrument gradually became evident. The player largely credited with this development was New Yorker Eddie Lang, whose work with violinist Joe Venuti exhibits the earliest examples of a sophisticated single-note style.

ular idea failed to take off, by the time of Orville Gibson's death in1918, the company that bore his name enjoyed a reputation second only toMartin.

Surprisingly, perhaps, the Gibson company flourished in the years following the death of the founding father, introducing a number of developments that would have a major impact on the future of the guitar. Many of these pioneering progressions were the work of Lloyd Loar, who joined the Gibson company in 1920 (*see also* page 50). In his early days with the company Loar was one of the first instrument designers to experiment with magnetic pickups – but this development would not come to fruition for another decade. In 1924 he was crucial in the design of a succession of legendary production archtop guitars. The first of these models was the highly successful Gibson L-5 with its two violin-style "f-holes" – an instrument that all but replaced the very popular banjo's role in dance bands (*see* page 60).

The Gibson archtop tradition continued in 1934 with the birth of the Super 400, Gibson's top of the range archtop instrument. It was during the '30s, spurred on by successful developments at Rickenbacker, that Gibson began to give serious attention to the electrification of its guitars – a process that would flow quite naturally from their success as the creators of the archtop guitar.

OTHER ARCHTOP MAKERS

The success of the Gibson L-5 was so significant that many other guitar makers followed suit. Gibson's most important rivals during the '30s were probably Epiphone. Founded in New York in 1928 by Epominondas Stathopoulo, the son of a Greek immigrant, Epiphone first built banjos but then established a solid reputation with the Emperor and Deluxe models, both of which found widespread use among jazz musicians. When Stathopoulo died in 1942, much of the company's early promise disappeared. Many of their finest craftsmen left and in 1957 the company was sold to Gibson. Since then the Epiphone brand has become something of a lower-cost diffusion range for Gibson guitars.

Among the most highly rated of all the archtop makers was John D'Angelico who established a small workshop in New York City during the '30s. Finely hand-crafted instruments, his two models – the Excel and the New Yorker – could be described as Art Deco in styling, with the two-bar trapeze tailpiece, pickguard and machine heads all exhibiting an intricate "stepped" design. Not only are they among the most beautiful guitars ever made, but the warmth and clarity of their tone also attracted players of the calibre of Chet Atkins (*see* page 94). Following D'Angelico's death in 1964, his assistant Jimmy D'Aquisto continued the tradition with his own range of New Yorkers.

**BIGGEST-SELLING COUNTRY ARTIST
OF THE '90S, GARTH BROOKS**

THE SOLID- BODY ERA

40

1ike its acoustic counterpart, there are many approaches to the construction of the solid-body electric guitar. Although most instruments have similar

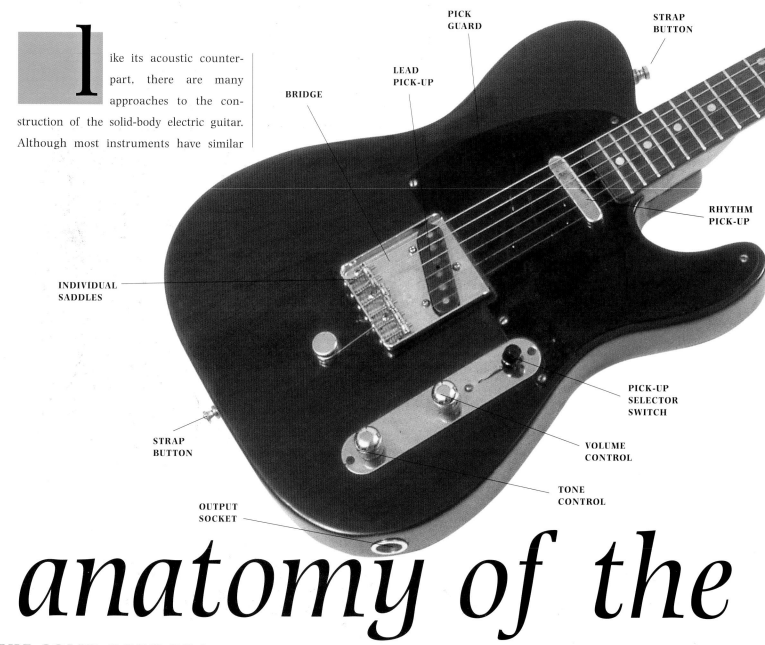

PICK
GUARD

STRAP
BUTTON

LEAD
PICK-UP

BRIDGE

RHYTHM
PICK-UP

INDIVIDUAL
SADDLES

PICK-UP
SELECTOR
SWITCH

STRAP
BUTTON

VOLUME
CONTROL

TONE
CONTROL

OUTPUT
SOCKET

anatomy of the

features, the materials used for today's guitars can differ greatly. Most bodies are made from kiln-dried hard woods, such as mahogany, ash, maple, walnut or alder. Necks are usually narrower, but otherwise differ little from those of acoustic instruments, although greater access to the upper frets provides greater flexibility for lead playing, and

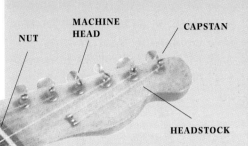

MARKER DOT

FRET MARKER

NUT

MACHINE HEAD

CAPSTAN

HEADSTOCK

some fingerboards are capable of a full two-octave range per string.

One major area of contention among guitar makers revolves around the way in which the neck is fixed to the body. The Fender approach, used by most other manufacturers, is to bolt the neck to the body. This makes construction more straightforward and also allows the angle of the neck to be tilted to fit a player's own preference. Gibson guitars have the necks glued permanently to the body. Other manufacturers favour "straight-through" necks, with the body centre – on which the bridge and tailpiece are mounted – and neck carved from a single piece of wood, and the treble and bass bouts glued on separately to the sides. Makers and players argue the merits of all three systems, although most would agree that the straight-through method is capable of producing the greatest sustain.

Alternative Materials

Since the aluminium resonator guitars were first produced in the early '30s (*see* page 63), makers have sought out alternative materials to the traditional hardwoods used in guitar production. In some cases it was a genuine search for improvement; in others it was to find ways of reducing production costs. Danelectro solids of the '50s were notable not only for their extraordinary shape and 32-fret fingerboards, but the fact that the bodies were built from hardboard glued around a wooden frame. These guitars tend to be more sought after by collectors than by players.

During the '60s Dan Armstrong experimented with making plastic-bodied instruments and achieving greater levels of sustain. The '70s saw a revival of interest in metal, with Veleno producing guitars entirely from aluminium. Kramer aroused a good deal of interest with their aluminium necks, but while nobody who heard these guitars doubted the improvements in volume and sustain, many players didn't like the "cold" feel of the neck.

The most successful materials experiment came in the '80s when American engineer Ned Steinberger attempted a radical overhaul of traditional guitar design. Initially working with bass guitars, Steinberger produced unique small-bodied, headless instruments from a carbon-based epoxy resin which he referred to as "graphite". It seemed to have

everything going for it: it was twice the density of wood – therefore producing greater volume, sustain and an even tone – had ten times the strength of wood, but was also extremely light. Some of the success of these outstanding instruments was undoubtedly due to visual appeal as much as sound and, excellent though they are, sadly they are too often viewed as a relic from one of the less distinguished decades. As the novelty of the shape wore off, Steinberger began producing more conventional-looking instruments and at the end of the '80s his company was taken over by Gibson.

As the Earth's natural resources become ever more scarce there is an inevitability that instruments made from the most sought-after woods will become increasingly costly. As a result, more and more guitar makers in future are likely to turn their attentions towards synthetic alternatives.

JOHN ABERCROMBIE PLAYS A REVOLUTIONARY STEINBERGER GUITAR

41

electric guitar

all electric guitars are fitted with some sort of pick-up so that they can be amplified. At its simplest, this can be a coil of fine copper wire wound many times around a bar magnet. The pick-up

the more windings there are, the higher the output will be. However, a high output can also lead to distortions of the original signal, so a balance has to be found.

In 1955, following in their great tradition, one of Gibson's engineers, Seth Lover,

used in a variety of combinations. Single coils give a better definition, but twin poles created a fatter, warmer sound.

The major factor governing the sound produced by a pick-up is its position on the guitar. Identical units placed immediately in front of

guitar hardware

is positioned beneath the steel strings of the guitar where it generates a magnetic field through which the strings pass. When they are struck this causes a disturbance to the magnetic field, generating pulses of electrical energy within the coil. These very low voltage pulses are passed through to the amplifier where they are greatly magnified to produce the signal that finally emerges from the loudspeaker.

Although there are many different types of pick-up, they can be divided into two generic categories – single coil and twin coil. Until the '50s all pick-ups were made from a single coil and worked as described above. There are many factors that govern the way a pick-up sounds, but the basic formula is simple: the stronger the magnet and

developed a new type of pick-up which was aimed at overcoming problems of electrical interference that plagued existing pick-ups. His solution was to build a unit that featured two coils instead of one. The coils were wired in series, so that the current flowed from one directly into the other, but the second coil was wired up "out of phase": any extraneous noise was therefore theoretically cancelled out before reaching the amplifier. To prevent the signal produced by the vibrating strings from also being cancelled out, individual pole pieces were fitted into each coil – the polarities of those in the second coil were reversed, inverting the signal arriving at the second coil, and so preventing phase cancellation of the signal.

Both types of pick-up are widely

the bridge and at the foot of the neck will produce entirely different results. The bridge pick-up creates a harder treble sound well suited to lead work; the pick-up closer to neck is often referred to as the "rhythm pick-up".

TREMOLO ARMS

A feature of electric guitars since they were first produced, a tremolo arm is a mechanical device incorporated into a bridge or tailpiece design. In practice it is a metal arm linked to a spring which when pushed down makes the strings longer, and thereby lowers the pitch of the note. When the arm is released the strings (in theory) return to their original positions. By moving the arm gently back and forth the player can create a mechanical vibrato effect. From the early '50s, there were only two widely used tremolo units: Bigsby arms were fitted to Gibson and Gretsch instruments; Fender produced their own version. The problem with these mechanisms was that after use they rarely returned exactly to their original position, often putting the guitar out of tune. The first man to successfully address this problem was a New Zealander named Floyd Rose, who in the early '80s developed a locking tremolo system. This mechanism uses a nut and bridge piece which locks the strings at

**LES PAUL AND THE GIBSON
MODEL NAMED AFTER HIM**

42

each end with an Allen key. Fine tuning is made by adjuster screws behind the bridge saddle. This means that the tremolo always returns to its locked position, unless one of the strings stretches or breaks (which will put the entire guitar out of tune).

With most leading manufacturers now using his system, the locking tremolo has made Floyd Rose a very wealthy man – indeed, his invention has all but rendered alternative systems redundant.

Strings

Although strings were traditionally referred to as "cat gut", they were invariably made from dried sheep intestines. Towards the end of the nineteenth century the use of steel strings became increasingly common on American acoustic guitars and by 1920 they were prevalent. Differences among steel strings are characterized by what is known as the "string wrap". Whilst the top two or three strings are generally made from a single thread of wire, the remainder comprise a wire inner core with a second piece of wire wound tightly around the outside. The nature of this wire wrapping has an effect on the sound and playability of the strings.

There are three types of string winding: roundwound, flatwound and groundwound. Roundwound strings are by far the most commonly used on electric and acoustic instruments. These strings are wound using conventional round wire, giving the characteristic ridge-like feel. They also produce the brightest treble sound. Flatwound strings – a core enveloped by a flat ribbon of metal – are often used on archtop guitars. They give a smooth feel but produce a less bright tone. They are less long-lasting, having a tendency to crack easily, however their main advantage is that they cut down the noise of the fingers moving across the strings. Groundwound strings are an attempt to combine the advantages of the other two types. Their conventional round windings are ground down so that the surface is partially flat.

Strings are not only wound differently, but also come in different sizes ("gauges"). Lighter strings are easier to hold down and bend, and are less harsh on the fingertips; heavier strings produce greater volume and sustain.

Although the six-stringed guitar has been the norm for almost 200 years, a number of alternatives have been produced. Twelve-string guitars have been in existence since the '20s, and remain popular among a minority of guitarists, and are prized for their characteristic "jangly" sound. In 1964 jazz guitarist George Van Eps had a seven-string model produced by Gretsch from experimental designs he had developed with Epiphone two decades earlier (*see* page 90). The seventh string was a lower bass string tuned to B. Although this idea failed to catch on, in the late '80s Steve Vai's collaboration with Ibanez saw the production of the similarly stringed Universe (*see* page 122). Although players who have mastered these instruments claim unprecedented versatility, the six-string standard looks likely to continue providing enough scope for most guitarists.

43

TWO GUITARS IN ONE: JIMMY PAGE OF LED ZEPPELIN PLAYS A GIBSON DOUBLE-NECK

the first amplifiers were built towards the end of the '30s. They were designed to allow guitars fitted with pick-ups to be heard over the more dominant acoustic instruments found in dance bands. The early models used valve technology similar to that of radios and electronic phonographs but were capable of producing a volume rarely above 10 watts.

As the demand for louder amplified music grew towards the end of the '40s it soon became clear that existing amplification was insufficient to fill larger venues. Leo Fender (*see* page 53) was among the first engineers to produce a dedicated guitar amplifier. In 1949 he and his engineer Don Randall produced the Fender Super amplifier. By the middle of the '50s Fender had produced a number of classic designs, such as the Bassman and Twin Reverb, some of which are still available in modified forms. During this period the self-contained amplifier and loudspeaker combination – usually referred to as a "combo" -

BRITISH-MADE MARSHALL AMPS HAVE DOMINATED ROCK FOR 30 YEARS

became the most widely accepted format. Towards the end of the '50s the British Vox company produced the AC30, which remains as much a classic of its type as the Fender Twin. Such models were popular with blues and early rock musicians not only because of the warmth of their tone, but because of the way they sounded when the valves were overdriven. This latter facility was by no means a deliberate design feature at the time, but a happy accident that helped to define much of the classic rock guitar sound.

During the early '60s, as guitar groups became more popular and performed in larger venues, power once again became a problem. One solution was put forward by British engineer Jim Marshall who produced a 100-watt amplifier which was connected to a cabinet containing four 12-inch (30.5 cm) speakers. This allowed the sound characteristics of the lower-powered amplifiers to be used in much larger venues. Consequently, guitarists like Jeff Beck (*see* page 96) actively started to integrate two of the engineers' traditional enemies – distortion and feedback – into their playing style. Thus the Marshall "stack" replaced the combo throughout much of the heavy rock era.

By the '70s, valve technology – long since abandoned by radio and hi-fi producers – fell from grace as manufacturers began to use solid-state transistor circuitry. The appeal was that transistors were cheaper to produce and more predictable. Although the new technology appealed to those of limited means, former valve users were reluctant to change. The rea-

PETE TOWNSHEND OF THE WHO TRASHES HIS MARSHALL STACK

son was not difficult to understand. When valves overloaded the sound became warmer and distorted, and fed back smoothly; when transistors overloaded, the tone produced was

amplification

44

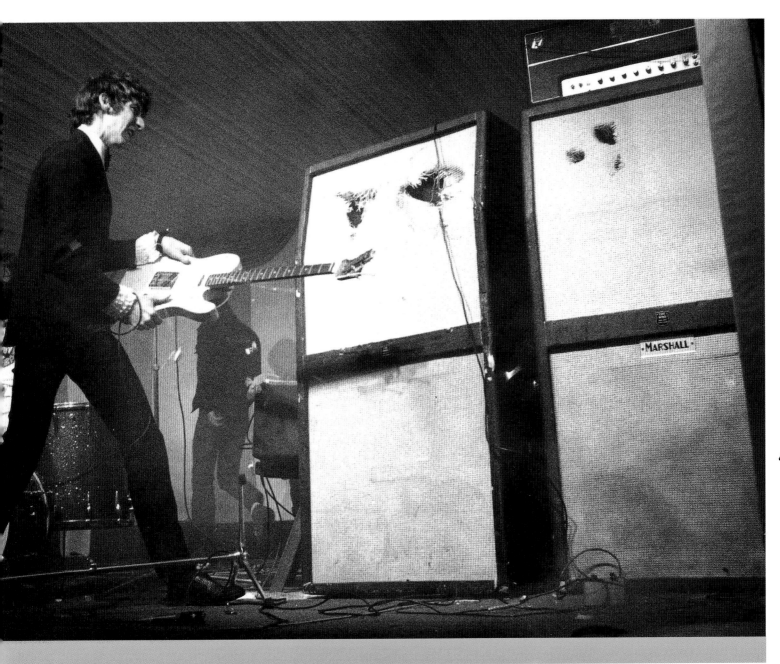

made up of grating harmonics or an extremely unpleasant howling whistle. Some designers tried to compensate by introducing analogue distortion, but it just wasn't as effective as the real thing. Nevertheless, solid-state circuitry found its following, especially among bass guitarists and other players who value a cleaner tone. Transistors are capable of dealing with a wider range of frequencies than valves, and also distort less at higher volumes, making them more suited to pure amplification purposes, such as PA systems or studio monitors.

So by the early '80s it had become clear that the "old-fashioned" valve sound was important to many electric guitar players, irrespective of what style of music they liked to play. This led some amplifier manufacturers to pursue a third direction – the valve/solid-state hybrid. The companies' rationale was simple: many characteristics of the valve sound came from the pre-amplifier section – the input volume and tone controls. The power amplifier – which boosts the preamp volume – can be achieved easily using solid-state

technology, boosting an original valve sound.

It would seem that most guitarists prefer to keep their set-ups as simple as possible, satisfied with a guitar, a few effects and a combo. In recent years, however, the emergence of a good deal of peripheral guitar technology has spawned a new type of techno-literate guitarist with rack-mounted amplifier and effects, both of which can be programmed and operated via MIDI (musical instrument digital interface) footswitching, or even from external sources such as a computer or sequencer.

effects

almost from the moment that use of the electric guitar became widespread in the '50s, engineers and musicians looked for new ways to produce radically different sounds. Some electronic effects were built into the amplifier, others came in the form of a plug-in foot pedal – a battery-operated unit inserted between the guitar and amplifier, which enabled the guitarist to switch the effect on and off by activating a footswitch. Technology has now advanced to include multiple-effects pedals – high-quality, digital units capable of producing a full range of sound-processing effects all of which can be programmed and combined in a variety of ways.

Numerous sounds which are now taken for granted as a part of the modern musical repertoire can only be achieved with some sort of add-on unit, making sound-processing a necessity for most types of music.

REVERBERATION

Reverberation was one of the first effects to capture the imagination of guitarists, who often found it built into early amplifiers. It is a natural effect caused by soundwaves bouncing off the surrounding environment and produces a warm, ambient sensation of the sound "spreading" out. Simulated reverb effects were originally created by the use of a small spring that was vibrated by the guitar signal. This "clanking" sound can be heard on numerous twangy rock 'n' roll instrumentals of the late '50s. Spring reverb remained the norm until

replaced by high-quality electronic digital units in the '80s. Nowadays, even the most basic reverb unit allows you the luxury of programming parameters, based on the attributes of natural reverberation, such as the size, shape and sound-damping features of an imaginary room.

ECHO EFFECTS

Many of the most commonly used effects are produced by repeating a delayed signal. Echo, like reverb, is the natural acoustic result of a sound being reflected from a distant surface. The first echo units were essentially simple tape-recorder mechanisms using a loop of magnetic tape that passed over a record head and then a number of independent playback heads. The pioneer in this field was the British-made Watkins Copycat, first produced in 1954.

"Slap-back" echo, a single fast repeat, was widely used by early rock 'n' rollers, both on guitar and vocals. In later years guitarists like Queen's Brian May used longer delays of several seconds to build and play over thick layers of sound, an approach that reached a natural conclusion with Robert Fripp, who used two Revox A77 tape recorders linked together to create soundscapes built from delays of 10 seconds or more. This system became widely known as "Frippertronics". Like reverb, echo effects are almost entirely digitally produced now.

FUZZ AND DISTORTION

Whether produced by an amplifier or external unit, distorted sound has been at the heart of electric guitar-playing since the mid-'60s. The principle is simple: a signal is fed into a low-output pre-amplifier where the volume is boosted to the point of distortion; the treated signal is then boosted by a "clean" power amplifier.

The first external mechanism to create this sound was the "fuzz" pedal, intended for guitarists who liked the effect of valve distortion, but wanted to be able to produce a similar result at lower volumes. The first fuzz box was designed by Gary Hurst for the British Sola Sound company. Called the Tone Bender, it was used by Jeff Beck on the Yardbirds' 1964 single 'Heart Full Of Soul' and further popularized by Jimi Hendrix (*see* page 108) and Eric Clapton. By the '70s all manner of sophisticated overdrive units were available, many aimed at providing not only distortion but a simulated valve sound for those using solid-state amplifiers.

WAH-WAH PEDAL

One of the most famous guitar-based effects is the wah-wah pedal (*see* below). A tone filter which is rocked back and forth inside a foot pedal, it can be used to provide a variety of tonal distortions. Jimi Hendrix was responsible

for popularizing this technique, his album *Electric Ladyland* demonstrating some particularly expressive uses. Frank Zappa often used the wah-wah as additional tone control, finding a setting he liked and leaving the pedal in that position. Funk guitarists in the early '70s used the effect heavily. Muting the strings and strumming a rhythm whilst rocking the footpedal produces a sound characterized by Isaac Hayes' music for the film *Shaft*.

PHASING

An odd effect known as phasing occurs when the same signal is played back from two different sources at the same time. A soundwave can be seen as a string of peaks and troughs. If an inverse signal is played at the same time – that is, a peak on one signal coincides *exactly* with an equivalent trough on the other – the effect is known as "phase cancellation" and the sound won't be heard. However, if they are out of alignment by even the smallest fraction of a second the result is a "sweeping" sound. This effect was discovered accidentally in the late '50s, but not deliberately used until 1967 when it was heard on the Small Faces' psychedelic-tinged 'Itchycoo Park' single. The greater the delay between the two signals, the more dramatic and "metallic" the sweep becomes. This effect is known as flanging.

DOUBLE TRACKING

Delay effects were originally created by recording a signal on two tape machines, and then playing them back at the same time. The inconsistencies in speed and pitch between machines helped to create the overall sound. This can be emulated by adding pitch modulation to disturb the delayed signal. ADT (automatic double tracking) and "chorus" effects add variations in pitch to a delayed signal, creating the effect of doubling up a performance.

FRANK ZAPPA VIEWED THE WAH-WAH PEDAL AS AN ADDITIONAL TONE FILTER

i t's pretty well impossible to imagine what much of the popular music produced over the past 50 years would sound like had the electric guitar never been developed. But although a common image of the electric guitar only really drifted into the public consciousness with the first generation of rock and roll stars of the 1950s, the electrification process can be traced back to a good 30 years earlier.

By the end of the 1920s, the steel-string guitar – especially the louder models like the revolutionary Gibson L-5 (*see* page 60) – had become a well-established feature in a majority of jazz and dance bands. It was from this point that a new tradition of exceptionally gifted jazz guitarists emerged. Eddie Lang in the US was the first player to demonstrate the potential of the guitar as a solo instrument outside of the classical sphere. Indeed, in the eys of many critics he was largely responsible for inventing the single-note solo in jazz. A few years later, on the other side of the Atlantic, Django Reinhardt (*see* page 116) also stunned his audiences with single note runs of staggering complexity.

As the popularity of this new generation of players grew, so too did the demand for louder instruments. Most of the early experiments revolved around increasing the size of the body or new design innovations, like the National guitars which used an aluminium resonating panel (*see* page 63). In spite of these efforts, however, soloing could only cut through in small-group situations. A new solution was needed.

THE FIRST ELECTRIC INSTRUMENTS

Although it's generally accepted that Gibson's Lloyd Loar had experimented with pick-up design in the early 1920s, the first significant breakthrough came in 1931 when Paul Barth and George Beauchamp joined forces with Swiss-born Adolph Rickenbacker to form their own Ro-Pat-In company (which would later became the Electro String Company, home to the famous Rickenbacker brand name). Beauchamp, himself a well known guitarist, had already played an important role in the design of the National resonator guitar and also worked with Barth in an attempt to produce an electrical amplification system. Their experiments came to fruition in 1931 with a pair of lap-steel "Hawaiian" guitars – the A22 and A25 models. Commonly known as "Frying Pans" because of their shape, these instruments were powered by a pair of large horseshoe magnets with six individual pole pieces that passed under each of the six strings. Although these models were not technically guitars in the conventional sense, they were nonetheless the first commercially produced electric instruments.

The Frying Pan first went into production under the Ro-Pat-In brand name. The body and neck of the prototype models were made from a single piece of maple, but by the time they were made available to the public cast aluminium was used instead. This was not an entirely successful development as the use of aluminium apparently resulted in problems keeping the instrument in tune. Later in the decade Rickenbacker made lap-steel guitars from strong bakelite plastic which proved to be more successful. Variations on the Frying Pan design remained in the Rickenbacker catalogue until well into the 1950s.

THE GROUND-BREAKING RICKENBACKER FRYING PAN

electric firsts

PIONEERING THE ELECTRIC GUITAR

It may seem strange to imagine that a lap-steel instrument was used to pave the way for the electrification of the guitar, but during this period, the conventional "Spanish" guitar was only then beginning to establish itself as a popular musical instrument. Although the Frying Pan had hardly set the music world alight, within a year Rickenbacker and his two colleagues had introduced the first genuine electric guitar. Known simply as the "Electro-Spanish", this instrument was a basic hollow-bodied arch-top design fitted with the same horseshoe magnet pick-up that head been used on the Frying Pan models. As with many great innovations, the Electro-Spanish was not a huge commercial success and was only produced in limited numbers between 1932 and 1935. Nevertheless, it holds a significant place in the history of the electric guitar and was a major influence on many of the models that followed, especially the first generation of electric instruments produced by Gibson.

ONE OF RICKENBACKER'S FIRST PRODUCTION ELECTRIC INSTRUMENTS

EDDIE LANG IS CONSIDERED BY MANY TO BE THE FATHER OF JAZZ GUITAR

49

CHAPTER FOUR

a fter Rickenbacker's early triumph, the period leading up to the mid-'30s saw most of the brand-name guitar manufacturers trying out their own experiments fitting magnetic pick-ups to acoustic guitars. None of these instruments sold in any great quantities until Gibson launched its first electric guitar in 1935.

Marketed in their trade catalogue as "another miracle from Gibson", the ES-150 was the first electric guitar to go into large-

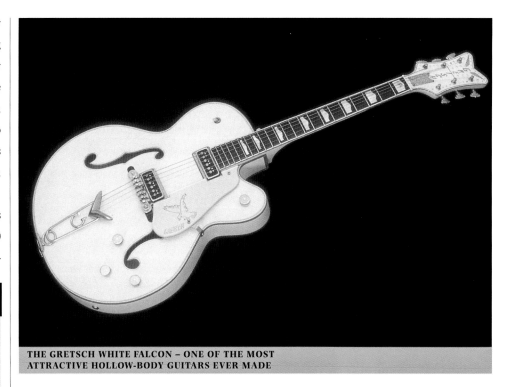

THE GRETSCH WHITE FALCON – ONE OF THE MOST ATTRACTIVE HOLLOW-BODY GUITARS EVER MADE

Lloyd Loar

Although his name may not be as widely known as those of Gibson, Martin or Fender, the American acoustic engineer Lloyd Loar is a very significant figure in the history of the electric guitar.

Loar joined Gibson in 1919, two years after the death of founder Orville Gibson. Some of his earliest experiments involved magnetic pick-ups and amplification. As well as having designed the revolutionary Gibson L-5 (see page 60), Loar is also known to have developed the first electric double bass, although this never actually went into production.

After leaving Gibson, Loar formed his own Vivi-Tone company in 1933. Although he failed to survive as a businessman, he did produce a series of highly rated arch-top guitars, some of which were fitted with pick-ups.

50

scale production. A revamped version of the popular budget L-50 archtop, the ES-150 hit the mark when it captured the imagination of jazz guitarist Charlie Christian (see page 100). More than any other musician, it was Christian who was responsible for establishing the electric guitar as a serious musical proposition.

The Gibson ES-150 had a hollow mahogany body with a spruce top and featured traditional Gibson-style "f-holes", a long pickguard and bakelite volume and tone controls. The narrow "bar" pick-up was positioned at the foot of the fingerboard which created a smooth, mellow tone that – partly through the

recordings of Charlie Christian – established the archetypal jazz guitar sound which has endured ever since. In 1940 the bar pick-up was replaced by a larger rectangular unit – the forerunner of the famed P90 pick-up. The ES-150 remained in production intermittently until 1956.

OTHER HOLLOW-BODY ELECTRICS

Throughout the '40s Gibson continued adding models to their range, sometimes making magnetic pick-ups an optional feature for standard Gibson archtops. Notable models were the ES-

production
electric guitars

CHAPTER FOUR

CHARLIE CHRISTIAN, FATHER OF THE ELECTRIC JAZZ GUITAR

300 produced from 1942 which featured a single pick-up mounted diagonally in front of the bridge. This could not only give the guitar a harder treble tone but the slanting of the unit also accentuated the ratio between treble and bass. This idea was taken up by Fender on their first solid-body electrics at the start of the following decade.

Another Gibson model to find favour with jazz musicians was the ES-175, produced from 1949, which featured a unique sharpened "Venetian" cutaway. Echoes of the ES-175 shape could be seen three years later when Gibson launched its first solid-body instrument – the Les Paul Gold Top (*see* page 68).

After the successful emergence of the first solid-body instruments, the vogue for hollow-body guitars understandably diminished. However, Gibson and other guitar makers such as Rickenbacker and Gretsch continued to produce hollow-body electrics throughout the '50s and '60s. Many of the most popular models remain in production to this day.

THE GIBSON ES-175 FROM THE LATE '40S – STILL POPULAR IN JAZZ CIRCLES

The Jazz Age

In the '20s the role of the guitar in jazz was still largely restricted to rhythm work. Django Reinhardt (*see* page 116) progressed the cause during the '30s playing the revolutionary Selmer Maccaferri guitar, the enlarged body and specially designed D-shaped sound hole making the instrument capable of greater volumes than regular guitars.

It was Charlie Christian (*see* page 100) who revolutionized not only jazz but the role of the guitar. Using the Gibson ES-150 he made massive strides forward with a style that owed more to the soloing of saxophonist Lester Young than any of his guitar-playing contemporaries. Through his extraordinary playing he gave a new generation of guitarists (not only in the jazz field) a glimpse of the instrument's potential to achieve the same volumes as a saxophone or trumpet.

A genuine virtuoso whose recording career lasted barely four years, Charlie Christian was one of the forerunners of bebop in the early '40s. In fact, until the emergence of Wes Montgomery (*see* page 112) in the '50s, Charlie Christian was viewed as the starting-point of study for every aspiring jazz guitarist.

by the end of the '40s the idea of the electric guitar had long passed the novelty stage, finding itself not only in large dance bands, but at the centre of burgeoning musical styles, as could be heard in the music of the early electric R&B guitarists like Muddy Waters (*see* page 124) and Elmore James, or emerging country stars such as Chet Atkins (*see* page 94) and Merle Travis. However, a fundamental problem of the early electric guitars – which were, after all, little more than acoustic guitars with pick-ups fitted – was that if the amplifier volume was too great, sound from the loudspeaker would cause the body of the guitar and strings to vibrate on their own.

This created a howling noise referred to as "feedback". Whilst rock players in the '60s learned to harness this sound as part of their playing styles, to the early electric players it was simply a nuisance. The logical solution to this problem, it seemed, was to increase the body mass of the instrument – without a working soundbox its capacity for vibration would be greatly reduced. During the '40s a number of unrelated parties therefore set about designing and building a solid-body electric guitar.

No one can say without doubt who got there first, but there are a number of candidates whose research work was unquestionably important. Designer-engineers Lloyd Loar (*see* page 50) and O.W. Appleton are well known to have experimented with solid bodies and magnetic coils. In the early '40s, country-jazz guitarist Les Paul created his own "Log" guitar using a Gibson neck attached to a solid piece of pine on which the pick-ups and bridge were mounted – the bouts from an Epiphone hollow-body archtop were added to the side to give it a broadly normal appearance. Although this was not a true solid-body instrument,

solid

Paul's experiments had been aimed at preventing feedback (*see* page 68).

A more significant claimant was engineer Paul Bigsby, who in 1948 produced a solid-body instrument designed with country guitarist Merle Travis. Bigsby and Travis had first collaborated three years earlier when the guitarist had requested some improvements to the vibrola (an alternative tremolo device) on his Gibson guitar. Bigsby came up with a completely new design for a vibrato arm – commonly (though wrongly) known as a tremolo – which was widely used over the next 20 years.

This Bigsby-Travis guitar represented an important development for a number of reasons. The shape of the body and headstock was clearly influential – some of the lines were echoed in the early Fender guitars over the next decade. Also influential were the thinline bird's-eye maple body and the fact that it featured a "straight-through" neck. Since at least a dozen of these instruments were produced, it could reasonably claim to have been the first "production" solid-body electric guitar.

THE FENDER FACTOR

Whilst these pioneers all played a crucial role in the development of the solid-body electric guitar, it was the foresight and ambition of one man that would establish the instrument as the most significant in the second half of the twentieth century. That man was Leo Fender. In 1946, the Fender Electrical Instrument Company was founded, producing electrified lap-steel guitars and amplifiers. Two years later, Leo Fender – with one of his employees, George Fullerton – set about creating the production-line solid-body electric guitar that became a legend. Their design first saw the light of day in April 1950 as the Fender Esquire, later renamed the Broadcaster and finally the Telecaster (*see* also page 65).

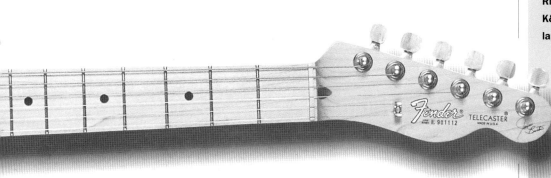

THE DISTINCTIVE FENDER TELECASTER, THE FIRST PRODUCTION SOLID-BODY ELECTRIC

Leo Fender

Born in Anaheim, California in 1909, Leo Fender developed a fascination for electronics during his childhood. Having already run his own radio repair shop, during the early '40s he formed K&F with Rickenbacker designer "Doc" Kauffman. K&F produced their own amplifiers and lap-steel guitars. In 1946 Fender broke away to form his own company, opening up a shop and small factory in nearby Fullerton, California. It was from this base that he created his innovatory range of guitars and amplification. In 1965, after a decade of intermittent illness, Fender became convinced that he had only a short time to live and sold off his business to CBS for $13 million. Shortly afterwards, a change of medical treatment restored him to perfect health. He rejoined his former company in a consultative capacity, and during the '70s was responsible for some outstanding Music Man guitars, such as the Stingray. In 1980 Fender rejoined his old friend George Fullerton to form G&L Music Sales, producing dramatic designs such as the Comanche, as well as refinements to his classic designs. He died in 1991. (*See also* pages 65 and 71.)

bodies

at first the Fender Telecaster was not a massive commercial success and it was treated by the musical trade as a novelty item. Nonetheless, the fact that the Fender factory at Fullerton was turning Telecasters out in reasonable quantities prompted Gibson to produce a new Les Paul model in 1952.

With its dramatic opulent finish, the Les Paul Gold Top was an altogether more luxurious beast that made Fender's Telecaster look spartan by comparison. Fender was sufficiently worried by the threat it posed that he felt compelled to design his own "luxury"

model, the Stratocaster, arguably the most famous electric guitar ever made (*see* page 71).

Although their fortunes varied along the way, the Fender Telecaster, Gibson Les Paul and Fender Stratocaster guitars are now viewed as classic designs, immediately recognizable to guitarists and music-buying public alike. The two Fenders have remained in production ever since, differing little from those groundbreakers that first rolled off the production line almost 50 years ago.

The Les Paul – during its early life, at least – experienced mixed fortunes. Sales of the Gold Top had peaked by 1956 and two years later, Gibson, fearing that the gaudy decoration may

have been too ostentatious, replaced it with the more conservative-looking Les Paul Standard (*see* page 69). The Les Paul design, in its various manifestations, has remained in production ever since. The late-'50s Standards are now such prized collector's pieces that they are more likely to be found resting in a bank vault than performing in a smoky blues club.

Although many other guitar makers did produce excellent solid-body instruments during the '50s and early '60s there was a clear rivalry between Gibson and Fender from the outset. Indeed, besides the three best-known models, they made most of the other noted solid-body guitars of the period –

THE STRATOCASTER – PERHAPS THE MOST FAMOUS GUITAR OF THEM ALL

the battle

Fender's Jazzmaster, Jaguar and Musicmaster models, and Gibson's SG, radical Flying V and Explorer (*see* page 78). This perceived dominance of the market was often played out with a sense of the old masters versus the new kids on the block, the rivalry filtering through to players themselves who would ally themselves to one camp or the other.

New Music From A New Guitar

Although country musicians were the pioneers of the solid-body electric guitar, it is with the various forms of blues and rock music that the instrument is most strongly linked. In the '50s it was the R&B boom that helped to establish a role in modern music. The sounds made by great Chicago electric bluesmen like Muddy Waters (*see* page 124) and Howlin' Wolf had a major impact on the young blues and rock players of the early '60s. During the same period, the gradual evolution into the rock 'n' roll era gave the electric guitar a special youth cachet, the likes of Elvis Presley – hips and guitar in full swing – adding a touch of notoriety. This continued over the next two decades as the emergence of loud rock music helped to maintain a healthy gap in taste and attitude between teenagers and their parents. The electric guitar became a useful symbol of the distance between the two generations.

Towards the end of the '50s, a number of popular solo guitarists emerged, achieving widespread popularity with a variety of "twangy" electric guitar instrumentals. It was an era that established the likes of Duane Eddy, Hank Marvin, Dick Dale and Link Wray. Although these players may not always have seemed like virtuoso musicians (at least on their most popular recordings), the sound of a simple tune played on an electric guitar turned on an entire generation of would-be strummers, like the reaction to the singing cowboys 30 years earlier.

In the first half of the '60s a young generation of British-based, white, blues-influenced musicians came to prominence. This first wave of rock guitarists included players of the calibre of Eric Clapton, Jeff Beck (page 96) and Peter Green, all three among the most venerated players in rock history. However, the greatest star of the solid-body electric guitar burst onto the scene in 1967: in all too short a life Jimi Hendrix gave a glimpse of the electric guitar's potential in the music of the future. Hendrix influenced his peers and successors like no one since Charlie Christian at the end of the '30s (*see* pages 108 and 100).

By the '70s, rock was so popular that it began to break itself down into sub-genres, all of which had their own stars and followers. Since then, however, in spite of the popularity of pyrotechnically gifted players like Eddie Van Halen, the music-buying public has seemed less inclined to appreciate instrumental virtuosity for its own sake. Whatever fashion has prevailed – be it heavy rock, progressive rock, punk, death metal, or grunge – the guitar has nevertheless remained at its very core.

TOM MORELLO OF RAGE AGAINST THE MACHINE WITH HIS CUSTOMIZED GUITAR

of the big three

a

lthough it may sometimes have seemed so, the history of the electric guitar has by no means been a two-horse race. There have been many other fine American manufacturers over the years, classic names such as Gretsch (*see* page 74), Rickenbacker (*see* page 81) and Epiphone producing fine models into the '60s; Kramer, Guild and Ovation (*see* page 82) in the '70s and '80s; and Jackson, Charvel and Paul Reed Smith throughout the past decade. Noted European makers such as Selmer, Vox, Hoffner and Burns have also left their own distinct marks on guitar history. However, in recent

Change came about in 1985 when Fender underwent a management buy-out and began a new two-tiered approach to production. This initiative saw the quality of their standard US models increase noticeably while they simultaneously produced their own Squier range of instruments in Japan. Later, as production costs began to rise in Japan, less industrialized countries were used for manufacturing, creating a complex multi-tiered system by which the top-range instruments were produced in the US, standard quality instruments in Japan, and budget models in Korea and Mexico. This proved to be both successful and popular with Fender buyers, reinstating a

the supporting players

years, the greatest strides have been made by makers based in the Far East, who have successfully turned around a reputation for producing cheap imitations of classic American designs.

For Fender in particular the copy issue became a problem in the early '80s. Until then, although many a novice had started on a cheap unplayable plywood "Stratocaster", these copies had been too poor in quality to pose any serious threat to the genuine makers in the US. However, during the mid-'70s, some felt that a decade of corporate CBS management had gradually eroded Fender's production standards. During the following decade the world suddenly woke up to the realization that the copies being manufactured by companies like Tokai were not that far behind the originals in terms of quality, and at only a fraction of the price represented excellent value for money.

consistency in quality among the top models and allowing novices or those with little money to own genuine, well-made Fender guitars – even if they weren't the real American thing.

JAPANESE ORIGINALS

From the '70s, some of the better-known Japanese guitar makers began to build up a reputation for their own designs. The Yamaha SG2000, built between 1973 and 1988, was perhaps the first guitar to prove to the world that instruments to equal the American masters could be made in Japan. Other highly

regarded Japanese brand names have included Tokai, Westone and Aria, the last of which introduced their own tiered production system, creating cheaper instruments in developing Far Eastern countries.

Perhaps the most successful Japanese guitar manufacturer of recent times has been Ibanez, whose already strong reputation was further boosted by well-publicized associations with such guitar gods as Steve Vai (*see* page 122) and Joe Satriani. Ibanez has a vast range of guitars available and some of the top-end models outrank their US counterparts, both in quality and cost.

STEVE VAI PLAYS AN IBANEZ JEM – A MODEL HE HELPED TO DESIGN
inset: **VAI PERFORMS IN SEVILLE WITH BRIAN MAY OF QUEEN**

W hen the electronic fuzz and wah-wah effects caught on during the mid-'60s, it was hardly surprising that some manufacturers would think that what the modern guitarist really needed was a guitar with built-in sound effects. During the '60s and '70s guitars found their way onto the market with hot-wired effects like distortion, delay and tremolo. The British Shergold company even produced the Modulator guitar to which a variety of plug-in effect modules could be attached as required. Perhaps the most dramatically useless idea was a guitar built by Guyatone in Japan which featured

a primitive drum machine with five preset rhythms. Very handy!

More successful were the attempts to create hybrid instruments. Probably the first such example to go into production was a guitar-organ built by Vox. This British company had already achieved worldwide success not only with its AC30 amplifier, but the Continental organ, which was used by numerous pop groups in the mid-'60s. In 1966, in true Frankenstein style, Vox installed the circuitry from a Continental into the body of a standard Vox Phantom guitar. Featuring ten controls and six switches set into an already small body, the guitar-organ was heavy and looked

extremely cluttered. It was also mains powered, a fact that might well have deterred some safety-conscious players. Although it may have "worked" successfully, the Vox guitar-organ, and others that followed in its wake, are now little more than footnotes in recent guitar history – but the idea was far from forgotten.

During the '70s, the synthesizer, like the organ during the previous decade, became the hippest new noise on the block. It was clearly only a matter of time before someone thought to create a hybrid guitar synthesizer. However, unlike those producing some of the crankier designs of the previous decade, the most enthusiastic purveyor of this new type of instrument was also one of the leading Japanese technology companies – Roland.

The first models to go into production were the GS-500 and GR-500 in 1977. Both units were required for the system to work. The

hybrid guitars

THE GIBSON DOUBLE-NECK REACHED A PEAK OF POPULARITY IN THE '70S

GR-500 was essentially a standard Roland synthesizer without a keyboard; the GS-500 was a regular solid-body guitar which was connected to the first unit. This system, like the improved models that followed, was no gimmicky toy, but a serious modern musical instrument that could reward any musician prepared to rethink his or her playing technique.

During the '80s, from these beginnings, a number of complex and sophisticated hybrid instruments were unleashed by bold, forward-thinking or just plain mad inventors. Among the most noteworthy were the Synthaxe and Stepp "guitars", both of which could be used to control external MIDI sound modules, such as synthesizers, samplers or drum machines. These have been impressive but were too costly for most to even contemplate. Players of the calibre of Pat Metheny and Allan Holdsworth have demonstrated some of the possibilities of these systems.

One of the main reasons why all of these ideas failed to catch on in a big way was that the guitar itself was viewed as part of the technology. An important aspect of the guitarist's psyche that most of the synth-based manufacturers had failed to take into account was the relationship between the player and his or her *own* guitar. With this in mind, Roland's next move was the introduction of the MIDI pick-up. Attached in front of the bridge of any standard instrument, it could be connected to a conversion unit, via which it was possible to trigger external MIDI sounds with a high degree of accuracy. But in spite of this considerable technical achievement the MIDI guitar remains a minority pursuit. Indeed, it's probably true to say that without Roland's continued persistence, the idea wouldn't have even made it into the '90s.

WHAT NEXT?

The electric guitar has dramatically altered the music of the past half-century. Indeed, most of the music it inspired would not even have been possible without the development of magnetic pick-ups, amplification and sound processing effects. But since the Fender Broadcaster first hit the production lines in 1950, how many genuine innovations have been made to the guitar itself?

Admittedly, every major manufacturer has experimented with new shapes, from Ted McCarty's Flying V and Explorer designs in 1958 – both of which proved to be way ahead of their time – through the double-necked Gibsons that emerged in the early '70s, to the dramatic Steinberger "headless" guitars moulded from graphite, that were first built in 1982 (*see* picture). It is also true that Ovation's bowl-backed acoustic guitars (*see* page 82) created a new benchmark in the production of steel-string acoustic guitars. However, as we move into the new millennium, it does seem rather strange that the most popular and desirable guitars remain those which are based not only on designs but also the materials first used a half a century ago.

There have also been many attempts to overhaul the sound and even the role of the guitar in the past, but interesting though some of these ingenious experiments have been, they have never achieved widespread popularity, though thankfully this has never stopped some of the most creative minds from trying to break new ground.

The recent reluctance of many guitarists to abandon tradition and embrace new technology may be partly due to the limiting fashionability of using the latest gadgetry. But one clear advantage that modern guitarists do have over their keyboardplaying counterparts is the knowledge that their own instrument won't suddenly be out of date (or even have lost that much of its value) within the space of just a few months. But then again, perhaps it's something altogether simpler: maybe those early pioneers such as Leo Fender just got it right first time.

JAZZ-ROCK STAR ALLAN HOLDSWORTH WITH HIS HEADLESS STEINBERGER

59

STAR GUITARS

introduced in 1922, the Gibson L-5 holds a pivotal position in the history of the modern guitar. Designed by engineer Lloyd Loar – who also pioneered the magnetic pick-up (*see* page 50) – the L-5 was the first archtop to feature a pair of violin-style tuned "f-holes" cut into the upper and lower bouts, rather than a conventional circular sound hole under the strings (*see* picture). This innovation, along with the "Virzi-tone" sound producer built into the body of the early models, helped to create a strong, full, warm sound which projected chord work through the brass-dominated dance bands of the period.

The L-5 was an immediate and overwhelming success, exerting a sizeable influence not only over rival guitar manufacturers, but also on the development of American popular music. Although the volume produced by the L-5 was not nearly sufficient for single-note work to be heard in large band settings, it was

considerably louder than the banjo or ukulele, which until then had been used more commonly in jazz bands. The L-5 helped to define the role of the guitar at this time, and banjo players deserted to it in droves. By the '30s the vast majority of jazz bands featured a guitar rather than a banjo.

This period also saw players like Eddie Lang taking the first tentative steps towards viewing the guitar as a serious solo instrument. In spite of the fact that Django Reinhardt (*see* page 116) championed the European-made Selmer Maccaferri, almost all of the early American jazz pioneers played a Gibson L-5.

During the first 11 years of production, the L-5, with its famed dark sunburst finish, which Gibson had christened "Cremona Brown", scarcely changed. In 1934 the body was

> **THE HISTORIC GIBSON L-5, DESIGNED BY LLOYD LOAR**

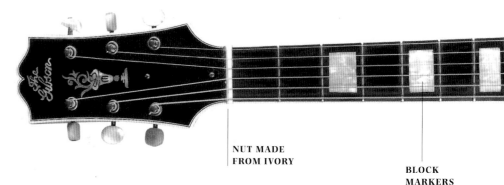

NUT MADE FROM IVORY

BLOCK MARKERS

gibson L-5 — (1922)

enlarged by an inch to 17 inches (43 centimetres) and a cross-bracing system added to further boost strength and volume. The first major change took place in 1939 when Gibson produced the L-5P, with a cutaway on the lower bout improving access from the fifteenth to the seventeenth fret.

The suffix "P" stood for "Premier", which until 1948 was how Gibson described their cutaway instruments – in 1948 the name was changed to L-5C, the letter "C" indicating a cutaway from then on. The original L-5 stayed in production until 1958; the cutaway model was discontinued in 1982, but re-introduced briefly in 1994.

The L-5 also provided a blueprint for another significant Gibson archtop instrument

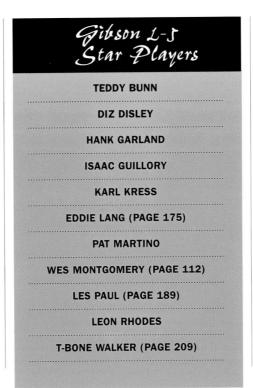

Gibson L-5 Star Players

TEDDY BUNN

DIZ DISLEY

HANK GARLAND

ISAAC GUILLORY

KARL KRESS

EDDIE LANG (PAGE 175)

PAT MARTINO

WES MONTGOMERY (PAGE 112)

LES PAUL (PAGE 189)

LEON RHODES

T-BONE WALKER (PAGE 209)

that followed – the Super 400, launched in 1934. So-called because its list price was $400 (a sizeable investment in post-Depression America), this model was fitted with optional pick-ups, marking the manufacturer's transition into the age of the electric guitar. With a maple body of almost 46 cm (18 in), an almost 32-cm (12.5-in) upper bout and nearly 65-cm (25.5-in) neck, it was possible to produce even greater volume than the L-5. In 1937, Gibson further increased the size of the upper bout to just over 34 cm (13.5 in).

In 1951, standard electrified versions of both guitars were made available: the L-5SEC quickly established itself as the guitar of choice for the majority of notable jazz players over the coming two decades.

RAISED PICK GUARD

FLOATING BRIDGE

TRAPEZE TAILPIECE

F-HOLE

61

the predominant trend among guitar makers of the '20s was to create louder instruments. In the era that preceded the development of the magnetic pick-up, designers sought a variety of ingenious solutions, one of the most innovative of which was developed by the Dopyera Brothers, a family of Slovakian immigrants living in California. The "resonator" guitar, with which the family name remained closely linked, has its own unique place in the history

of the instrument. The best-known model is the original National Style O.

The impetus to design the resonator came about when banjo maker John Dopyera was approached by vaudeville guitarist George Beauchamp. His request was simple: he wanted a louder instrument. Dopyera's creative solution was to integrate the acoustic principles that drive a regular loudspeaker. He built a guitar with a floating aluminium "cone" fitted into the top of the guitar's body and fixed to the bridge. Vibrations from the

strings were passed through the bridge saddles and transferred to the cone which "resonated" back and forth in a similar way to a loudspeaker. The sound created was a distinctive metallic jangle. Although it wasn't to the liking of all guitarists, it could produce far greater volume than any conventional guitar. Resonator guitars have often been used as bottleneck instruments, and are most widely played by folk, blues and country musicians.

The first resonator guitars were built in 1926 for the National guitar company, in

national style O

(1926)

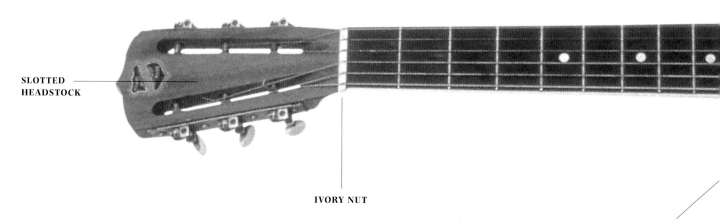

SLOTTED HEADSTOCK

IVORY NUT

NECK JOINS BODY AT TWELFTH FRET

NATIONAL STYLE 0 RESONATOR FROM THE LATE '20S

which one of the Dopyera brothers – Louis – had invested. The following year, however, John, Rudy and Ed Dopyera broke away to form their own Dobro (DOpyera BROthers) company, producing an alternative resonator guitar. The principal difference between guitars produced by the two companies was that most of the National models not only featured aluminium resonators but they also had aluminium bodies; the Dobro-branded guitars were conventional flat-top instruments built from wood with the resonator panel being fixed into the top of the soundboard.

The split between the two companies resulted in lengthy legal wrangling. During the Depression, National struggled to survive and in 1932 they were bought out by Louis Dopyera, who merged National and Dobro into a single company. But the resonator guitar never quite took off as well as expected. Towards the end of the decade National turned their attention to the coming electrical age, and the rights to the Dobro name were sold off to the Regal company. During the '60s, Mosrite

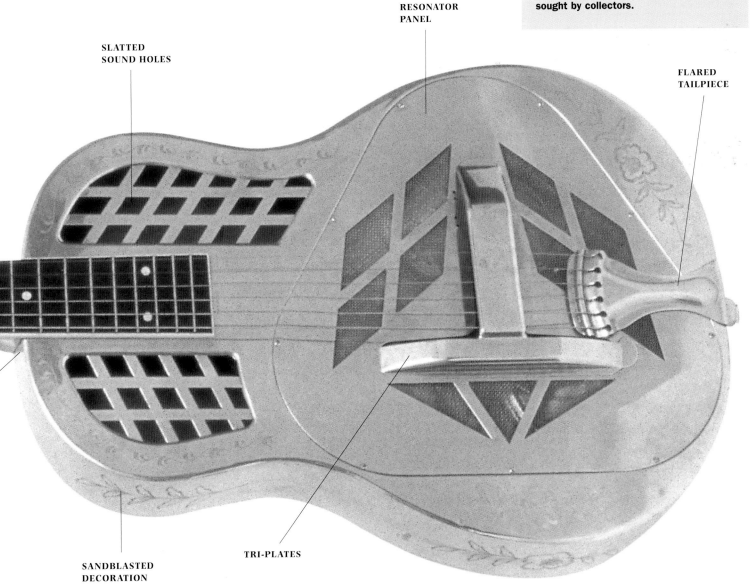

SLATTED
SOUND HOLES

RESONATOR
PANEL

FLARED
TAILPIECE

SANDBLASTED
DECORATION

TRI-PLATES

Variations

Resonator guitars have appeared in a number of different designs. The earliest models, produced by National in 1926, were known as "triplate" resonators, featuring three aluminium cones, the centres of which were connected to one another, and to the bridge saddle. The best-known National guitar is the original Style O, which has a large, single resonating cone. Although many wood-bodied resonators have been produced, it is the early metal-bodied instruments that are ranked among the most attractive guitars ever made because of the intricate sand-blasted decorative motifs they often featured. Consequently, they are widely sought by collectors.

64

SLIDE PLAYER BONNIE RAITT, ONE OF THE FINEST EXPONENTS OF THE STYLE "O"

produced Dobro-branded resonators, successfully creating 12-string and bass versions. Later in the decade, Emil Dopyera, the son of Ed, began making resonators under the company name Original Musical Instruments. This company changed hands several times in the '80s until it was acquired by Gibson in 1993, who have since continued to market both wooden and metal resonator guitars under the famous Dobro brand.

Over the years, many different guitar companies have produced variations on the resonator principle. Nonetheless, the idea is so strongly linked with the name of the Dopyera brothers that resonator guitars – irrespective of the way in which they are branded – are more often generically referred to as "dobros".

The resonator, although perhaps a footnote in the history of the guitar, has retained a sturdy loyal following over the years, especially in the blues and country fields of music.

fender telecaster

(1950)

ASYMMETRIC HEADSTOCK

BOLT-ON NECK OF SOLID ASH

as early as 1947 engineer Paul Bigsby and country musician Merle Travis had produced a small number of influential solid-body electric guitars. However, it was three years later that Leo Fender, formerly the owner of an electrical repair shop, created the first mass-produced instruments. Engineer George Fullerton joined Fender in 1948. Together they set about design-ing a full-production solid-body electric guitar. Although Bigsby may have got there first, it was Fender's vision that resulted in the development and eventual mass-popularity of the electric guitar. Although Bigsby is now best remembered for his vibrato unit (also designed for Merle Travis), the influence of the Bigsby guitar can be seen in the styling of Fender's first designs, especially in the asymmetric head-stock.

The first model Fender produced – albeit in tiny quantities – was a single-pick-up instru-ment called the Esquire, which appeared in April 1950. A few months later a similarly

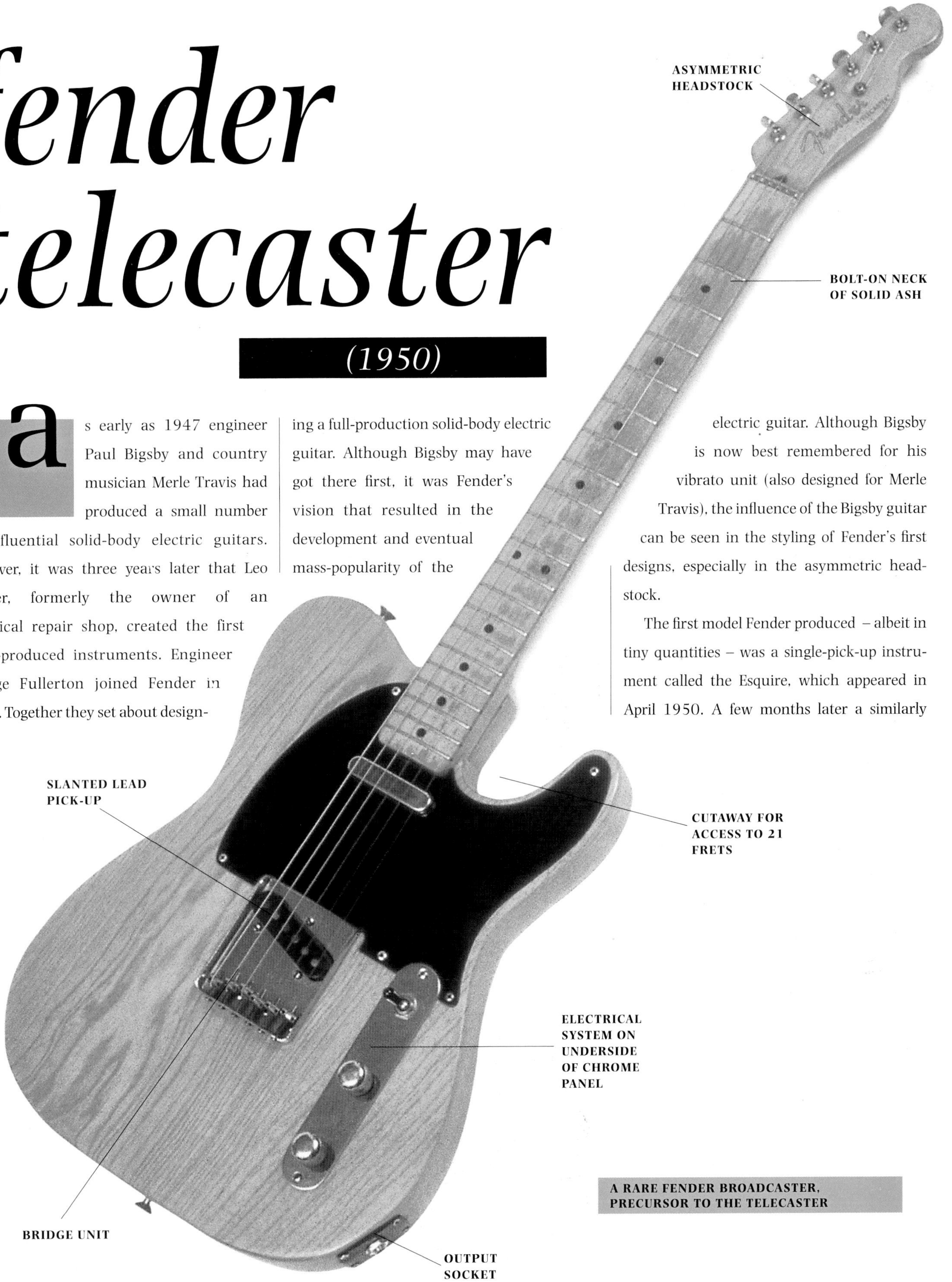

65

SLANTED LEAD PICK-UP

CUTAWAY FOR ACCESS TO 21 FRETS

ELECTRICAL SYSTEM ON UNDERSIDE OF CHROME PANEL

A RARE FENDER BROADCASTER, PRECURSOR TO THE TELECASTER

BRIDGE UNIT

OUTPUT SOCKET

66

small run of twin-pick-up Esquires was made. Fender took these guitars to one of the national trade shows, but was met with something approaching incredulity. Quite simply, few took the maker or the instrument seriously – fewer still could see any commercial potential for a solid-body electric guitar.

In November 1950, undeterred and wanting to differentiate between the two models, Fender renamed the twin-pick-up guitar the Broadcaster. This was the first instrument that he put into general production. But there were further problems to face: early the following year Fender was informed that Gretsch already produced a drum kit called the Broadkaster, and he was legally obliged to change the name of his guitar. It was Fender's salesman Don Randall who thought up the new name – the Telecaster. Remaining necks that bore the Broadcaster motif had the name cut out leaving just the Fender logo – these rarities are known by collectors as "No-casters".

Without a formal distribution network, most of the early sales were made either at bandstands or direct from the factory. One of the first guitarists to take to the Telecaster was country player Jimmy Bryant, and to this day this guitar remains the most popular country electric by a considerable margin. A unique feature of the instrument that began to attract guitarists was the cutaway that allowed unrestricted access to the upper register. Gibson cutaways, such as the popular ES-175, allowed reasonably free movement up to the eighteenth fret – the Telecaster extended the range of the guitar to 22 frets.

Part of the enduring appeal of the Telecaster is its sheer no-frills simplicity. The original finish was only available as plain vanilla, and there were no fancy contours or neck inlays. They were guitars aimed at the working musician. Fender's second-in-command George Fullerton defended the basic design: "Did you ever see a working cowboy? He's dirty and got rough boots on and heavy leather on his pants... we kind of looked at guitar players as being working cowboys."

Of course, there has to be more than an austere design to explain why this guitar has remained so popular (and in production) for almost 50 years. That reason is the unique Telecaster sound. The bridge and pick-up are a part of a single self-contained unit. The strings pass through the body of the guitar from the

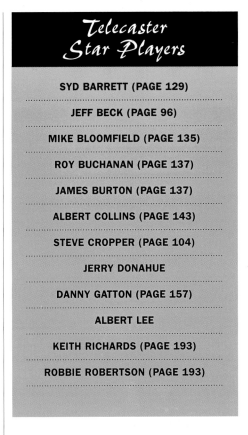

Telecaster Star Players

SYD BARRETT (PAGE 129)

JEFF BECK (PAGE 96)

MIKE BLOOMFIELD (PAGE 135)

ROY BUCHANAN (PAGE 137)

JAMES BURTON (PAGE 137)

ALBERT COLLINS (PAGE 143)

STEVE CROPPER (PAGE 104)

JERRY DONAHUE

DANNY GATTON (PAGE 157)

ALBERT LEE

KEITH RICHARDS (PAGE 193)

ROBBIE ROBERTSON (PAGE 193)

67

back, anchoring the bridge unit firmly to the body and increasing the sustain. The hallmark Telecaster sound is the "biting" treble of the back pick-up. This is produced through the slanting of the pick-up so that the sound from the top string is taken from a point much closer to the bridge saddle than the bottom string.

MANIC STREET PREACHERS: TELECASTERS
REMAIN AS POPULAR AS EVER

**HEADSTOCK
WITH GIBSON
"BELL"**

gibson had already estab-
lished itself as an early
leader in the electrification
of the guitar with Lloyd
Loar's experiments with pick-ups in the '20s
(*see* page 50), and the eventual development of
the ES-150 – in 1934 the first production line
electro-acoustic guitar. However, the success of
Leo Fender's Broadcaster created panic in a
company which only a few years earlier had
laughed when guitarist Les Paul tried to sell
them his prototype solid-body, the Log.

So it was that "the kid with the broomstick

guitar", as Gibson management had named
Paul, was recalled and invited to collaborate
on the design for a new solid-body instrument.
In 1952, the first of the legendary models to
bear his name came off the production line –
the Gibson Les Paul Gold Top.

Although the Les Paul is now viewed as
something of a design classic, the guitar was
not a great success. Fearing that the bright gold
finish was off-putting for working musicians, in
1958 Gibson produced the more subdued Les
Paul Standard – an identical model with a more
conservative three-tone sunburst finish. By this

**"CROWN"
INLAYS**

gibson les paul

(1952)

**POSITION
PICK-UP
SELECTOR
SWITCH**

**SINGLE COIL
"PAF" PICK-UPS**

**SUNBURST
FINISH**

**RAISED
PICK GUARD**

**FIXED
TAILPIECE**

**GIBSON LES PAUL STANDARD – ONE
OF THE "BIG THREE"**

Variations

Over the past 45 years, there have been a number of Les Paul variations. Some, such as the single-pick-up Junior and Special models, featured cutaways on either side of the body, and are thus not immediately recognizable as Les Pauls.

Later variations incorporated certain changes to hardware and finish, such as the three-pick-up Custom and Artisan models, or the Anniversary, Heritage and Studio editions.

time Fender dominated the market, and in 1961, after producing only 2,000 instruments, Gibson abandoned the Les Paul design.

A peculiar reversal of fortunes began in the early '60s when the Les Paul Standard found itself popular with a new generation of young blues guitarists. Players such as Mike Bloomfield and Eric Clapton valued its "thick" sound and remarkable sustain, and as the decade unfolded these relatively rare instruments began to command very high prices. In 1968 Gibson brought out a reissue Les Paul Gold Top. Although this was a great success for Gibson, it seems somewhat surprising that it was not until 1975 that the Standard was made available again.

The design of the Les Paul guitars leant heavily on the well-established traditions of Gibson archtop models, such as the immediately recognizable symmetrical headstock (*see* picture). It also incorporated many of Les Paul's own designs, such as the glued-in neck and trapeze tailpiece. The body was made from mahogany with a 22-fret rosewood fingerboard. The electrics consisted of a pair of single-coil P90 pick-ups, each with adjustable pole pieces. Tone and volume controls were provided for each pick-up and a toggle switch allowed either or both pick-ups to be activated.

SLASH OF GUNS N' ROSES WITH HIS LOW-SLUNG STANDARD

70

RETRO-ROCKER LENNY KRAVITZ, AN
AVOWED LES PAUL MAN

Les Paul Star Players

DUANE ALLMAN (PAGE 127)

JEFF BECK (PAGE 96)

DICKEY BETTS (PAGE 132)

PAUL BUTTERFIELD

BERNARD BUTLER

ERIC CLAPTON (PAGE 141)

GRAHAM COXON

ROBERT FRIPP

PETER FRAMPTON

ACE FREHLEY

BILLY GIBBONS

PETER GREEN (PAGE 160)

STEVE JONES

FREDDIE KING (PAGE 173)

PAUL KOSSOFF (PAGE 174)

LENNY KRAVITZ

JEFF LYNNE

HARVEY MANDEL

BOB MARLEY

GARY MOORE

JIMMY PAGE (PAGE 114)

CARL PERKINS

JOE PERRY

RANDY RHODES

BRIAN ROBERTSON

MICK RONSON

SONNY SHARROCK

SLASH

JOHNNY THUNDERS (PAGE 202)

JOE WALSH

NEIL YOUNG (PAGE 216)

t he Fender Stratocaster is probably the most significantly popular electric guitar ever built. In the field of rock music it is not an exaggeration to say that nearly every notable player has at some time used a "Strat".

There were two factors that brought about the development of the Stratocaster. One was the fact that Leo Fender would go out of his way to elicit feedback from his customers – the musicians who used his instruments night after night. He was desperate to know exactly what they did and didn't like about the Telecaster. The other factor was the serious threat posed by the launch in 1952 of Gibson's Les Paul solid-body. With its exotic gold finish

and plush archtop contours, the bare simplicity of the Telecaster seemed rather dull and ugly by comparison. In short, as Fender salesman Don Randall said: "We felt the need to upgrade and provide something that gave them a little competition."

It was clear to Fender and his colleagues that they needed to produce an upmarket alternative to the Telecaster. Rather than beefing up his original model – which was beginning to establish itself – he chose to design a new instrument from scratch.

Crucial to this development were the comments given by western swing guitarist Bill Carson. An early user of the Telecaster, Carson liked the instrument, but he could also see many areas for improvement. He provided

Switching

The original Stratocasters had a three-way pick-up selector switch, however some players found that by forcing the toggle between locking positions they were able to use combinations of the front or back two pick-ups. This produced an unusual sound which has often been referred to as "out of phase". In fact, the two signals are not technically out of phase, it is the interaction of two closely related signals which causes the cancellation or emphasis of certain frequencies. One of the Strat's star players, Mark Knopfler, combines the bridge and middle pick-up to achieve his characteristic sound. In 1977 Fender finally acknowledged this effect by fitting a five-way selector switch.

fender
stratocaster

(1952)

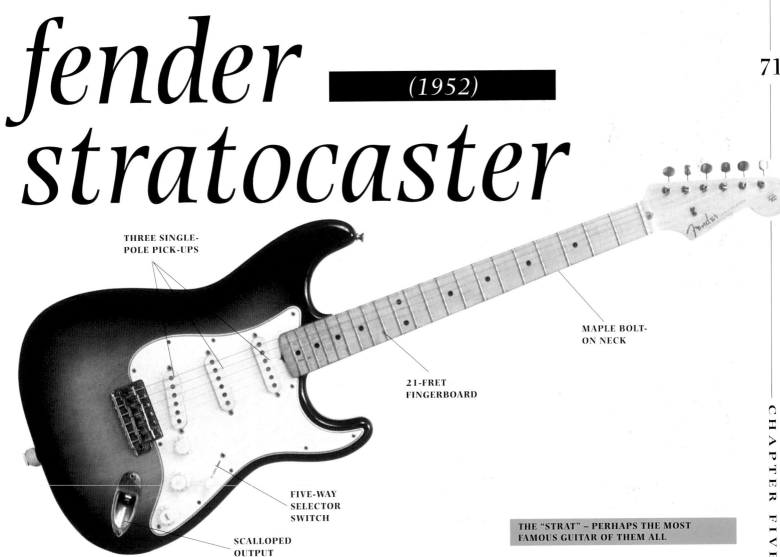

THREE SINGLE-
POLE PICK-UPS

MAPLE BOLT-
ON NECK

21-FRET
FINGERBOARD

FIVE-WAY
SELECTOR
SWITCH

SCALLOPED
OUTPUT
SOCKET

THE "STRAT" – PERHAPS THE MOST
FAMOUS GUITAR OF THEM ALL

CHAPTER FIVE

CHAPTER FIVE

Fender worked closely on the design with draughtsman Freddie Tavares. The twin-horned shape, while revolutionary for a guitar, was in fact an extension of their design for the Precision bass, the first solid-body electric bass – another of Fender's revolutionary achievements. The lower "horn" on the Stratocaster's body was cut away to give access to the 22-fret fingerboard – much like the Telecaster. However, the asymmetric upper bout, which protruded almost as far as the twelfth fret, gave the instrument a vital balance which the Telecaster lacked.

The Strat, with its smooth curves and sheared surface that made it more comfortable to play, quickly established itself as the premier solid-body electric guitar. Fender took a further jump ahead of his competitors in 1959 when he presented his wares to the Frankfurt Music trade show, which few non-European companies attended at that time. So it was that Fender guitars began to sell in Europe to such an extent that by the middle of the '60s the company is thought to have exported more instruments than all other American manufacturers put together.

At the beginning of the electric era Gibson had a heritage of no fewer than 60 years of guitar-making whereas Fender had none at all. It was partially this lack of traditional knowledge that gave Fender his revolutionary approach to guitar-making. He faced each new problem as an engineer (which he was) rather than as a luthier, which meant having to find solutions from scratch.

Whatever arguments are put forward as to who was responsible for "inventing" the solid-body electric guitar, there can be no doubting that Leo Fender was the single most important figure in the past 50 years of guitar-making. The enduring popularity of the Stratocaster remains a unique testament to his brilliance and foresight.

Fender with his own specification for a dream instrument. Carson wanted a guitar with individually adjustable bridge saddles, four or five pick-ups, and a vibrato or tremolo arm that could be heavily detuned in either direction *and* return to position with the guitar still in tune. Most radical of all, however, he wanted the shape modifying so that it was comfortable when played either standing or sitting down – the sharp edges at the back of existing guitars dug into the ribs when played over long periods.

KULA SHAKER'S CRISPIAN MILLS PLAYS A STRAT

Some of the models produced by the Gretsch company during the '50s are among the most attractive and collectable of all vintage guitars. Especially highly rated are the series of instruments endorsed by Chet Atkins, one of the legends of country music (*see* page 94).

The Gretsch company was founded in 1883 when German immigrant Friedrich Gretsch opened up a music store in New York City. During the early '30s his son Fred began to manufacture steel-string guitars from a small factory in Brooklyn. The association with Chet Atkins developed in the early '50s when the company's in-house demonstrator Jimmie Webster – himself a well-respected country picker – approached Atkins with a

EDDIE COCHRAN, ONE OF ROCK 'N' ROLL'S FIRST GUITAR HEROES

gretsch

(1955)

74

BIGSBY-DESIGNED VIBRATO ARM

DECORATIVE F-HOLES

PICK-UP SELECTOR SWITCH

DE ARMOND DYNASONIC PICK-UP

OVERALL VOLUME CONTROL

GRETSCH "CHET ATKINS" TENNESSEAN

view to his endorsing Gretsch guitars. Until then Atkins had always used D'Angelico guitars, and was evidently perfectly happy to keep using them. It was only when Webster offered him the chance to design his own instrument from scratch that "Mr Guitar" agreed.

The first Chet Atkins model was the 6120, launched in 1954. This was a hollow-body archtop instrument, featuring "f-holes", twin De Armond pick-ups with independent volume controls and overall volume and tone controls, and a three-way selector switch. The finish was in the ranch style "amber red": the country link was reinforced not only by the Gretsch "G-brand" but the beautifully ornate "cowboy" fingerboard inlays.

At Atkins' own suggestion, the guitar was equipped with a Bigsby vibrato arm, and metal bridge and nut fittings. In 1962 the 6120 appeared with a new "thinline" double cutaway body. Although the new instruments were hollow-bodied, they no longer had operational sound holes – the "f-holes" were painted on as a design feature.

In spite of the country association, the 6120 and other models in the Chet Atkins series – such as the Country Gentleman and Tennessean – also gained a wide following among the early rock 'n' roll musicians like Eddie Cochran. Atkins maintained his link with Gretsch right up to 1981 when he signed a new endorsement deal with Gibson which resulted in a signature nylon-string electro-acoustic guitar and, in 1987, the Gibson Country Gent.

The collectability of vintage Gretsches – including classics like the White Falcon and Double Anniversary, and the rarer White Penguin – is more down to their appearance than their sound or playability. The sharp corners of the Gretsch wide body made it uncomfortable for some guitarists. Other drawbacks were that the bridge saddles had no individual adjustability for intonation, and that the electrics were not always laid out in the most logical way.

According to some collectors, vintage Gretsches also tend to be less robust than some contemporary models, with their glues and bindings sometimes deteriorating and resulting in costly repair work. During the lifetime of the company, Gretsch also produced acoustic and solid-body instruments, but it is for their hollow-body electrics that they are famed.

In 1967 Gretsch sold the company to Baldwin, which continued production of Gretsch guitars until 1981 when the Brooklyn factory was closed down. But in 1989 the brand name copyright was returned to the Gretsch family, after which a new range of instruments based on the classic '50s designs was produced in Japan.

THUMBNAIL FRET MARKERS

ZERO FRET

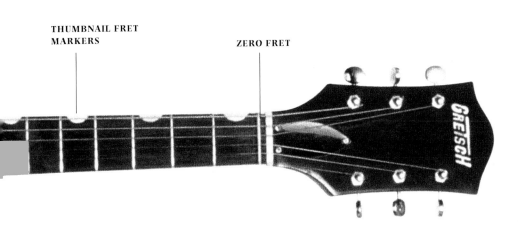

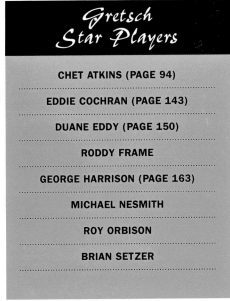

Gretsch Star Players

CHET ATKINS (PAGE 94)

EDDIE COCHRAN (PAGE 143)

DUANE EDDY (PAGE 150)

RODDY FRAME

GEORGE HARRISON (PAGE 163)

MICHAEL NESMITH

ROY ORBISON

BRIAN SETZER

chet atkins series

gibson ES-300 series

(1958)

1958 was a busy year for Gibson. Not only did it see the launch of a daring range of revolutionary solid-body instruments, but also the unveiling of the ES-335, the first of a series of guitars which combined the characteristics of a hollow-bodied instrument with some of the advantages of a solid body. Although the Electric Spanish hollow-bodied instruments had long been established, they could be problematic when played at high volumes, the sound of the loudspeaker causing the strings to vibrate in sympathy, creating a loop of unpleasant feedback. The ES-335 attempted to overcome this problem by using a solid block of hard wood which was connected to the neck

BRITISH ROCK 'N' ROLLER DAVE EDMUNDS PLAYS A GIBSON ES-335

Gibson Model Codes

Unlike Fender, who during the '50s and '60s only produced a single standardized version of their designs, Gibson archtop and hollow-body instruments were available in a wide variety of variations, which can be identified from the suffixes used:

CODE	STYLE
ES	Electric Spanish – hollow-bodied instruments with single fitted pick-up.
T	Narrow "thinline" body thickness.
C	Cutaway in the bout.
D	Two fitted pick-ups.
SV	Stereo and Varitone wiring.

and passed through the centre of the body, preventing it from acting as an acoustic chamber. The upper and lower bouts (*see* page 28) were hollow, each with its own "f-hole". The ES-335 was also the first of Gibson's electric guitars to feature a symmetrical cutaway either side of the neck joint. Shortly after the ES-335, Gibson launched ES-345 and ES-355 models, both of which had the same unique body shape, but were offered with different visual features and alternative electrical systems, such as stereo wiring and the notorious six-way Variphone tone selector switch, which did not prove very popular with guitarists.

The sound produced by the ES-300 series is warm and mellow. Over the years it has proved to be a popular choice with jazz musicians. Rock and blues players have also made extensive use of these instruments, prizing their pure and lengthy sustain. Among the most noted users is bluesman B.B. King, who famously refers to whatever ES-355 he happens to be using as "Lucille" (*see* page 110). Gibson didn't seem to crack the feedback problem to King's satisfaction, since he is known to have stuffed towels into the f-holes to prevent the body vibrating at exceptionally loud festivals. Nonetheless, he was happy to endorse the instrument, his own signature model appearing during the early '80s.

The ES-335 has remained in production since it was first launched in 1958. Like other guitars of this vintage, collectors and players alike have been known to argue the debatable merits of models produced during dif-

ferent periods. Guitars dating from between 1958 and the early '60s are the most eagerly sought, especially the "blonde" models of which only 200 were built originally. The sound of the early versions is also highly rated. They were at first fitted with the same "stud" tailpieces that were used on Les Pauls at that time. These units were plugged through the top of the guitar into the central body block. During the early '60s, Gibson replaced them with "trapeze" style tailpieces which supported the strings from the base of the guitar. Some players felt that this "improvement" reduced the ES-335's legendary sustain.

The influential symmetrical shape of the ES-300 series can be seen in the Gibson SG ("solid guitar") which first appeared in 1961.

MULTIPLE "PARALLEL" BINDING

PICKGUARD

FLOATING BRIDGE

BIGSBY VIBRATO ARM

FORTY YEARS OLD AND STILL GOING STRONG – THE GIBSON ES-355

by the end of the '50s, a pattern of dominance had emerged in the market for the solid-body electric: there were only two major names – Fender and Gibson. Although Gibson's Les Paul was well established, the two main Fender guitars – the Stratocaster and Telecaster – had established their own unassailable markets. With sales of the Les Paul beginning to flag, Gibson, a company with a proud heritage that went back to the nineteenth century, were struggling to compete with rivals who were barely 10 years old.

So it was that Gibson company president Ted McCarty set out to prove to the guitar world that, in his words, "Gibson was more modern than all the rest." To this end, in 1958 he designed and launched three new models, all of which constituted a radical departure from traditional guitar design.

Construction

The original Flying V design featured a 22-fret rosewood fingerboard, the unique line of the body giving unmatched access to the upper register. Deviating from the traditional mahogany used on the Les Paul models, the body of the Flying V was made from the lighter African limba wood (sometimes also known as korina). The two pick-ups were standard Gibson PAFs (an abbreviation for "Patent Applied For"). The guitar had a volume control for each pick-up and an overall tone filter. The original model featured a front-mounted socket in the bottom corner – on some models this was part of the scratchplate, otherwise known as the fingerplate.

The three new instruments – the Flying V, the Moderne and the Explorer – were certainly dramatic, their designs incorporating strong modernist lines rather than the traditional curves usually associated with the guitar. Bold as it was, however, McCarty's experiment was an immediate failure, all three instruments receiving a hostile reception from retailers and players alike. Although they were typically well-crafted, high-quality instruments – nobody would have expected anything less from Gibson – in their original forms, none stayed in production for more than a couple of years. Indeed, the Moderne – whose shape was rather like a Flying V cut along the body below the pick-ups – never even made it to the production line. It wasn't until 1980 that a limited-edition "re-issue" was made available.

The Explorer fared little better – fewer than 100 were made and it was withdrawn within a year. The oddly balanced shape found its strong lines toned down by gentle curves in 1963, when it re-emerged as the Firebird. However, the Explorer's later popularity in the '70s, when it, too, was

THE FLYING V – TOO RADICAL FOR GUITARISTS OF THE '50S

HUMBUCKING PICK-UPS

TAILPIECE

OUTPUT SOCKET

gibson flying V

(1958)

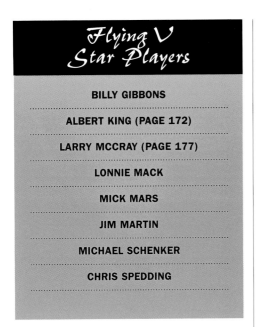

Flying V
Star Players

BILLY GIBBONS

ALBERT KING (PAGE 172)

LARRY McCRAY (PAGE 177)

LONNIE MACK

MICK MARS

JIM MARTIN

MICHAEL SCHENKER

CHRIS SPEDDING

re-issued, showed that its design also had been ahead of its time.

The Flying V has proved to be the most enduring of Ted McCarty's designs, even if at the time it failed to stem the growing popularity of the Fender Stratocaster. Like the Explorer, few (little more than 100) original Flying Vs were made and production ended in 1960. However, by the middle of the decade, it had established something of a cult reputation among rock and blues guitarists, and original models started to accrue considerable value. Consequently a variation on the original design went into production between 1967 and 1979. This was replaced by the V2, which featured "V"-shaped pick-ups. Finally, in 1983, Gibson re-introduced the original Flying V design.

The Gibson story during this period shows a traditional guitar maker struggling to stamp its mark on a new market. The shapes that Gibson unleashed in 1958 were unquestionably bold, but, as future manufacturers would often discover to their cost, few guitarists actually want a radical new design. That said, McCarty's futuristic attempt at redefining the solid-body guitar has, to some extent, been vindicated by the growing popularity of his original designs over the years.

K.K. DOWNING OF JUDAS PRIEST, ONE OF A SELECT GROUP OF FLYING V ROCKERS

In 1961, Gibson found themselves in safer waters as they produced a popular new variation on the original Les Paul design – the Les Paul SG ("Solid Guitar"), now viewed as a classic in its own right. Les Paul disliked its new symmetrical body shape, which took the sharp cutaway of the Les Paul and duplicated it on the upper bout, and asked for his signature logo to be removed. From then on it became known as the Gibson SG.

Swiss-born immigrant Adolph Rickenbacker formed the Electro String Company in 1931, along with Paul Barth and George Beauchamp, two employees of the California-based National company. Beauchamp had formerly been instrumental in the development of the resonator guitar (*see* page 62) and was also one of the pioneering names in the development of the magnetic pick-up. The Rickenbacker brand name was assured a place in history by having produced some of the first electric guitars, but after Beauchamp's death in 1940, Rickenbacker struggled to compete with the dominant Gibson Electric Spanish ranges. In 1953 he sold his company to a Californian businessman named Frank C. Hall. Although this transition brought an end to a pioneering era, under Hall's guidance the company produced a number of significant "classic" instruments.

In 1954 Rickenbacker launched its first solid-body instrument – the Combo. The shape showed a stark contrast with the guitars being produced by Gibson and Fender. Although the line was not highly successful, it proved to be the first appearance of the classic Rickenbacker body shape which would become so popular during the '60s. In 1958 the Capri series was launched, showing a refinement of the Combo shape with a "sharpening" of the features. It was when this basic shape was applied to a thinline, hollow-body instrument that the "classic" Rickenbacker emerged.

The first great player to make widespread use of Rickenbacker guitars was James Burton, who came to fame playing on the hits of Rick Nelson. He also tested out prototypes for new models. But it was in the early '60s that the Rickenbacker hollow-body instruments achieved a new level of popularity when the short-scale 325 models were used by John Lennon and George Harrison of the Beatles.

The Rickenbacker 360-12 hollow-body

THE JAM: PAUL WELLER (LEFT) AND BRUCE FOXTON (RIGHT) WERE BOTH RICKENBACKER PLAYERS

Export Models

Although the success of the Beatles help to make Rickenbacker an international name, the original guitars were difficult to come by outside the US. In 1964 a British agent launched the Rickenbacker range in the UK, but requested a number of alterations, the most dramatic being the replacement of the distinctive "slash" sound hole with a traditional f-hole. To differentiate them from the standard US models they were given new numbers: the 325, 335 and 345 models were known respectively as the 1996, 1997, 1998. The "export" Rickenbackers are now rare collector's pieces.

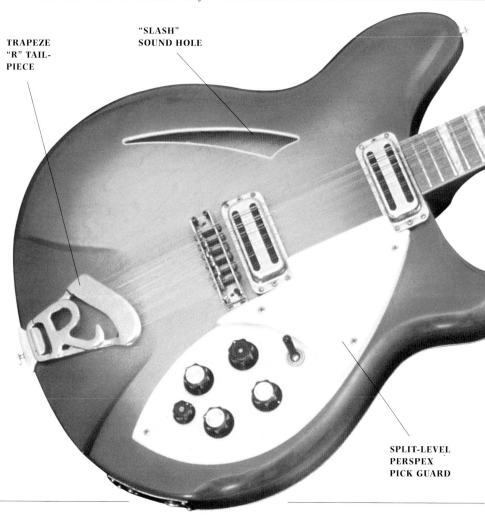

TRAPEZE "R" TAIL-PIECE

"SLASH" SOUND HOLE

SPLIT-LEVEL PERSPEX PICK GUARD

(shown below) was the first popular electric 12-string guitar, and is perhaps the most significant instrument in their later history. During the Beatles' 1964 US tour George Harrison was presented with one of the first production models. Shortly afterwards he began using it on recording sessions, one of its earliest uses being the opening chimes of the single 'A Hard Day's Night'. The following year, Roger McGuinn formed the Byrds and the 360-12 formed the basis for their entire sound.

Rickenbacker Hollow-Body Star Players

PETER BUCK (PAGE 137)

GEORGE HARRISON (PAGE 163)

JOHN LENNON

ROGER McGUINN (PAGE 178)

WENDY MELVOIN

PAUL WELLER

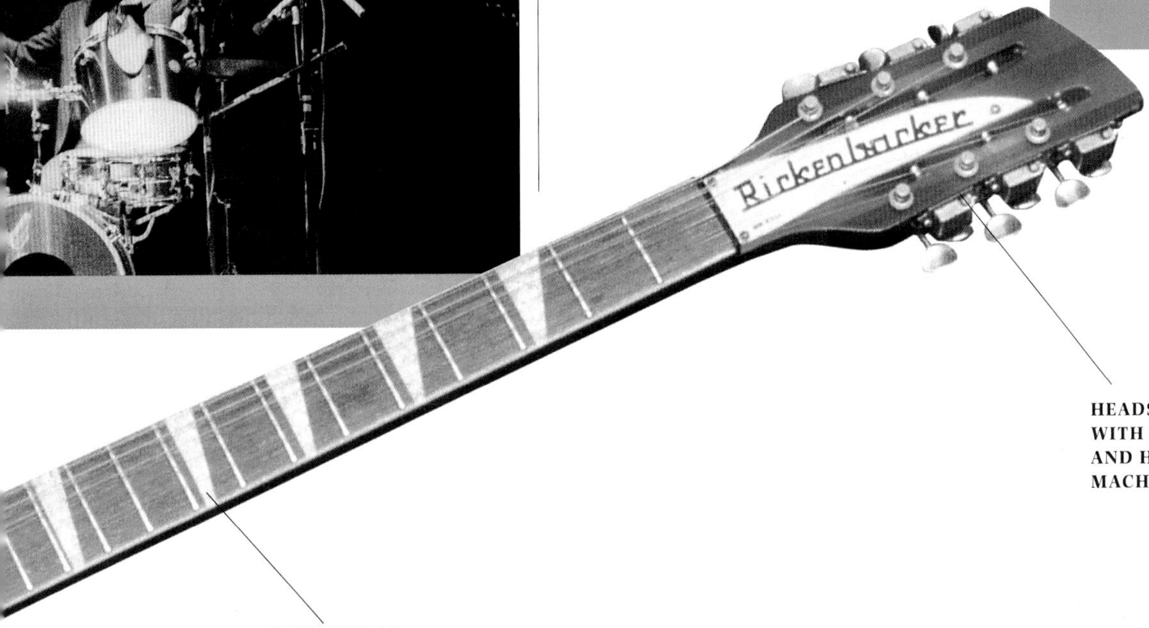

81

**HEADSTOCK
WITH VERTICAL
AND HORIZONTAL
MACHINE HEADS**

**TRIANGULAR
INLAYS**

(1964)

rickenbacker hollow-bodies

t he American Ovation company is the most significant manufacturer of acoustic guitars to have emerged since the war. The company was founded in 1966 as a division of Kaman Aerospace, a company owned by a wealthy industrialist called Charles Kaman, who had made his fortune in designing and manufacturing helicopter blades. A keen musician, Kaman used his extensive engineering expertise to produce a design that would revolutionize the world of the steel-string acoustic and electro-acoustic guitars.

The fundamental design principle saw a complete overhaul of the traditional acoustic guitar body. The back and sides were replaced with a single, one-piece bowl, crafted using a newly developed fibreglass called Lyrachord. With no joins or body strutting needed to support the top of the guitar, the sound could no longer be trapped in the corners of the soundbox. This duly created a purer tone and greater volume.

The Balladeer was the first Ovation guitar to be launched. The early models, produced in 1966, featured a top made from sitka spruce with a cross-bracing system on the underside. The neck construction was also unique. It was built from mahogany with a maple fingerboard, and a steel truss rod was set inside an aluminium channel passing the full length of the fingerboard.

In 1970, the Balladeer was made available as an electro-acoustic instrument. It was here that Ovation found their greatest success. A traditional problem for live performers is that the miking-up of an acoustic guitar poses all kinds of logistical difficulties for the sound engineer – variations in tone and volume, depending on the position of the guitar in relation to the microphone, feedback and sound spillage from other instruments. One attempted solution had been to fit pick-ups which clamped on the inside of the sound hole. However, this meant only the string vibrations were picked up, creating a sound more like a semi-acoustic electric guitar.

Ovation's solution was to create a unique electro-acoustic instrument which had six individual piezo-electric transducer pick-ups on the underside of the bridge saddle. Crystals in each piezo unit generated electrical energy when placed under mechanical strain, such as the vibrations of the strings from the bridge above, as well as the sound from within the "bowl" coming from below. The overall effect was to create a far more natural acoustic guitar sound when the instrument was plugged

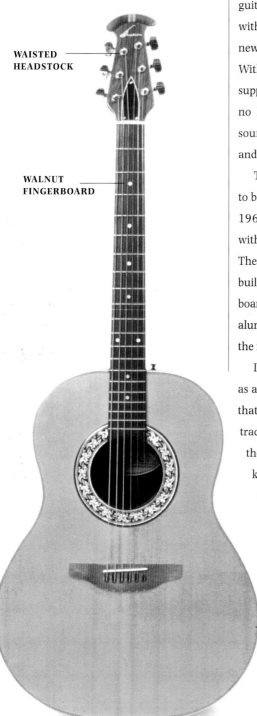

WAISTED HEADSTOCK

WALNUT FINGERBOARD

BODY BOWL MADE FROM LYRACHORD

Variations

They have created steel-string, nylon-string and 12-string instruments, all available as acoustic or electro-acoustic guitars. They have also experimented with a variety of combinations of natural and man-made materials. From 1978, Ovation produced its most noted (and expensive) range of guitars – the Adamas. This range of instruments featured the Lyrachord body bowl, still used for all Ovations, but the top was made from a laminate of birch, carbon fibres and plastics. The central sound hole was replaced by 22 smaller holes of varying size towards the front of the body.

(1970)

ovation

82

JOAN ARMATRADING: THE OVATION IS NOW VIRTUALLY
SYNONYMOUS WITH THE TERM "ELECTRO-ACOUSTIC"

into an amplifier. It also guaranteed the player a consistency of sound irrespective of venue.

Since the development of the Balladeer, Ovation has largely dominated the professional electro-acoustic market, and by the beginning of the '80s Ovations had become as common a feature on the wish-lists of aspiring players as Stratocasters or Les Pauls. They remained out of the price range of many non-professional users until Ovation launched the Matrix budget range, and then expanded into the Applause diffusion line.

balladeer

Ovation Star Players

CHAPTER SIX

RELATIVES AND ODDITIES

UNUSUAL GUITARS

84

from the seventeenth century on, the guitar went through a large number of structural changes. Luthiers experimented with almost every aspect of the guitar's construction, attempting to obtain bigger sound, better tone and increased range from the basic instrument. These experiments ranged from eccentric one-offs built purely for novelty to designs that were still being played and built in the early twentieth century, but most of these guitars are no longer played outside specialist ensembles.

THE OLD WORLD
The Lyre Guitar and Harp Guitar

Two of the most spectacular and unusual guitars developed in the eighteenth and nineteenth were the lyre guitar and harp guitar. The lyre guitar had a single neck between two wing-like appendages that were as long as the neck but part of the body. Its design was based on Ancient Greek classical art.

The harp guitar had two or three necks, each with six or seven strings and its own

sound hole. Only one neck could be played at a time. An example of this would be the instrument built in 1862 by Josef Petzval (something of a specialist in this type of guitar) which had two necks, one with 31 frets and six strings, the other with 12 frets and six bass strings.

THE LYRE, ONE OF THE GUITAR'S MANY UNUSUAL RELATIVES

The design of these instruments seemed to be more for decorative than practical purpose – an example of function following form.

The Keyed Guitar

The keyed guitar was a bizarre, isolated development in which a small keyboard was added to the low end of the soundbox. The keyboard had an enclosed mechanism of hammers; to produce a note, the key corresponding to the desired string was pressed. These guitars were fashionable for a short time in the eighteenth century.

Other Experiments

To improve tone and volume, extended soundbox guitars were attempted – for instance, with an elongated tapering body extending to twice the length of the neck. In the early nineteenth century a few guitars appeared with cut-outs to facilitate access to the top frets.

Guitars with sympathetic strings added also appeared. These strings were not plucked but resonated in sympathy with the soundbox of the guitar. José Porcel was thought to have been the first person to implement this idea. An example from 1867 has 19 sympathetic strings with their own bridge, positioned at an oblique angle to the usual six strings.

There was even a bowed guitar, known as the *guitar d'Amour* or *arpeggione*, developed and played by one J.G. Staufer, who is also credited with the first adjustable bolt-on neck. This neck allowed the raising and lowering of the action by adjusting the height of the neck relative to the body.

While most of these developments were abandoned as soon as they proved impractical or unpopular, three variations of the guitar sustained a longer lifespan. These were the (classical) bass guitar, the terzguitar and the quartguitar.

The bass guitar was a standard guitar with an extra two to six bass strings, which could be on the same neck as the normal strings, or on a separate fretless neck. This instrument was also known as the arch-guitar, double-necked guitar, theorbo-guitar or harp guitar. The design originated in Italy at the end of the sixteenth century and was used as a solo instrument in chamber ensembles. It was the most long-lived of the three, but fell into disuse in the first part of the twentieth century.

The terzguitar and the quartguitar were both smaller than the modern classical guitar, the quartguitar being the smaller of the two; it was tuned a fourth higher than normal. The terzguitar was a tuned a minor third higher. Both were used with normal guitars in chamber ensembles.

The Zongora

This is a guitar from Northern Transylvania in Romania, used in a very unconventional way, which was mentioned by classical composer Belá Bartók in his research into folk music. It is used solely as a rhythm instrument and the notes played do not change to accommodate the melody. Traditionally it has only two strings, tuned D-A, although more modern versions have three strings, the tunings of which are changed depending on the melody to be accompanied.

THE GUITAR IN LATIN AMERICA

There were no known native equivalents to the guitars the Spanish and Portuguese sailors brought to the New World; the only known plucked string instrument indigenous to Latin America was the mouth bow used by some tribes of Indians. The European influence on the local Indian music was all-pervasive as the Spanish and Portuguese established political control over these new territories, with the native population enthusiastically adopting and adapting the instruments their conquerors brought with them. Each different Indian tribe's musical traditions mixed with that of the Spanish and Portuguese and that of the large imported African population to produce a rich mosaic of regionally distinctive folk musics. This also gave rise to regionally defined variations of the guitar's form, which led to the evolution of new types of guitars, with new types of tuning and new kinds of ensembles for the instruments.

Mexico

As well as the normal "classical" guitar, Mexico has the *guitarron*, a four-string bass guitar used mainly in mariachi ensembles, although the Tex-Mex band Los Lobos have used it in an acoustic pop setting. This guitar has a very deep body and high action and is played with its table almost horizontal; these attributes ensure difficulty in playing anything more than the simplest of bass lines and so limit the instrument's popularity.

The instrument known as *vijuela*, *juarana* or

85

LOS LOBOS – STARS OF TEX-MEX

CHAPTER SIX

86

BOSSA NOVA PLAYER CHARLIE BYRD

juaranita is a six-string guitar, of the same shape but smaller than the conventional classical guitar. It is also used in mariachi bands, and is tuned higher than the normal guitar. The mariachi ensemble plays a kind of music that is unique to Mexico; it generally consists of guitars, *juarana*, *guitarron*, Mexican harp and trumpet.

Another Mexican variation is the *huapanguera*, a large five-course guitar of eight or ten strings. Its name is derived from the music it is normally used to accompany, the huapango, a kind of son (country song) of southern Mexico.

Cuba

Cuban music is incredibly rich and diverse. While the more modern dance forms are well known, there is also a tradition of guitar music which makes use of guitars such as the *tres*, a small guitar with three pairs of strings; a seven-string guitar called the *armónico* invented by Compay Segundo (it also has the third string double strung); the *laoud*, a small twelve-string guitar that is actually very similar to a lute; and the seis, a twelve-string guitar, as well as the normal guitar, with both gut and steel stringing. These guitars can be found in ensembles consisting of percussion, guitar and double bass – with the optional addition of piano and trumpet as circumstances permit – playing the more traditional forms of Cuban music such as the *son* and *guajira*.

Brazil

Brazil is also musically a very rich and diverse country and is home to one of the most famous types of guitar-based music, the bossa nova. Antonio Carlos Jobim was the master composer of this type of music. Stan Getz's version of his 'Girl From Ipanema' (featuring Joao Gilberto on guitar) was an international hit in the early '60s, stimulating much external interest in Brazilian music, especially from American jazz musicians (*see* Laurindo Almeida in A–Z). Other noted players and composers of the bossa nova are Luis Bonfa and Oscar Castro-Neves. Charlie Byrd, an American jazz guitarist, became well known for his adoption of the style.

As well as the normal six-string guitar, Brazil also has the *violáo*, which can have between four and 14 strings, but usually 10. The singer, composer and instrumentalist Milton Nascimento, who has worked with Wayne Shorter and Pat Metheny, occasionally uses this type of guitar.

Venezuela

Venezuela's national instrument could well be the *cuatro*, a small four-string guitar that is capable of great expressiveness. It is used as both a lead and a rhythm instrument, and its greatest players are virtuosos. Its predecessor was probably the *cavaquinto*, a fifteenth-century guitar of Portuguese origin. Variations of this guitar can be found in Colombia, Jamaica and Mexico. In Trinidad and Tobago it is used as part of calypso bands. Outside these areas it is not well known, though it would have been heard elsewhere as part of the band backing Hugo Blanco, a player of the South American harp who made what would now be known as easy listening records in the late '50s.

Other South American Guitars

The *charango* of the Andes is an unusual hybrid of the guitar and mandolin, dating from the mid-eighteenth century and still in use. It is a very small instrument, shaped like the Spanish guitar, but with a small thin soundbox, and anywhere from five to 18 frets. The back of the soundbox is traditionally made of an armadillo shell, but is now more commonly carved from a single piece of wood. It has between four and 15 metal, gut or nylon

strings arranged in four or more commonly five courses. Its tuning varies from area to area, the most common being A minor (E-A-E-C-G) and E minor (B-E-B-G-D). It is also known as the *chillador*, *kirkinchu*, *kirki* (in Peru and Bolivia), and the *tatu* and *mulita* (in Argentina).

It is possible to divide contemporary use of the charango into rural and urban traditions. The rural tradition of Bolivia and Peru prefers a wooden, flat-backed instrument with five double or triple courses of thin metal strings, usually strummed to produce a characteristic rich treble sound. The urban *mestizo charango* tradition uses a deeper-sounding instrument, usually curve-backed with nylon strings and a low octave string in the central course. The instrument is plucked as well as strummed. In both traditions the *charango* is used solo and in ensembles.

Another less common guitar of Andean South America is the *guitarilla*. The version

SOUTH AMERICA IS HOME TO MANY VARIATIONS ON THE BASIC GUITAR FORM

used by the Chipaya Indians of Bolivia has five double strings, six frets, is tuned D-A-F-C-G and comes in three sizes. The Chipaya are unusual in that they use no other instruments apart from the *guitarilla* which they normally play in duos.

Other South American guitars include the tiple, the *requinto* and the *mejorana*. The *tiple* is a small guitar found in Colombia, Guatemala, Puerto Rico and Venezuela. The name is actually the Spanish word for "treble" or "soprano", a reflection of its role in string ensembles. In the Colombian Andes it has four courses of three metal strings, tuned to the four upper strings of the guitar, but with the middle string of the three lower courses tuned an octave lower.

The Guatemalan *tiple* is slightly larger than its Colombian counterpart, and sometimes has a fifth course. The requinto is a small four-string guitar found in Ecuador, Mexico and the Colombian Andes. It is tuned D-G-B-E and played with a plectrum. The Mexican *requinto* is slightly different and is used with the main guitar in *mestizo* serenades. It is tuned a fourth higher than the normal guitar. The *mejorana* is a small, short-necked, five-stringed guitar from Panama.

Two examples of string ensembles using these instruments are the Andean *murga* and the Guatemalan *zarabanda*. The basic *murga* is a trio with the *bandola* or *requinto* providing the melody, the *tiple* providing chords or counter-melody and the normal guitar providing both bass and chordal accompaniment. Additional instruments are sometimes added, particularly an extra *bandola* playing the melody in parallel thirds or sixths. The *zarabanda* is normally made up of fiddles, guitars, *bandolin*, *tiple* or *guitarilla* and South American harp. In some of the larger ensembles percussion and accordion may also be added.

87

OTHER WORLD GUITARS
Hawaii

Hawaii was the original home of the ukulele, a small four-string guitar first seen in the late nineteenth century, based on the Portuguese *machete*. After the turn of the century it was fashionable in America and Britain as a parlour instrument, a kind of forerunner of the home organ, particularly in the '20s. This popularity was no doubt due to its small size, light weight, low cost and undemanding playing technique. Outside Hawaiian music, its most famous exponents are probably George Formby in Britain and the TV entertainer Arthur Godfrey in the US, who caused another surge in the popularity of the instrument in the '50s. There are a few varieties of the ukulele, including tenor and baritone versions, and the "taro-patch fiddle" which is actually a version with four double courses of steel strings. The modern version has nylon strings and a variety of tunings, the most common being the North American tuning of A-D-F#-B.

The ukulele was for a time known as the "Hawaiian guitar", but

SPANISH GUITARS ARE DEEPLY ROOTED IN SPANISH FOLK TRADITIONS

GEORGE FORMBY, "THE UKULELE MAN", BROUGHT WIDESPREAD POPULARITY TO THE INSTRUMENT

that name is now normally applied to a very different instrument. Around 1830, the Spanish guitar was brought to Hawaii by Mexican cattle drovers (cowboys!) and by the mid-nineteenth century native Hawaiians had adopted the instrument and absorbed it into their own musical idioms. The normal tuning of the guitar was replaced by open tunings (also known as "slack key" tuning) with the strings of the guitar tuned to the notes of a major triad.

A guitarist by the name of Josef Kekutu was reputed to have been the first to place the guitar across his knees and slide a comb or penknife along the strings to produce the glissando effects that make Hawaiian sound so distinctive. In the early twentieth century, Hawaiian music became popular in mainland America and guitar manufacturers started to

guitar rapidly. This instrument is known as the pedal steel guitar. The form of these instruments is now so different to the normal guitar that it is only through its history that it can be defined as a member of the guitar family.

The Far East and Asia

The guitar was less influential in the colonies of the Far East, but an interesting example is the *luc huyín cám*, a Vietnamese version of the Spanish guitar that first appeared in the '30s. It has from four to six strings, tuned lower than normal, and is still in use. Its most unusual characteristic is the two bass frets between which the wood is scooped out deeply enough to allow the player pull the strings with the fretting hand, a technique normally associated with players of a local instrument called the *dán nguyet* (moon-faced lute). Other unique developments of the guitar in the Far East are the Javanese *kroncong*, an instrument of Portuguese-Indonesian extraction, and the three-string guitar used by the Montese people of Mindanao in the Philippines.

THE HAWAIIAN LAP STEEL GUITAR – ELECTRIFICATION PREDATED THE REGULAR SPANISH GUITAR

make guitars especially designed for Hawaiian-style playing, usually with a raised nut and higher action than normal guitars. These instruments came supplied with a steel bar for slide-playing, resulting in this type of guitar becoming known as the "steel guitar", although they were also known as Hawaiian guitars.

Rickenbacker produced the first electric steel guitar (the "frying pan", a lap steel) in 1931. The first electric steel guitar mounted on legs was produced by Gibson in the '30s. Some of these instruments had more than one neck, each neck having a different tuning. Around this time country and western bands started using them. In an effort to make playing chromatic harmony easier, arrangements of knee levers and foot pedals were added that allow the player to alter the tuning of the

The seven-string guitar

There is a small but significant school of American jazz guitarists who espouse the use of a seven-string guitar. The pioneer of this instrument was George Van Eps, a master of chordal acoustic jazz guitar who started his career in the '30s swing era playing in the bands of Benny Goodman (above), Bud Freeman and Jack Teagarden. Two modern players are Howard Alden and Steve Masakowski. Masakowski's guitar is a very exotic custom model with the extra string tuned to a low A, five extra frets for extended range and a headless neck. In rock Steve Vai has also used such guitars.

THE ELECTRIC BASS GUITAR

There have always been guitars to fulfil the function of the bass voice, but due to the difficulties of building an acoustic instrument that could function convincingly in that role, they were not widely adopted until recently. The physics of low frequency vibration meant that acoustic bass guitars would be either prohibitively large, or prohibitively quiet. In popular music in the first half of the twentieth century, if a specific bass instrument was required, the double bass (or to a lesser extent the tuba) was employed. However, the double bass, evolved from the viol de gamba and unrelated to the guitar or cello, has several inherent idiosyncrasies that were exacerbated as pop music began to evolve, and in particular, became amplified. The qualities that make it unsatisfactory for modern pop include the fact that the basic technique required to play it in tune is formidable and takes several years to perfect; the instrument is very physically demanding, and bad technique is rewarded by severe tendonitis; and it is very difficult to amplify. But its acoustic volume could no longer compete with the increasingly amplified guitar and the new high-volume environments made it even more difficult to play the instrument in tune. It is also a very large but very delicate instrument, so just getting it to the gig at all is problematic! The first electric basses were actually double basses with a solid body of such reduced volume that they are sometimes known as stick basses. Rickenbacker started making this instrument in the mid-'40s. One of its first

THE FENDER PRECISION – THE FIRST ELECTRIC BASS GUITAR

players was Smiley Burnette, the bassist with Gene Autry's band (*see* A–Z). Variations on the theme are still available today, and are popular with bassists playing salsa and Latin-jazz, among whom it is sometimes known as the baby bass.

While this development helped to reduce travel and amplification difficulties, it still left the tuning problem, as well as some less obvious problems. Many bands would have a guitarist who would also double on the upright bass when required. The problem was that they also normally sang backing vocals, and playing the double bass made this almost impossible, especially with the microphones of the period. So when in 1951 Leo Fender came up with the idea of an electric bass guitar that solved all of these problems in one fell swoop, it was no wonder the instrument was adopted with such alacrity that for a long time the generic term for the instrument was the "Fender bass".

Fender's design revolutionized bass playing, as well as making the singing bassist possible (imagine Paul McCartney or Sting jumping around a stage with a double bass). The electric bass allowed a virtuosity and inventiveness in the bass part that was unprecedented in pop music and resulted in many new styles of music and ways of playing. A whole specialist school of bass guitar has evolved and the bass player is no longer just a guitarist who plays bass; players such as Jack Bruce, John Entwistle, James Jamerson, Carol Kaye, Jaco Pastorius, Stanley Clarke, Marcus Miller, Darryl Jones, Mark King and too many others to mention here have ensured its place as an instrument in its own right. The bass is now played with the thumb (rare amongst modern players), with two or more fingers (fingerstyle), with a plectrum or by slapping and "popping" the strings. (Now generically known as "slap" bass, this technique was orig-

Leo Fender's bass classics

Introduced in 1951, the first Fender bass was a simple but effective design known as the Precision model; it was called this because its fretted fingerboard allowed the player to play in tune "with precision". The fretting of the instrument was the same as the guitar's, albeit of a longer string length (34 inches) which was dictated by the physics involved. Its strings were tuned the same as the bottom four strings of the standard guitar. It had one magnetic pick-up designed so there was no fade out in the sound caused by the strings vibrating out of the magnetic field of the pole pieces of the pick-up. Ten years later, Fender designed the Jazz bass in an effort to make a more versatile bass to compete with the refinements other manufacturers introduced on their own models. The Jazz bass had a redesigned, narrower neck (still 34-inch scale), a restyled body for greater comfort and two pick-ups for greater tonal variation. Fender produced still another classic in the mid-'70s for a company called Musicman. This was the Stingray, and had a restyled headstock, with one hum-bucking pick-up and active electronics on board. While Fender did design other basses, including five- and six-string models ahead of their time, none attained such popularity as these three, all of which are still in production.

inally pioneered by Larry Graham, the bassist with Sly and the Family Stone.) Each of these techniques has a distinctive sound, the style used being dictated by the musical circumstances.

The Fender Precision bass was soon copied by other manufacturers, who expanded on his basic design, adding their own refinements and variations. These included classic designs by: Rickenbacker (the 4001, as played by Chris Squire of Yes); Gibson (whose bass models never obtained the popularity of their guitars even though John Entwistle played a Gibson Thunderbird); Hofner (whose violin bass was made famous by Paul McCartney); and Alembic (championed by Stanley Clarke). Fender himself designed another two classic basses, the Jazz bass and the Musicman Stingray (see box). Modern materials have led to exotic designs such as the Steinberger headless bass (as played by Robbie Shakespeare), and graphite necks have become common. More ergonomic designs have surfaced to ease the physical problems to players caused by the weight and large body size of older designs, an example being the basses of the German company Warwick.

Modern musical requirements have also led to further developments: in an effort to match the increased lower range of synthesizer basslines, basses with an additional low string tuned to B or C were developed. As bass players were given more solo space, they wanted an increased higher range, so an additional higher string was added. As a result, five- and six-string basses are now a common sight, an example being the Ken Smith six-string bass developed for Anthony Jackson. The bass may even be a dedicated solo instrument in an ensemble including another bass – an example being Foley McCreary, who played piccolo bass in Miles Davis' band in the late '80s. (The most unusual bass currently used has to be the two-string bass customized and played with a slide by Mark Sandman of the band Morphine.)

In an attempt to get a sound more similar to the double bass, Jaco Pastorius took the frets off a Fender Jazz bass and invented the fretless electric bass. Semi-acoustic and acoustic bass guitars with piezo-electric pick-ups have also been developed in an effort to get a more woody sound. Ironically, this has produced a resurgence in interest in the double bass, which is still the preferred bass instrument in

91

CHAPTER SIX

jazz groups, bringing the evolution of the bass guitar full circle.

Amplifier and speaker design has also evolved to cater for the bassist. In the '40s there were no specialist amplifiers for the bass, and the speaker cones of the day could not accurately reproduce very low frequencies. Fender was again one of the first manufacturers to address this problem, producing his Bassman amplifiers and combos. The modern diversity of bass guitar is reflected in the diversity of amplification available for it, from the simplest practice combos to esoteric designs with aluminium speaker cones.

DISTANT RELATIVES
The Banjo

The banjo does not belong to the guitar family; it has an evolution independent from that of the guitar, which resulted in many physical and constructional differences between the two instruments. It is based on an instrument taken to the New World in the seventeenth century by West African slaves, which was known in French colonies as the *banza* and in English areas as the *banjer*. This had a long flat neck and hide sound table covering a gourd body. The contemporary banjo comes from commercial adaptations of the original

THE BANJO EVOLVED INDEPENDENTLY OF THE GUITAR

instrument which were made in the early to mid-nineteenth century.

The banjo has a body made of laminated wood resembling a drum-shell or tambourine covered with a sound table made of a material similar to a drumhead (historically skin or parchment, but now usually plastic) which is tensioned by an array of screws and brackets around the body. The skin tensioning system can be of great complexity on high quality instruments. There is normally no covering on the reverse side of the instrument, but on some designs a wooden resonator is added to increase volume. The banjo has four full-length strings and one shorter one (known as the thumb string) connected to a tuning peg halfway down the neck, originally of gut but since the twentieth century made of steel.

The tuning of the strings changed a number of times during evolution, but the contemporary banjo is normally in what is known as C tuning (G-C-G-B-D) or G tuning (G-D-G-B-D). The tuning of the sound table does not appear to be standardized. Originally, the banjo did not have raised frets; this refinement was not introduced until the 1880s. A number of variations were developed in the late nineteenth and early twentieth century, including bass,

tenor, piccolo, guitar and mandolin models.

The banjo was used predominantly by the black population (most of whom were in slavery) until the mid-nineteenth century, when it was introduced into white urban culture by players in the popular "minstrel" shows. Its use became widespread in the 1870s as a parlour instrument, and from 1890 to 1930 was exceedingly popular, both solo and in ensemble. A large amount of music was published for it, including transcriptions of classical music.

Modern players of the banjo include Pete Seeger, an exponent of Southern and rural styles; Earl Scruggs, a master of the bluegrass style (famous for the *Beverly Hillbillies* TV show theme – *see* Lester Flatt in A–Z); and Alison Brown, a young virtuoso who has introduced the banjo to more contemporary settings.

The Mandolin

This is an eight-string instrument of the lute family that is widely used in guitar ensembles and may be considered a guitar by this association. The name "mandolin" comes from the Italian for "little almond". It is found in various forms around the world, in particular as the *bandolin* from South America, which has a flat back and five pairs of strings. The *bandolin*

92

is used in the Guatemalan *zarabande*, the Colombian *murga* and also in Venezuela with the *cuatro* as an accompaniment to the *fulia* and *corrido* songs.

One of the most famous modern players of the mandolin is Bill Monroe, who in the '40s fused together elements of dance, religious and folk music of the south-eastern highlands of North America to develop what is now known as bluegrass music. A bluegrass band is a string ensemble that includes the fiddle, five-string banjo, mandolin, steel guitar, lead and rhythm guitar and double bass. The most interesting modern player of the instrument is Béla Flick, another young virtuoso who is using an electric version of the instrument in new musical hybrids, including versions of classic bebop tunes of the '40s!

The Balalaika

The balalaika is a long-necked, three-string lute or guitar, with a distinctive triangular soundbox. It is the predominant folk instrument of Russia and was of Tartar origin, becoming popular in the eighteenth century. The instrument was improved and standardized largely through the efforts of V.V.

THE BOUZOUKI, NATIONAL INSTRUMENT OF GREECE

Andreyev, a balalaika player who was active in the late nineteenth and early twentieth century. As a result of his work the balalaika comes in six different sizes ranging from piccolo to bass versions.

All versions of the instrument have three strings, a flat back and a thin, slightly arched body normally made of spruce. The most common type is the prime balalaika which is tuned E-E-A. Balalaikas are normally used

singly to accompany dancing and singing, but balalaika orchestras do exist and indeed have toured outside Russia.

The Bouzouki

The bouzouki is a Greek long-necked, fretted string instrument that first appeared in the nineteenth century. It is based on the Turkish *bozuk*, a type of lute with a carvel-built or carved resonator and movable gut frets. The modern bouzouki is also carvel-built (without the wooden strips overlapping), but has metal frets and either three or four courses of double strings. The three-string version is tuned E-B-E, the four string type D-G-B-E. Both are played with a plectrum, but the four-string version did not appear until late '40s.

During the first half of the twentieth century the bouzouki was used for virtuoso improvisation and accompaniment to the *rebetiko*, a type of music and song of the low life. It was at this time so strongly perceived as an anti-establishment instrument, associated with an environment of crime and hashish-smoking, that the Greek government actively persecuted players.

The initial method of improvisation on the bouzouki was based on the melodies and modal methods of Asia Minor and the Near East, but the influence of Western harmony gave rise to the need for a more diatonic approach. It was originally a single-line instrument and not really suitable for playing chords; the four-string model was developed as a result of the need to satisfy the harmonic and chordal demands of the new Western influence. The most well-known use of the bouzouki is probably Mikis Theodorakis' music for the 1964 film *Zorba The Greek*, through which the instrument was introduced to a larger international audience. The bouzouki is still the folk instrument of choice in the Greek-speaking world.

93

A RUSSIAN NAVAL BALALAIKA ORCHESTRA PERFORM ON BOARD THEIR SHIP

LEGENDS OF THE GUITAR

OF THE

GUITAR

CHET ATKINS
1924–

94

Country music's greatest virtuoso guitarist, Chet Atkins is one of the architects of the Nashville Sound. At the heart of his playing style lies an awesome fingerpicking technique and sophisticated syncopation of muted bass strings. This has been a major influence on every notable country player of the past 40 years – little wonder, then, that he is so widely known as "Mr Guitar", or more recently "Chet Atkins CGP – Certified Guitar Picker".

Born in 1924 in the Appalachian hamlet of Luttrell, Tennessee, Chet Atkins was surrounded by music from an early age, both his parents and grandfather having been musicians. His first great influence was his half-brother James (his elder by 12 years) who was already a well-established country performer having played with another of Chet's heroes, Les Paul.

A prodigious talent, at the age of 18 Atkins successfully auditioned to join the house band on Knoxville's WNOX radio station. Within months he was given his own daily solo spot.

By his early twenties he had worked on dozens of similar country radio stations, although his style of playing, which introduced elements of jazz to his country picking, was sometimes viewed as too arty for the down-the-line barn dance music he was paid to play.

Milestones

1924 Born June 20, Chester Burton Atkins in Luttrell, Tennessee.

1942 Leaves home to work as a musician on radio stations in Denver, Cincinnati and Chicago.

1950 Moves to Nashville and begins regular gigs at the Grand Ole Opry.

1953 Records first hit single 'Gallopin' Guitars'.

1973 Inducted into the Country Music Hall of Fame – at 49 years old, the youngest ever recipient.

1988 Wins a record-breaking ninth Country Music Association Award.

In 1947 he began his long association with the RCA label. Although his first few records were not as successful as had been hoped, the label felt he had the potential to be a new Merle Travis. Six years later they were rewarded with his first solo instrumental hit, 'Gallopin' Guitars'. That same year, Atkins' career shifted up a gear when he joined Mother Maybelle and the Carter Sisters. They were invited to play at Nashville's Grand Ole Opry.

Although Atkins has been a successful hit artist in his own right, much of his finest work has been heard accompanying others. In fact, it's no exaggeration to say that every major Nashville artist of the period – Hank Williams, Faron Young, Porter Wagoner, Waylon Jennings, to name but a few – enjoyed some level of involvement with the Chet Atkins sound. Such was the strength of his public association with the guitar that manufacturer Gretsch gave him his own signature models, one of which was the legendary "Country Gentleman" – named from one of Atkins' instrumental hits. He stayed linked to Gretsch until 1977, when he switched to Gibson, who also gave him his own signature model.

Classic Recordings

A Legendary Performer (compilation, 1952–1967)

A selection of Atkins' instrumental hits from the '50s and '60s which gives a good demonstration of his dexterous picking style.

Chester and Lester (1976)

Most of Atkins' best work can be heard when he is collaborating with others. This album sees him duelling with the legendary Les Paul.

Stay Tuned (1985)

A rare feast of guitar treasures. Atkins gives a set of simple, formulaic tunes the instrumental treatment with top-notch cohorts, including Earl Klugh, Mark Knopfler and George Benson.

CHET ATKINS, CGP (CERTIFIED GUITAR PICKER)

Much of Atkins' long-standing influence has come not only from the fact that he is country's greatest ever guitarist, but from his role in the music business as well. During the mid-'50s he began managing RCA's studios in Nashville's Music Row, and acted as a free-lance talent-spotter for the label. It was this period that saw him steer country music towards a newly sophisticated sound – it was christened the Nashville Sound.

Atkins was soon promoted to RCA's Head Of Operations for Nashville, making him coun-

Guitars

Atkins initially used D'Angelico guitars, but he switched to Gretsch when he was offered the chance to design a guitar from scratch. The first model to bear Atkins' signature was the 1955 6120 Hollow Body. This was followed by the most famous model, the Country Gentleman. In 1977 Atkins left Gretsch when he was invited to design a new series of electro-acoustic guitars for Gibson.

try's most important record executive – in time, Music Row would become as much a shrine for country fans as Chess Studios or Sun Studios are to fans of blues or rock 'n' roll. His significance to the development of modern country music was ratified in 1973 when, at the age of 49, he was indicted into the Country Music Hall of Fame. He is still the youngest person to receive such an honour.

Having long since become bored with the business side of music, in 1981 Atkins resigned from his executive position at RCA to concentrate on the thing he loved the most – playing the guitar. He still records and performs widely and has also produced a number of best-selling tutorial videos that illustrate the sheer complexity of his picking technique. Too often in the past, simple song formats have led to country players being overlooked by listeners of more "serious" types of music. Chet Atkins' pursuit of musical excellence stands alongside virtuosos in any genre.

JEFF BECK
1944–

More than any other contemporary guitar legend, Jeff Beck is perhaps the very essence of the cliché, the "guitarist's guitarist". Much to the chagrin of those who have tried to impose their will on his direction, Beck has shown time and time again that he will do what *he* wants to do, and commercial considerations don't necessarily get a look-in.

An art school student, Beck's professional career leapt out of the starting gate in 1965 when he joined the Yardbirds, Britain's premier blues band. He was given the thankless task of replacing Eric Clapton, a blues purist uncomfortable with the band's new-found pop success. Undaunted, Beck steered the Yardbirds through a transitional phase as they became one of the most original rock bands of the mid-'60s. Classic cuts such as 'Evil Hearted You', 'Shapes Of Things' and 'Heart Full Of Soul' capture Beck in all his youthful glory – a technical wizard whose playing seemed to based firmly on pure instinct.

Milestones

1944 Born June 24, In Wallington, Surrey, England.

1965 Joins the Yardbirds following Eric Clapton's departure.

1966 Leaves the Yardbirds after the arrival of Jimmy Page (see page 114).

1968 Forms the Jeff Beck Group with Rod Stewart and Ronnie Wood.

1972 Forms power trio Beck Bogert and Appice.

1975 Records *Blow By Blow* with Beatles' producer George Martin.

Classic Recordings

The Yardbirds (1966)
One of the great British albums of the mid-'60s. Beck's fuzzed-out tremolo experiments transform the Yardbirds from bluesboys to Britain's most thrilling rock band.

Truth (1968)
Jeff Beck Group debut mixes blues covers with originals like 'Beck's Bolero'. Showcases Rod Stewart's vocals at their rawest and Beck's playing at its most resonant.

Wired (1976)
A jazz-rock dictionary of playing techniques that became required listening (and learning) for fledgling guitarists of the late '70s.

Not the most conformist of characters, Beck parted company with the Yardbirds while touring America in 1966, the addition of session man Jimmy Page to the line-up having affected the band's chemistry (*see* pages 114–15). While the Yardbirds came apart (to re-emerge two years later as Led Zeppelin), Beck engaged on a solo career that over the next 30 years would be glorious, difficult and bizarre in broadly equal measures.

Signed up by pop impresario Mickey Most for his new RAK label, Beck cut a series of extraordinary singles which brought him brief pop stardom. Hits included an instrumental version of 'Love Is Blue' and the party perennial 'Hi Ho Silver Lining', which revealed his vocal talents to be less advanced than his guitar work. Sensibly retreating, he formed his own Jeff Beck Group in 1968, with vocalist

Rod Stewart and guitarist Ronnie Wood (who switched to bass for the gig). Playing extensively throughout Britain and the US over the next year they showed themselves to be the only real competition for Led Zeppelin in the blues-based heavy rock stakes. But it didn't last long – Beck's unpredictable behaviour affected their success in reaching the audience they deserved. Stewart and Wood teamed up with ex-members of the Small Faces to form the Faces – they would become perhaps the greatest live band of the '70s.

Beck devoted much of the '70s to session work and jazz-rock fusion. Among those benefiting from his tasteful contributions were Stevie Wonder – indeed, Beck's spine-tingling solo on 'Lookin' For Another Pure Love' from the *Talking Book* album is surely one of the finest ever consigned to tape.

Those who favour Beck in his "guitar hero" mode usually cite *Blow By Blow*, produced by George Martin, or *Wired*, on which he shared the limelight with synthesist Jan Hammer. Both albums showcased a growing interest in jazz, even if his fusion take of Charles Mingus' 'Goodbye Pork Pie Hat' would not have amused too many purists. Although he has continued to play as a hired hand since the '80s, sessioning with Mick Jagger, Buddy Guy (*see* pages 106–7) and Kate Bush, to name but a small sample, his own releases have become more sporadic, if not downright mercurial – 1993 saw the release of *Crazy Legs*, a bizarrely out-of-character tribute to little-known '50s rockabilly guitarist Cliff Gallup.

The rollercoaster ride that has been Jeff Beck's career has undoubtedly been compounded by a genuine compulsion to follow his own muse rather than satisfying managers, record labels or fans. Although admirably uncompromising, he continues to enjoy a smaller scale of commercial success than many of his considerably less capable peers.

Guitars

Beck seems to view guitars largely as tools of the trade. As such he has never remained loyal to one particular model. Much of his early work saw him use Gibson Les Paul Standards played through a combination of Marshall amplifiers and Fender speakers. The latter part of his career has seen a shift in favour of Jacksons or the Fender Stratocaster, for which he was given his own "signature" model in 1991.

JEFF BECK, AN UNCOMPROMISING MUSICIAN

JULIAN BREAM
1933–

Although there remains one pre-eminent name in the world of the classical guitar – the great Andrés Segovia – if one musician can be said to have carried on in the master's tradition it is Julian Bream.

Born in London in 1933, Bream was first taught to play guitar by his father, an amateur musician. However, it was exposure to records by Segovia that fired his passion for the instrument. His first formal lessons were taken with exiled Russian guitarist Boris Perrot. He took a major step forward in 1947 when Segovia first played in London. Bream not only attended the recital but received some personal tuition from the master himself. That same year he gave his first solo performance.

Bream's formal music education consisted of studying the piano and cello at London's principal music establishment, the Royal College of Music. It seems strange to imagine that, in spite of the work of Segovia, even then the guitar was not on the curriculum in music schools (*see* The Torres Revolution and the Classical Guitar). In fact, there was no professor of the guitar at the Royal College until 1960, when Bream's friend and collaborator John Williams (the other great post-Segovia guitarist) was offered the position.

On leaving music school Bream was obliged to do a period of National Service in the army. He chose to join the Royal Artillery primarily so he could join the regiment's dance band. It was here he had his first experience of the electric guitar, but it was not one that he would repeat too often during this career. His first classical recital was in 1951 at London's Wigmore Hall. Like Segovia's previously, Bream's early concert career drew a large part of its repertoire from the player's own transcriptions of music written for other instruments, a fine example being his 1957 recording of works by J.S. Bach, most of which were originally written for the organ.

By the end of the '50s, Bream had established a worldwide reputation for his playing. During the following decade his public fame and the respect held for him within the music world enabled him to make perhaps his greatest, lasting contributions to the classical guitar. Throughout the '60s Bream commissioned some of the finest post-war composers to produce pieces for the guitar. In fact, many of the works written specifically for Bream are standard parts of the modern classical repertoire. Lennox Berkeley wrote *Sonatina* in 1958, Benjamin Britten wrote *Nocturnal* in 1964 – other composers adding their weight to the growing canon have included Richard Rodney Bennett and Hans Werner Henze.

As he began his career, Bream also took up the lute, primarily to offer him a second source of income when guitar work dried up. In fact, Bream has brought the same scholarly approach to this instrument, to point where he is now widely considered to be the finest lutenist working in the world.

While Bream and John Williams are widely spoken of in the same breath – there are many who rate Williams every bit Bream's equal as a player – it is the latter's work in broadening the classical repertoire, either as a commissioner, transcriber, or archaeologist of obscure works from the past, that makes him the most valuable classical guitarist of the post-war era.

Milestones

1933 Born June 15 in London.

1944 Begins guitar lessons.

1947 Sees Segovia's British debut; attends Segovia master classes.

1951 Makes his professional concert debut at London's Wigmore Hall.

1955 Records debut album – *Anthology Of English Song* with tenor Peter Pears.

1958 Makes US debut at New York's Town Hall.

Classic Recordings

Arnold and Guiliani (1961)
First recording of Malcolm Arnold's *Guitar Concerto, Opus 67*, which was directed by Arnold himself. The flip side contrasted Giuliani's *Concerto in A major, Opus 30* composed at the start of the nineteenth century.

20th Century Guitar (1967)
A landmark in classical guitar, specially commissioned compositions by Benjamin Britten, Frank Martin, Heitor Villa-Lobos, Hans Werner Henze, and Reginald Smith Brindle.

Julian Bream 70s (1973)
Works written for Bream by noted composers Richard Rodney Bennett, William Walton, Alan Rawsthorne and Lennox Berkeley.

Guitars
Julian Bream plays guitars built by Hauser, the German company formed by Hermann Hauser (1882–1952), which was one of the first non-Spanish guitar makers to find favour in classical music.

98

**BREAM IS PERHAPS THE MOST SIGNIFICANT
CLASSICAL GUITARIST SINCE SEGOVIA**

CHARLIE CHRISTIAN
1916–1942

Whilst Django Reinhardt (*see* pages 116–17) had pioneered and mastered the use of the acoustic guitar as a solo instrument during the '30s, it was Charlie Christian who made a similar leap forward for the newly developed amplified guitar. Part of the mystique surrounding Christian is the unbelievable impact he made during such a brief career. The entire body of his recorded works were produced within a period of barely three years before his tragic death in 1942 at the age of 25.

Charlie Christian was born into a musical family. His father had been a professional singer and guitarist, and all four of his brothers were also musicians. He became adept on the trumpet, double bass and piano before realizing that the guitar was his forte, although it was as a bassist that he first found paid work in 1934.

It was seeing Eddie Durham playing an amplified arch-top guitar in the Jimmie Lunceford band in 1937 that first aroused Christian to the possibilities offered by the instrument. Spotted by jazz entrepreneur John Hammond, he was recommended to Benny Goodman, who showed little interest in auditioning him. According to jazz mythology, Hammond organized Christian to gatecrash one of Goodman's shows – enraged at first, then hearing the audience response to Christian's playing, Goodman gave him the job. Within a year he was widely recognized as the finest jazz guitarist working in America. (Belgian-born Django Reinhardt's reputation had reached epic proportions, but it would be another six years before he was to cross the Atlantic.) Barely four years later – after redefining the meaning of jazz guitar – he was dead, having contracted pneumonia while convalescing from tuberculosis. It was said that Christian was a victim of the pace of the Big City life, to which this Oklahoma farm-boy never happily adapted.

Although Christian remained with Goodman until his death, it was his extra-curricular activity during his final year that cemented his position as one of the most influential figures of his time. He became a key player in the regular after-hours jam sessions at Minton's Playhouse in Harlem, New York, which brought together a new generation of gifted, technically brilliant young musicians like Charlie Parker, Dizzy Gillespie, and Thelonious Monk. It was the birthplace of

Milestones

1916 Born July 29 in Dallas, Texas.

1934 First professional gig with the Alphonso Trent band.

1937 Meets pioneering electric guitarist Eddie Durham and acquires his first electric guitar; jazz entrepreneur John Hammond introduces Christian to Benny Goodman, whose band he joins.

1939 Pioneers bebop at legendary after-hours jam sessions at Minton's Playhouse in Harlem, New York.

1940 Diagnosed as suffering from tuberculosis; he ignores doctor's advice and continues touring with Goodman until he becomes too ill to perform.

1942 Dies March 2 from pneumonia while convalescing in Staten Island sanitarium.

CHARLIE CHRISTIAN PLAYING A GIBSON ES-150 FITTED WITH A SINGLE PICK-UP

bebop – a movement that would permanently change the face of jazz.

Considering his influence in the development of jazz guitar and new musical direc-

In spite of being musically active for barely three years, Christian recorded extensively. Unsurprisingly for a player of his stature, almost everything he ever recorded remains relatively easy to obtain.

Charlie Christian Live (1940)

(with the Benny Goodman Sextet) Electric live performance that showed off Christian's blueprint for his "riff-run-riff" approach to jazz guitar.

Solo Flight (1940)

Recorded with Goodman, although this time with his orchestra. Never before had the electric guitar been used so effectively in such a setting.

The Harlem Jazz Scene (1941)

Recorded with trumpeter Dizzy Gillespie, and featuring the keyboard genius of Thelonius Monk. The recording may not be the very best, but it captures bebop taking its first tentative steps.

however, he was viewed as nothing less than a genius. It was not until the arrival of Wes Montgomery in the late '60s that a similar influence on jazz guitar would emerge (*see* pages 112–13).

As with other great bebop players of the period, through the legacy of his recordings, the power and emotion of Charlie Christian's playing continues to thrill each successive generation of guitarists.

Guitars

Christian is perhaps best remembered as one of the first men to see the potential of the electric guitar. He used Gibson's Electric Spanish ES-150 to the exclusion of all other models. The single pick-up ES-150 was Gibson's first full production electric guitar.

tions, Charlie Christian remains a slightly controversial figure. Whilst his sweeping, high-speed flurries and complex use of harmony redefined the electric guitar as a solo instru-

ment, some critics of the past have claimed that he simply adapted the style of saxophone genius Lester Young to another instrument. For the guitarists who followed in his footsteps,

Ry COODER
1947–

pair, both naturally curious to experiment with new musical forms, began a brief but rewarding collaboration under the name the Rising Sons. Although Taj Mahal vanished from LA before they could complete their intended recording

In trying to evaluate the music of Ry Cooder one is faced with the problem of the sheer diversity of his expertise. That he is one of the finest guitarists of his generation is beyond dispute. However, the fact that he has managed to assimilate the widest variety of jazz, country, blues and rock styles with such brilliance is little short of miraculous.

A largely self-taught player, Ryland Peter Cooder first picked up the guitar at the age of three. In his teens, he developed an interest in traditional blues forms while listening to old recordings of Josh White. Living in Los Angeles, as a teenager he gravitated towards the Ash Grove – the home of the LA blues scene. It was here that he met ragtime blues legend Reverend Gary Davis, an association that led him to investigate bottleneck guitar and other traditional instruments such as the mandolin and banjo.

It was also at the Grove that the 17-year-old Cooder met another guitarist, Taj Mahal. The

102

Milestones

1947 Born March 15 in Los Angeles, California.

1967 Begins session career on Captain Beefheart's *Safe As Milk*.

1969 Plays on the Rolling Stones' *Let It Bleed* album; is rumoured to be the replacement for Brian Jones.

1970 Records his acclaimed debut solo album.

1982 Album *The Slide Area* makes UK Top 20, his biggest ever chart hit.

1988 Earns a Grammy for children's album *Pecos Bill*, narrated by Robin Williams.

THE TERM ECLECTIC DOESN'T DO JUSTICE TO THE BREADTH OF RY COODER'S MUSIC INTERESTS

debut, the mysterious bluesman remained a significant influence on the young Cooder.

By the time he was 20 Cooder was a well known figure on the West Coast blues scene, and had already established himself as an in-

Guitars

On his "electric" recordings, Ry Cooder uses a Fender Stratocaster. Most of his acoustic work has been played on a Martin D-45, although on occasions he has been known to use a National Style O resonator or Dobro.

demand session player. One of his first free-lance jobs was as a hired hand on Captain Beefheart's 1967 debut *Safe As Milk*. Although the recording process was said to be chaotic, and the Captain was not the easiest person to get along with, the end result was an impressive one, paving the way for the ground-breaking *Trout Mask Replica*. For the next two years Cooder seemed to work with just about every West Coast artist from popsters Paul Revere and the Raiders to the eminent Randy Newman.

Cooder first came to the attention of a wider public in 1969 when he was brought to London by producer Jack Nitzsche to work on the Rolling Stones' *Let It Bleed* album. So successful was the association that he was even rumoured to be first choice as replacement for the Stones' late guitarist, Brian Jones. But it was the other paid work he undertook while in England that would have a greater impact on his future. Working with Nitzsche, he recorded the soundtrack to the film *Candy*. It was first of many soundtracks he would compose and record over the next three decades.

With his stock as a session man running so high, the Reprise label offered Cooder the chance to record his own solo album. His 1970 debut, *Ry Cooder*, provided a showcase for his blues and folk inclinations, covering a wide selection of twentieth-century American songs. Although less successful in some other ways, it showed the attention to the smallest detail that would characterize his future recordings, and that would earn him a reputation as something of an academic of historical American musical forms.

Cooder's debut also hinted at the eclectic choice of styles and materials that was to follow. Future albums would see him tackle classical guitar (*Boomer's Story*, 1973), gospel (*Paradise And Lunch*, 1974), Hawaiian music (*Chicken Skin Music*, 1976), old-time jazz (*Jazz*, 1978), and rock 'n' roll (*Bop Till You Drop*, 1979), each one masterfully researched, performed and

Classic Recordings

Chicken Skin Music (1976)

Cooder plays alongside Hawaiian "slack" guitarist Gabby Pahinui and Tex-Mex accordion maestro Flaco Jimenez. Extraordinary covers of Jim Reeves hit 'He'll Have To Go' and Ben E. King's 'Stand By Me' are the stand-out tracks.

Music By Ry Cooder (1995)

Double CD featuring sounds from 11 soundtracks, including *Paris, Texas* and *Thelma And Louise*, on which Cooder's trademark bottleneck blues are well to the fore.

Buena Vista Social Club (1997)

Masterful collaboration with veterans Compay Segundo, Ibrahim Ferrer and Ruben Gonzales, brought together by Cooder who plays on some tracks.

recorded. These albums saw Cooder amass an unexpected and substantial following in Europe, peaking with *The Slide Area*, which hit the British Top 20. Impressive as all of these works undoubtedly are, however, his thirst for experimentation has confounded those critics who have been unable to make the necessary mental leap from, say, a Bix Beiderbecke tune to The Drifters' 'Money Honey' on successive albums.

It is, however, in his parallel career composing music for cinema soundtracks that Cooder has perhaps been most consistently successful. It is not so surprising that a man who displays such a deep and varied knowledge of the mechanics of so many different musical styles would also have a natural understanding of creating mood and atmosphere. In fact, since the early '80s Cooder's slide bottleneck playing has become almost obligatory for certain types of road movie, such as the widely admired *Paris, Texas*, on which he uses the simplest of slide devices to echo the barren landscapes seen throughout the film.

STEVE CROPPER
1942–

Milestones

1941 Born October 21, in Willow Springs, Missouri.

1951 Family moves to Memphis where he first hears black R&B music.

1961 His band, the Mar-Keys, enjoy their first hit.

1962 Forms Booker T and the MGs with Booker T Jones.

1980 Reaches widest ever audience in the Blues Brothers Band.

1992 Booker T and the MGs inducted into Rock and Roll of Fame.

During the '60s the guitar solo was the measure by which a guitarist was usually judged. Often it was a case of the faster and flashier the technique the better. In the more enlightened '90s we have come to accept that space and taste can tell us far more about a player's worth. Steve Cropper might not have topped many guitarists polls at the peak of his career in the mid-'60s. And yet three decades on he is widely rated as one of the masters of his instrument.

It was while still at university that Steve Cropper enjoyed his first flush of success. When his old high-school band the Royal Spades – renamed the Mar-Keys – produced the instrumental hit 'Last Night', Cropper quit his engineering course to concentrate on music. Playing around the Memphis area, the Mar-Keys became the original house band for the Stax and Volt labels, not only recording under their own name, but acting as backing band for the label's burgeoning vocal talent.

The Mar-Keys' formula was simple but effective: stabbing horns played over Cropper's crisp rhythm phrasing and Donald "Duck" Dunn's loping bass lines. It was a unique sound that helped to define what became known as Southern Soul. Indeed, for many

Guitars

The Steve Cropper classic treble sound that slices through the mix on hits by Booker T and the MGs, Sam and Dave, and Otis Redding, can *only* be achieved with a Fender Telecaster playing on the back pick-up. In recent times he has also used Peavey guitars.

years – given the musical company he kept – many listeners assumed that he must have been a black musician, rather than a clean-cut, middle-class American.

Leaving the Mar-Keys, Cropper moved towards studio work, writing and producing hits for the Stax label. At the same time, he put together a new studio band featuring Dunn and the prodigious keyboard talents of 16-year-old Booker T Jones. They called themselves the MGs. The legend was created one hot summer afternoon in 1962. A session had been scheduled to record a singer named Billy Lee Riley. When Riley failed to turn up, the MGs whiled away the time jamming around a simple blues progression. Startled by what he was hearing, Stax owner and session engineer Jim Stewart switched on a tape machine and recorded the jam. He was impressed and thought the results were releasable. He encouraged the band to play on. This time they fooled around with a riff Jones had been working on – within a few hours one of the all-time classic R&B instrumentals, 'Green Onions', had been born.

A chart hit the world over, Booker T and the MGs (as Stax christened them) followed up with a succession of hip grooves that appealed to black and white audiences alike – a rare achievement in the pre-integrated Deep South of 1962. Hits like 'Soul Dressing', 'Boot-Leg', 'My Sweet Potato', 'Groovin'', 'Soul Limbo' and 'Time Is Tight' made the MGs the most successful instrumental R&B band of all time.

And yet there so much more to Steve Cropper's story than this. Functioning as the Stax house band, the same line-up backed up

virtually every soul artist who recorded for the label right through to the late '60s. The Stax and Volt roster at this time reads like an A to Z of soul and R&B – names like Otis Redding, Sam and Dave, Rufus Thomas, Carla Thomas, Eddie Floyd, William Bell and Johnnie Taylor, to name but a few.

Many of the biggest Stax hits were written and produced by Cropper, and featured his sparse, measured rhythm work. Some of his most successful compositions include timeless soul classics like 'Dock Of The Day', 'Midnight Hour' and 'Knock On Wood'. Examples of his work can be heard on the awesome nine-CD box detailing singles released on the Stax and Volt labels between 1959 and 1968.

In the late '70s Cropper and Dunn joined forces with Levon Helm (of the Band) to play in the RCO All-Stars – a kind of '60s R&B soul review. This led to their recruitment as members of the Blues Brothers Band, lending a rare authenticity to the film starring John Belushi and Dan Aykroyd. The film, *The Blues Brothers*, and its soundtrack were a massive success, which spawned some live tours and a further two albums before Belushi's death.

STEVE CROPPER – THE FINEST RHYTHM PLAYER
OF THEM ALL

The Complete Stax/Volt Singles (1959-1968)

Nine-CD boxed set detailing the early history of one of the most important R&B/soul labels. The house band on most of these recordings was either the Mar-Keys or Booker T and the MGs – both featuring Steve Cropper. Music doesn't get much better than this.

Booker T And The MGs: Greatest Hits (compilation, 1962-1969)

The tightest house band in music history playing at its peak. Just buy it.

With A Little Help From My Friends (1971)

Cropper's tasteful-in-the-extreme solo debut that showcases his spartan style – the complete antithesis of what one would usually expect when a guitarist steps into the limelight.

105

In 1988 the three surviving MGs (drummer Al Jackson was murdered in 1975) reunited for a series of shows, and in 1992 they received the ultimate music industry accolade as they were inducted into the Rock and Roll Hall of Fame.

That same year they acted as the house band for the Bob Dylan tribute concert held at New York's Madison Square Garden. Here they were given the task of backing everyone from Eric Clapton, Stevie Wonder and George Harrison to Lou Reed, Johnny Cash and Neil Young. Suitably impressed by their virtuosity, Young then asked the group to accompany him as his backing band on his 1993 tours of Europe and North America.

Throughout his career, Cropper has always seemed happy to let others grab the limelight, and yet his unique ability for writing and playing simple, yet immediately recognizable, licks is second to none.

BUDDY GUY
1936–

The original young gun of the Chicago blues scene, even though he's more than 60 years old, and at an age when most bluesmen have already become venerated senior statesmen, Buddy Guy still plays and performs with a life-loving zeal that most players half his age would be hard pressed to match.

Guy was born and raised in Lettsworth, Louisiana. He learned to play guitar at the age of 13 on a home-built instrument. His earliest influence was John Lee Hooker. Unlike many of his peers, who struggled for years before gaining recognition, Guy was something of a prodigious blues talent. By the time he was 17 he was already performing with such notables as Slim Harpo, Lazy Lester and Lightnin' Slim.

It was when he decided to move to Chicago at the age of 21 that his career shifted into the next gear. Initially finding it a struggle to live, under the guidance of Muddy Waters (see pages 124–25) he honed his raw fret work so successfully that in 1958 he was able to beat

Otis Rush, Junior Wells and Magic Sam in a Battle of the Blues contest at the Blue Flame Club. As a result of this success he was signed up to the Cobra label, where he worked as a back-up player and was given the chance to cut some sides of his own.

In 1960, having impressed no lesser name than Willie Dixon, Guy joined the legendary Chess label, where he recorded with the likes of Muddy Waters and Howlin' Wolf. His association with Chess only lasted for five years, but it was during this period that he recorded some of his best work. In 1965 he moved to Sam Charters' Vanguard label, probably hitting his peak with fine albums like *A Man And His Blues* and *This Is Buddy Guy*. 1965 was also the year he formed a particularly fertile association with singer and harmonica player Junior Wells. The pair would record and perform together intermittently over the next 25 years.

The '70s were a difficult time for some blues artists. Often overshadowed by the growth of rock and the developing soul scene, the heyday of Chicago blues was well and truly a thing of the past. Whilst Guy continued to record and perform increasingly in Europe, where his regular performances at the Montreux jazz festival invariably stole the show, back in Chicago things were tougher. He chose to open up his own club, the Checkerboard Lounge, where he busied himself performing on a small stage most nights – and sometimes behind the bar. A small venue, the club attracted packed houses, including numerous visiting rock musicians, eager to see one of the greatest blues players working in a small club setting.

Milestones

1936 Born July 20 in Lettsworth, Louisiana.

1957 Moves to Chicago.

1958 Wins Battle of the Blues competition over Otis Rush.

1960 Signs to the legendary Chess label.

1965 Begins working with vocalist and harmonica player Junior Wells.

1984 Opens Buddy Guy's Legends blues club in Chicago.

Classic Recordings

The Complete Chess Studio Recordings (compilation, 1960-1965)

Guy's work for the Chicago label from 1960 finds his playing at its most dramatic with plenty of tremolo and sustained solos.

Buddy Guy and Junior Wells Play The Blues (1972)

Guy is firmly in the driving seat on this high-octane set. Guest stars include Eric Clapton and keyboard player Dr John.

Damn Right, I've Got The Blues (1991)

The album that secured Guy's position in the league of blues legends. Classic, gritty, '50s-style Chicago blues with a '90s production sheen.

The '80s saw Buddy Guy re-emerge with a new-found confidence. Blues was gradually gaining a new audience, aided by the emergence of new stars like Robert Cray, who infused elements of rock and soul and championed modern production values. The decade ended with the dazzling reinvention of John Lee Hooker, who at the age of 69 leapt back into the spotlight with *The Healer*, the biggest-selling blues album of all time.

Joining Hooker's British-based Silvertone label, Guy recorded his own "comeback" album in 1991. *Damn Right, I've Got The Blues* gave Guy his biggest-selling single album and established him as, arguably, the greatest living Chicago bluesman. He continues to perform all over the world.

Guitars

Although some of Guy's '70s work was played on Guild guitars, mostly (before or since) he has used a Fender Stratocaster with a Fender Twin Reverb amplifier.

**BUDDY GUY, THE GREATEST LIVING
CHICAGO BLUESMAN**

JIMI HENDRIX
1942–1970

As far as the electric era is concerned, one single name towers above all other guitarists – James Marshall Hendrix.

Hendrix was given his first electric guitar in 1954. He learned to play by listening to the first wave of great Chicago blues players such as B.B. King (*see* page 110), Muddy Waters (pages 124-25) and Elmore James. While he was in the US Army he formed his first band, King Kasuals, with fellow soldier Billy Cox, who would later play with Hendrix again in the Band Of Gypsies.

On leaving the army, he found work as a back-up player for touring rock 'n' roll artists. Among Hendrix's numerous credits were performances with Little Richard, Ike and Tina Turner, B.B. King and Jackie Wilson. In 1965 he moved to New York where he became a member of the Isley Brothers band. At this stage he was using the pseudonym Jimmy James.

In 1966 Hendrix decided to strike out on his own, forming the band Jimmy James and the Blue Flames. It was while performing at a club in Greenwich Village that he was spotted by Chas Chandler, former bassist with the Animals who was looking to start a career in management. Chandler convinced him that London would be a more suitable environment from which to launch himself. In October 1966, he formed the Jimi Hendrix Experience with drummer Mitch Mitchell and guitarist Noel Redding, who switched over to bass just to get the gig. Chandler immediately found the band a record deal and by the end of the year their debut single 'Hey Joe' was a Top 10 hit. Hendrix followed up this immediate success with a sequence of three peerless albums which redefined the electric guitar for every player who followed.

In 1967 Hendrix returned to his home country, where he still remained relatively unknown. The situation changed overnight following his performance at the Monterey Pop Festival. One of the lesser known names on the bill, he gave a performance that defied the eyes and ears of a massive outdoor crowd, ending a high-octane set by setting fire to his guitar.

Like many inspirational players, Hendrix would continue to be heard at his best in concert. Indeed, the lessons learned while he served his apprenticeship with rock'n'roll showmen like Little Richard became an unexpectedly valuable asset to his live show, his party pieces including playing the guitar behind his neck or with his teeth, as well as other moves of a more sexual nature.

With US military activity getting out of hand in Vietnam, the rock world would begin to take a vocal stand against the war. By the end of 1968 his shows would climax with his own version of the 'Star Spangled Banner', the US national anthem. Starting out as a simple unaccompanied solo, the piece ended with an effective recreation of the noises of warfare – exploding bombs, gunfire – all of them performed on a heavily overdriven guitar. This was captured for eternity at the Woodstock Festival in August 1969 – even if the rest of his set showed that he seemed then to be tiring of the rock 'n' roll treadmill.

This spectacle was widely perceived as a political gesture, although Hendrix himself was less than forthcoming about his views. Whatever he felt about the war in Vietnam was tempered by his respect as a former

Guitars

Hendrix is best remembered for using a Fender Stratocaster, although he also played a Fender Jaguar and Gibson Les Paul. A left-handed player, Hendrix used standard right-handed guitars with the strings reversed. The positioning of the body allowed him unique access to the volume and tone controls, which he integrated into his playing style. Amplification consisted of a series of Marshall heads hooked up to six 4 x 12 Marshall cabinets.

Milestones

1942 Born Johnny Allen Hendrix on November 27 in Seattle, Washington; four years later his parents rename him James Marshall Hendrix.

1961 Enlists in the US Army, as a paratrooper in the 101st Airborne.

1962 Forms King Kasuals with fellow soldier Billy Cox.

1963 Plays for two years in backing bands for the likes of Jackie Wilson, the Supremes, Little Richard, and B.B. King.

1965 Moves to New York to join the Isley Brothers backing band; forms Jimmy James and the Blue Flames and plays on New York club scene.

1966 Discovered by Chas Chandler (formerly of the Animals) playing in a Greenwich Village club

1967 Moves to London, where he forms the Jimi Hendrix Experience.

1968 Records groundbreaking *Are You Experienced?* album.

1969 Forms the Band of Gypsies with Buddy Miles and Billy Cox.

1970 Dies September 18 from drug overdose in London.

108

JAMES MARSHALL HENDRIX TAKING THE GUITAR INTO UNCHARTED TERRITORY

Are You Experienced? (1967)

One of the most important albums of the '60s, a treasure trove of blues and psychedelia that provided the blueprint for a new generation of rock musicians.

Axis: Bold As Love.(1967)

A mere six months after his debut, Hendrix cut back on the pyrotechnics to showcase his songwriting on a second certified classic.

Electric Ladyland (1968)

Double album set that featured cameos from Buddy Miles, Steve Winwood and Al Kooper, mixing succinct rock classics with spiralling blues jams to prove beyond all doubt that Hendrix was out there in a league of his own.

paratrooper for the military professional. Nonetheless his "protest" brought further unwanted pressure from black radical groups.

Towards the end of his life a never-ending search for new ways to develop took Hendrix into less popular areas. Disbanding the Experience, he formed the Band Of Gypsies with Buddy Miles and Billy Cox. Three virtuoso musicians they may have been, but the results were not widely viewed as the greatest listening experience. However, during the same period he seemed to spend most of his waking hours in recording studios, improvising alone or with anyone (literally) who happened to walk in. In a career which saw the release of only five albums during his lifetime, these recordings (and endless live tapes) have resulted in approaching 500 releases since his drug-related death in 1970.

In the space of just four years, Jimi Hendrix took the electric guitar into uncharted territory, setting new standards for rock and blues improvisation and influencing a generation of musicians like no one before or since.

109

B.B.KING
1925–

Not only one of the greatest blues guitarists of all time, B.B. King, whose career has lasted over half a century, is perhaps the most famous blues artist in the world. His legacy to the pantheon of modern guitar techniques is the extensive use he makes of string-bending, either as a playing device or as an alternative vibrato technique.

B.B. King was born in 1925 in Itta Bena, a small area outside Indianola, Mississippi. His parents parted when he was three and he moved with his mother to the nearby town of Kilmichael. Throughout much of his early life he was raised by a white family who employed him as a farmhand. It was here that he first picked up the guitar. His first influences were Charlie Christian and T-Bone Walker.

In 1946 King moved to Memphis to try to make a living as a musician. Before arriving at the blues he spent a good deal of time playing

Milestones

1925 Born September 16 in Itta Bena, Mississippi.

1946 Moves to Memphis to try to make a living as a musician.

1949 Gets own show on WDIA in Memphis.

1950 Debut single 'Three O'Clock Blues' for RPM is a million-seller.

1961 Signs to mainstream label ABC but is at his best in concert.

1970 Hits the Top 30 with all-star album *Indianola Mississippi Seeds*, also featuring Leon Russell, Joe Walsh and Carole King.

Classic Recordings

King Of The Blues (compilation, 1949–1989)
Four-CD career anthology drawing from King's first ever session for the Bullet label in 1949 right up to his version of 'When Love Comes To Town' with U2.

Live at The Regal (1960)
King captured in top form both as a singer and guitarist. One of the greatest live albums ever made.

Completely Well (1969)
A change of approach – King recording with white West Coast session musicians and scoring a hit with the gloriously orchestrated 'The Thrill Is Gone'.

gospel music. His first break came in 1949 when Sonny Boy Williamson II gave him an unpaid 10-minute slot on his KWEM radio show. Shortly afterwards King had his own show on WDIA in Memphis billed as "Riley King, The Blues Boy From Beale Street". Following sponsorship he became known as the "Pepticon Blues Boy", a name which was soon shortened to "blues boy", and finally just "B.B".

It was Ike Turner, then a session player, who brought King to the attention of RPM. His first single for the label, 'Three O'Clock Blues', sold over a million copies and topped the R&B chart for almost four months. King made over 200 recordings over the next 10 years with RPM, among them such classic electric blues compositions as 'Woke Up This Morning' and 'You Upset Me, Baby.'

By 1961, King was sufficiently famous nationally to sign for ABC, a mainstream pop label. Although this period failed to produce outstanding results in the studio, King did establish himself as a truly exceptional live performer, as can be heard on *Live At The*

THE BLUES BOY WITH THE EVER-FAITHFUL LUCILLE

110

Regal, which is simply one of the finest concert albums ever made.

Until the early '60s, the audience for blues music had largely been restricted to black America, or the hipper young urban whites. However, this situation changed when King and fellow blues players like Muddy Waters (*see* pages 124–25) were surprised to find themselves the subject of veneration by a new young generation of white blues musicians. In Britain, Eric Clapton, John Mayall, Brian Jones and Keith Richards had been inspired to produce their own takes on the works of the veterans. Thus, the electric Chicago blues of the '50s found itself a principal influence on the rock music of the mid-'60s.

Not slow to see that King had a potentially new young audience, manager Sydney Seidenberg successfully began to steer him towards the crossover market. This approach has typified King's career ever since. With his music and playing always firmly rooted in the blues tradition, he has been able to adapt himself to changes in fashion. During the '80s he even tried his hand at country and jazz crossovers, although neither are generally thought of as living up to his best work. Nonetheless, King remains one of the greatest living concert performers and continues to find himself a figurehead for successive generations of new musicians, particularly those in search of that elusive "authenticity".

111

Guitars

Although King used a Fender Telecaster for most of his RPM recordings, he is most closely associated with the Gibson ES-335, which he famously christened "Lucille". The 335 was first manufactured in 1958, but in 1981 Gibson repaid the compliment by producing a B.B. King signature 335.

WES MONTGOMERY
1925–1968

Wes Montgomery was the indisputable master of post-war jazz guitar. Alongside Django Reinhardt and Charlie Christian he remains one the three most influential guitarists in jazz history. A list of successors in whose playing he can be heard includes George Benson, Pat Metheny, Herb Ellis, John Scofield – indeed, pretty well every noteworthy jazz guitarist of the past 30 years.

Montgomery taught himself to play the guitar during his teenage years, inspired (and which post-war jazz guitarist wasn't?) by the single-string soloing of Charlie Christian (*see* pages 100–1). After a brief period of playing locally in his native Indianapolis, Montgomery left to tour with vibes legend Lionel Hampton's band in 1948. In spite of two years solid gigging on the professional jazz circuit, he returned home in 1950, unable to sustain a professional career. Throughout the '50s Montgomery worked by day as labourer and by night played in jazz clubs with his two brothers Monk and Buddy.

In spite of having won widespread admiration with his brothers, Montgomery's career looked to be going nowhere fast, until 1959 when, at the suggestion of Cannonball Adderley, producer Orrin Keepnews signed him up for the Riverside label. A succession of genre-defining performances were captured on recordings such as *The Wes Montgomery Trio* (1959) and the befittingly titled *The Incredible Guitar Of Wes Montgomery* (1960) which transformed him almost overnight into the most widely imitated jazz guitarist of the period. He suddenly found himself working with major league stars like John Coltrane and Wynton Kelly, and later organ legend Jimmy Smith, Milt Jackson and George Shearing.

The most unusual aspect of Montgomery's style was his use of the thumb to pick the strings. With the "attack" characterized by the absence of the traditional plectrum, Montgomery produced a mellower sound than had been heard before in jazz. At the same time he perfected Django Reinhardt's unison octave playing – a technique which adds a second note an octave above during soloing – and use of swiftly executed parallel chording. The unaccompanied track 'While We're Young' shows Montgomery's playing at its finest – sumptuous and rich with a seemingly endless capacity for reworking the most traditional of blues-styled sequences without ever resorting to cliché.

WES MONTGOMERY - AFTER CHARLIE CHRISTIAN, THE MOST SIGNIFICANT GUITARIST IN JAZZ HISTORY

Hopes ran high when Montgomery signed to the Verve label – home to so many jazz masters. For many of his most fervent followers these were soon dashed as he found himself in lush orchestral surroundings producing an

Milestones

1925 Born March 6 in Indianapolis, Indiana.

1948 Tours in Lionel Hampton band until 1950.

1959 Signs to Riverside label and records debut.

1960 Records *The Incredible Guitar Of Wes Montgomery*.

1964 Signs to Verve label and begins period of unprecedented commercial success.

1967 Appears on US television with trumpeter Herb Alpert; signs to Alpert's A&M label.

1968 Dies June 15 in Indianapolis following a heart attack.

112

Classic Recordings

The Incredible Jazz Guitar Of Wes Montgomery (1960)

One of the crucial guitar albums in any genre. A gently swinging set and though easy on the ear, an example of how Montgomery's improvisational skills and masterful tone changed the course of the guitar in jazz.

Full House (1962)

Exhilarating live recording that captures Montgomery at his most inventive and inspired.

Wes And Friends (1967)

Teamed up in a small group setting with vibe star Milt Jackson and pianist George Shearing, Montgomery briefly shows a return of the vintage flair that characterized his earlier work.

Alpert in 1967 – a year before Montgomery's death from a heart attack – allowed him to reach an audience that other jazz musicians could only dream about.

His early death left a gaping hole in the world of jazz guitar, which only the likes of George Benson and Pat Metheny – one of Montgomery's many young acolytes – have come close to filling. His influence has, if anything, grown in the years since his death – a fact illustrated by the Kool Festival all-star tribute concert held in his honour at New York's Carnegie Hall in 1985.

Guitars

Wes Montgomery's soft, mellow sound was produced using a Gibson L-5CES. The original L-5 archtop was launched in 1923, but underwent numerous changes until the late '40s, including electrification and cutaway bodies. Versions of the L-5 were produced until the '80s.

easy-listening style of jazz. Although Montgomery's mellow tone fitted neatly above the syrupy strings his playing lacked the sheer vitality of his Riverside recordings. It's not that his Verve work was bad, simply that stripped of the challenge of the small group situation Montgomery lacked the impetus to fire on all cylinders. However, his orchestral recordings were staggeringly successful in the commercial sense, and television appearances with Herb

JIMMY PAGE
1944–

Of the many British guitar heroes who emerged out of the blues boom, such as Eric Clapton, Jeff Beck (*see* pages 96–97) and Peter Green, it is ultimately Jimmy Page whose work has displayed the most variety and enduring appeal. And the influence of his band, Led Zeppelin, can be heard in the new wave of rock bands that have emerged during the '90s.

Page joined his first band, Neil Christian and the Crusaders, in 1960, when he was 16 years old. Even at that age his playing was already remarkably developed and it wasn't long before he began to find regular work playing on the London session scene. During the early '60s he gained a reputation for being one of the most versatile and hard-working guitarists around, often playing three or four sessions a day. Among the earliest beneficiaries

of his playing were the Who's 'Can't Explain', Them's 'Baby Please Don't Go' and Tom Jones' 'It's Not Unusual'.

In 1964, when Clapton left the Yardbirds, Page was offered the job of replacing him as guitarist, but he turned it down in favour of continuing his lucrative session career. Two years later, however, he had a change of heart and joined when bass guitarist Paul Samwell-Smith left. The Yardbirds now starred Jeff Beck

Jeff Beck (*see* pages 96–97)

JIMMY PAGE HAD BEEN A WELL-ESTABLISHED SESSION MAN LONG BEFORE HE BECAME A SUCCESSFUL ROCK STAR.

Guitars

Jimmy Page is closely associated with the Gibson Les Paul Standard, although he has also been famously captured live playing a Gibson double-neck with six and 12 strings. However, the Led Zeppelin classic, 'Stairway To Heaven', perhaps his most enduring single track, was played on a Fender Telecaster.

in the leading role, but the new combination didn't work and when Beck finally left in early 1968, the Yardbirds disintegrated, leaving Page on his own with rights to the name of the

Milestones

1944 Born January 9 in Heston, Middlesex, England.

1966 Joins the Yardbirds as bass player.

1968 The New Yardbirds become Led Zeppelin.

1980 Led Zeppelin split following the death of drummer John Bonham.

1994 Page begins partnership with Robert Plant.

1995 Surviving members of Led Zeppelin are inducted into the Rock and Roll Hall of Fame.

1998 Plant and Page release new album to critical acclaim.

114

band and a contracted tour of Sweden to fulfil. With Peter Grant as a manager, Page went about forming a New Yardbirds band for the tour. The musicians they found were session veteran John Paul Jones, drummer John Bonham and singer Robert Plant.

The band completed the Scandinavian tour as the New Yardbirds, but then began playing in England under a new identity – Led Zeppelin. Their debut album was recorded in the space of 30 hours and was released in early 1969. The sound was an awesome "heavy" blues, each musician giving virtuoso performances. The album was an immediate hit on both sides of the Atlantic, launching

what would become the most successful rock groups of all time.

At the heart of the Zeppelin sound lay the intricate guitar work and production skills of Jimmy Page. His brilliance on the acoustic can be heard on his altered-tuning version of the folky 'Black Mountain Side'. On this track Page uses what is known as the "D-A-D-G-A-D" tuning system (these are the notes the guitar is

JIMMY PAGE MADE REGULAR USE OF THE GIBSON DOUBLE-NECK ON STAGE

Classic Recordings

Led Zeppelin I (1969)

Sophisticated high-energy workout containing rock classics 'Communication Breakdown' and 'Dazed And Confused'. Established the band as a logical replacement for the pioneering Cream, and Jimmy Page as one of the most exciting and innovative musicians in rock.

Led Zeppelin II (1969)

Written on the road in hotel rooms and soundchecks, it became the definitive rock album of the late '60s, and includes 'Whole Lotta Love'.

Led Zeppelin IV (1971)

Also known as the "four symbols" album, from the runic imagery on the sleeve (the album has no formal title). Zeppelin's live shows' increasing subtlety and dynamism established them as the biggest band in the world. The track 'Stairway To Heaven' became one of the definitive rock anthems of the '70s.

115

tuned to from bottom to top) – a notoriously tricky tuning. However, it is his electric playing that has influenced so many, not least the gently picked arpeggios of Zeppelin's "theme tune", 'Stairway To Heaven'.

The band broke up following the death of John Bonham in 1980, but Page has continued to work at a pace ever since. After a false start in 1985 with Paul Rodgers' band the Firm, Zeppelin fans the world over were thrilled to hear of Page and Plant's new partnership in the early '90s.

However, it is with the eleven Led Zeppelin albums that Page's reputation will always rest. This is an extraordinary body of work – Led Zeppelin set a new benchmark for technical excellence in rock without ever seeming to be dull, self-important or over-indulgent. It is a benchmark that no other band has really come close to meeting.

DJANGO REINHARDT
1910–1953

Jean Baptiste "Django" Reinhardt was not only the first great virtuoso jazz guitar soloist, he was also the first non-American musician to make a notable impact on the world jazz scene. Born in 1910 to a nomadic caravan-dwelling gypsy family, Django Reinhardt was the son of an entertainer who worked in a travelling show between Belgium and France. As a child he learnt to play the violin and banjo before moving on to the guitar. However, it was at the age of 18 that a fire in his caravan famously disabled his left hand, leaving only the thumb and first two fingers functioning. Although most young musicians would have given up under the same circumstances, Reinhardt used his limitations to develop a unique technique which enabled him to performing lightning-fast single note runs the likes of which had rarely been heard before.

Influenced by early jazz pioneers like Louis Armstrong, Duke Ellington and guitarist Eddie Lang, Reinhardt began his professional career playing in the coffee houses of Montmartre in Paris. It was here that he was introduced to the popular young French crooner Jean Sablon in

Guitars

All three guitarists in the Quintet of the Hot Club of France used the Selmer Maccaferri guitar. Designed by the Italian Mario Maccaferri for the French instrument maker Henri Selmer, it was created with an in-built sound chamber allowing for the projection of greater volume – ideal for noisy jazz clubs with no amplification. When Reinhardt "went electric" in the late '40s he generally used Gibson guitars, such as an L-5 fitted with pick-ups.

1933. Reinhardt spent a fruitful year as Sablon's solo accompanist until he joined up with violinist Stéphane Grappelli in the Quintette du Hot Club de France.

Within a year, the Quintet – which also featured Louis Vola on bass and Roger Chaput and Reinhardt's younger brother, Joseph, on rhythm guitar – had built up an international reputation based largely on the interplay between the soloing violin and guitar. It was a unique sound that matched Grappelli's elegantly flowing lines with Reinhardt's high-speed, single-string runs and swift chord work. The Hot Club played widely throughout Europe, regularly topping the bill over visiting American stars. During the five years in which the Quintet were active they cut over 200 sides, most of which are now viewed as being among the high points of pre-war jazz.

When war broke out in Europe in 1939, Grappelli based himself in London. Reinhardt chose to return to his former gypsy life, travelling through France and Belgium. During this period he seemed to lose some of his passion for the guitar, taking an interest in other musical forms, and devoting much of his time to painting and fishing.

In 1946 Reinhardt received a cable from Duke Ellington, inviting him to perform in the US. Through a mixture of Hot Club recordings and word-of-mouth reports from American jazzmen returning from Europe, Reinhardt's arrival in New York was preceded by a reputation that was impossible to follow. Partly because he was playing electrified guitar for the first time, the concerts were not entirely successful and, disappointed by the reaction, he cut short his visit and returned to Europe.

In truth, Reinhardt's visit to the home of

Milestones

1910 Born January 23 in Liverchies, Belgium.

1928 Damages two fingers of his left hand in a caravan fire.

1933 Forms the Quintet of the Hot Club of France with violinist Stéphane Grappelli.

1939 Returns to itinerant life during war years.

1946 Makes US debut touring with Duke Ellington.

1953 Dies May 16 in Fontainebleau, France.

jazz had been an underwhelming experience for everyone. Whilst he had towered above his peers for much of the '30s, the end of the decade had already seen the emergence of the next generation: the electric guitar was now an instrument in its own right and in a fleeting career, over almost as quickly as it had begun, Charlie Christian had already redefined the role of the guitar in jazz (*see* page 100).

In later years Reinhardt struggled to keep up with the changing face of jazz. Whilst his leaning shifted towards bebop, its style and intellectualism was suited to neither his playing nor personality. By all accounts, Reinhardt had also found it difficult to adjust to life away from his gypsy roots, and was ill-equipped to deal with the by-products of success. The many apocryphal stories of his struggles with the modern world – he was once reputed to have permanently discarded a new car on the roadside after it had run out of petrol – have only served to reinforce his image as an "otherwordly" stranger. But although he could neither read nor write, his classic recordings of the mid-'30s reveal a latent musical literacy that was way ahead of its time.

Classic Recordings

**50th Anniversary
(compilation, 1934–1935)**

Reinhardt recorded few formal "albums" in his life. However, the many classic recordings made with the Quintet of the Hot Club of France between 1934 and 1939 have remained widely available in compilation form, for example on *50th Anniversary* (1934-35).

Among the most noteworthy recordings are his arrangements of standards like 'I'll See You In My Dreams', 'Stardust' and 'Sweet Georgia Brown'. Reinhardt's own compositions such as 'Nuages' and 'Djangology' have become jazz standards in their own right.

DJANGO REINHARDT, THE FIRST GREAT
JAZZ GUITAR SOLOIST

ANDRÉS SEGOVIA
1893–1987

More than anyone before or since, it was Andrés Segovia who brought widespread respectability to the guitar and helped the instrument gain acceptance in the elite world of classical music. Until then, despite the works of composers and musicians from Sor to Tárrega (*see* chapter on the Torres revolution and the classical guitar), the guitar was still considered a rather crude and limited "boudoir" instrument. All the more remarkable, then, is the fact that Segovia was a self-taught maestro – indeed he was always proud to declare that he had always been his own master and pupil.

Born in 1893, Segovia studied music in Granada against the wishes of his family, but abandoned all other instruments in favour of the guitar. Under his own extraordinary tuition, he refined many of the revolutionary developments in playing that had been made by Tárrega during the previous century, most notably the relaxation of Tárrega's rigid

Milestones

1893 Born February 21 in Linares, Spain.

1909 Makes professional debut in Granada, Spain.

1916 Tours Central and South America to widespread acclaim.

1924 Makes Parisian debut.

1928 Makes New York debut.

1987 Dies June 2 in Madrid.

right-hand technique. He also developed the range of possible guitar tones in his playing by striking the strings either with the nails or with nails and fingertips.

Remarkably, by the age of only 16 Segovia had already made his first professional recital in Granada, which he followed up with performances throughout Spain. In 1916 he made his first tour of South America, where his concerts were met with sensational acclaim.

In 1924 Segovia made his debut in Paris. Among the audience were Manuel de Falla and Albert Roussel, both of whom would compose seminal works for the guitar. Segovia's debuts in Moscow (1926) and New York (1928) were met with similar enthusiasm. Thereafter he toured widely throughout world, astounding audiences with an unprecedented virtuosity on an instrument which was still largely unfamiliar to the masses. Although Segovia never actively sought widespread popularity – indeed he spoke out against artists who pandered to mass appeal – he was one of the most popular soloists performing in the classical field.

It was Segovia's visits to South America that had wider implications for the development of the classical repertoire. It was here that he encountered some of the greatest composers of the period, such as the Brazilian Heitor Villa-Lobos. His 1929 piece *Douze Etudes* is widely thought to be the first composition for the instrument by a non-guitarist. The lack of knowledge of the instrument's limitations paved the way for the development of future composition that would place increasing technical demands on

Classic Recordings

Recordings (1927–1939)
A double CD capturing Segovia at the peak of his playing. Includes works by Castelnuovo-Tedesco, Sor and Bach.

The Master (compilation, 1950s)
Segovia later in his career. Includes works by Tárrega, Torroba and Sor, as well as transcriptions of works by Handel and Bach.

Considering Segovia's reputation, a relatively small amount of his recorded work remains in print.

the musician. Another notable composer to benefit from meeting Segovia was the Mexican Manuel Ponce (*see* page 27) who produced works such as *Twelve Preludes*, *Chanson* and *Concierto del Sur*, all of which were given their concert debuts by Segovia.

The importance of Segovia's role as the instrument's greatest ambassador during the first half of the twentieth century cannot be overestimated. Not only the greatest maestro the instrument has yet seen, he was responsible for making the guitar a truly international instrument. Also, in bringing a new repertoire to the classical stage, he could be viewed as being responsible for widening the twentieth-century tradition for guitar composition. Without his influence it is doubtful that such fine composers as Castelnuovo-Tedesco (*Cavatina*) and Rodrigo (*Concierto de Aranjuez*) would enjoy such widespread popularity throughout the world. His own transcriptions of works for other instruments (such as the vihuela and lute) and of works by composers of the stature of Bach, Mozart and Chopin also greatly increased the guitar's classical repertoire. Segovia considered his work as a crusade, as he wrote himself in his autobiography:

"From my youthful years I dreamed of raising the guitar from the sad artistic level in which it lay. Since then, I have dedicated my life to four essential tasks. The first: to separate the guitar from mindless folklore-type entertainment. My second purpose: to make the beauty of the guitar known to the public of the entire world. The third task: that of influencing the authorities at conservatories, academies, and universities to include the guitar in their instruction programs on the same basis as the violin, cello, and piano. And my fourth item of labour: to endow it with a repertory of high quality, made up of works possessing intrinsic musical value, from the pens of composers accustomed to writing for orchestra, piano and violin."

Also significant is Andrés Segovia's role in encouraging many young musicians such as John Williams, amongst others, in master-class courses at music academies in Italy and Spain.

Even though Segovia's greatest work was done over 40 years ago, he remains the single most important figure in the history of the classical guitar, and whilst a number of out-standing players have succeeded him, his own recordings of the standard classical repertoire are still held up as the benchmarks against which all newcomers are measured.

Guitars

Segovia started out using a guitar built by Spanish maker Benito Ferrer, switching to a model built by the Ramirez brothers in 1912. In the late '30s he began using guitars built by the German maker Hermann Hauser. Towards the end of his life he was known to have returned to Spanish-built instruments made by Fleta and José Ramirez III.

ANDRÉS SEGOVIA – A SELF-TAUGHT MASTER

119

FRANCISCO TÁRREGA
1852–1909

The revolutionary work by Torres in reinventing the guitar (*see* earlier chapter) brought about new possibilities in playing the instrument. The first man to build on those new beginnings was Francisco de Asis Tárrega y Eixea, the man who laid the foundations for the modern classical technique and first suggested that the guitar could be taken seriously as a classical instrument to rival any of its more noble rivals.

Francisco Tárrega was born in Villareal, Valencia in 1852. Although at the age of 10 he studied classical guitar with Julian Arcas, at the wish of his father he studied piano at Madrid's prestigious Conservatorio. A brilliant student, he was awarded first prize for harmony and composition. However, he soon returned to the guitar, the instrument on which he would become the dominant figure of the nineteenth century.

In 1869, Tárrega was fortunate enough to acquire a guitar built by Antonio de Torres, a luthier based in Seville. By 1877 Tárrega was making a living as a music teacher and concert guitarist. At his first performances in London and Paris during 1880 he was hailed as "the Sarasate of the guitar", Sarasate being the most eminent violinist of the period. At the end of the century Tárrega travelled widely throughout Europe, his virtuoso performances allowing the guitar to be viewed in a much more serious light.

He also composed many original pieces for the instrument, although they are by no means viewed as the most interesting new works of the period. On the other hand, his transcriptions of Beethoven (the *Addagio* and *Allegretto* from the *"Moonlight" Sonatas*) and Chopin's *Preludes* were valuable additions to the instrument's repertoire.

It was as a teacher and innovator that Tárrega won his reputation as a legend of the guitar. Many of the standard techniques used right up to the modern day originated from him. The most dramatic development was the positioning of the guitar on the left leg, a move which came about as a result of the increase in the size of its body. This position had been previously identified as preferable, but the narrow waists and overall smaller size of the older instruments had made it impossible to adopt with any comfort.

Tárrega also revolutionized right-hand techniques, bringing about the widespread use of the *apoyando* stroke, with which the finger pushes through the string and comes to rest on the next one. Previously, although this had been standard for the thumb, finger strokes had more usually been played *tirando*, the tips rising after the string had been struck. Whichever stroke was used, however, Tárrega was the principal voice to suggest that the little finger should *not* rest on the guitar body, but that the entire right hand should be poised free above the strings. This approach also came about through Torres' new designs which saw the height of the fingerboard raised so that it was no longer flush with the surface of the guitar body. This in turn required the bridge saddle to be heightened, which made the technique of the little-finger support extremely uncomfortable to use successfully.

Among the many guitarists who received personal tuition from Tárrega were fellow Spaniards Miguel Llobert, Maria Rita Brondi and Emilio Pujol, all of whom were among the most eminent practitioners of the instrument during the first half of the twentieth century.

In 1906, at the peak of his fame, Tárrega was struck down with paralysis of his right side. Although he continued to appear in public, he never fully recovered. He died in Barcelona in 1909.

Classic Recordings

Although recorded sound had been pioneered towards the end of Tárrega's life, not surprisingly there are no recordings of his work in existence. Like other classical pioneers who succeeded him, Tárrega broadened the classical repertoire with a mixture of transcriptions of other nineteenth-century composers' works for different instruments, and his own romantic compositions, the most notable of which are *Recuerdos de la Alhambra* and *Capricho árabe*.

Milestones

1852 Born Francisco de Asis Tárrega y Eixea in Villareal, Valencia, Spain.

1862 Studies classical guitar under Julian Arcas.

1869 Acquires a guitar bulit by Torres.

1909 Dies in Barcelona, aged 57.

Guitars

Francisco Tárrega was a champion of the new generation of guitars produced by Antonio de Torres Jurado. It was thanks largely to the work of Tárrega that the design and construction of the Torres model became a blueprint for the other classical guitars that followed.

120

**THE REVOLUTIONARY TÁRREGA OPENED UP
NEW POSSIBILITIES IN GUITAR-PLAYING**

STEVE VAI
1960–

If there is one man who embodies the art of the modern lead guitar – for better or for worse – it is American pyrotechnician Steve Vai.

Born in Brooklyn, New York in 1960, Vai first played the guitar at the age of 13, and was given lessons by Joe Satriani. His earliest influences included John Lee Hooker, Jimmy Page (*see* pages 114–15), Jimi Hendrix (pages 108–9), Roy Buchanan and Carlos Santana. A phenomenal learner, Vai studied music and composition on his own until he entered Boston's Berklee School of Music.

Vai first made an impact on the music scene in 1979 when he moved to Los Angeles to play second guitar in the Frank Zappa band. An ideal home for such a rigorous disciplinarian, Vai is known to have followed an austere 10-hours-a-day practice regime at various times. Working with Zappa introduced an element of eclecticism to his repertoire, as can be heard on his home-recorded debut album *Flex-able*. Indeed, with tracks like the intricate sci-fi spoof 'Little Green Men', first-time listeners could be forgiven for thinking that this *was* Zappa working under a pseudonym.

After Zappa, Vai began to carve out a reputation performing in the conventional rock mainstream, first stepping in to replace Yngwie Malmsteen in the band Alcatrazz on 1985's *Disturbing The Peace*. He followed this up by writing and playing on two very listenable albums by former Van Halen vocalist Dave Lee Roth before moving on to join Whitesnake in 1989.

Vai's ascension to the ranks of guitar god was assured when he recorded the award-winning and technically stunning *Passion And Warfare* album in 1990. A kaleidoscope of guitar wizardry, he displayed complete mastery of every imaginable rock-based style. Not only could some of the most awesome high-speed soloing be heard, but it displayed a rare intelligence in his understanding and use of dynamics. In some ways *Passion And Warfare* could be thought of as a digital equivalent to Jimi Hendrix's *Electric Ladyland*, but although Vai's skill in manipulating sound may come close, it seems to lack the effortless warmth that made Hendrix's playing so "human". Some critics find that Vai's skill is almost too evident at times.

Vai showed a little more restraint on 1993's sister album *Sex And Religion*. Although this cemented his reputation as top dog in a select league of contemporary guitar heroes over the likes of Eddie Van Halen and Joe Satriani, it simultaneously illustrated that, instrumental genius though he may be, his own compositions seem less impassioned compared to the fire of his playing. Unlike that of Van Halen, who is known for producing some of the most appealing rock albums of the '80s, Steve Vai's music is bought primarily for the stunning quality of the guitar work.

Vai has also involved himself in the development of new instruments, having worked with Japanese guitar makers Ibanez to produce the Jem and Universe models. These are highly playable (not to mention expensive) "rock" guitars of the "Superstrat" variety, both featuring three pick-ups, a two-octave fretboard and a scalloped fingerboard beyond the twentieth fret to facilitate *very* fast lead work by the technically accomplished.

Milestones

1960 Born June 6 in Brooklyn, New York.

1979 Joins Frank Zappa band.

1985 Joins Alcatrazz, replacing Yngwie Malmsteen.

1989 Joins Whitesnake.

1990 Records genre-defining, award-winning *Passion And Warfare*.

1993 Records *Sex And Religion*.

**STEVE VAI PLAYS THE IBANEZ JEM, WHICH
HE HELPED TO DESIGN**

MUDDY WATERS
1915–1983

Muddy Waters brought the music of the Mississippi Delta into the modern world, becoming the first great electric blues guitarist in the process. He was largely responsible for introducing R&B to white audiences, and in doing so laid the foundations for much of the rock music of the '60s and beyond.

Growing up in Clarksdale, Mississippi, McKinley Morganfield learned to play the guitar and harmonica at the age of 17. His earliest influences were Son House and Robert Johnson. Working on a local plantation, Muddy Waters (as Morganfield was known by then) made a name for himself locally both as a musician and as a moonshine bootlegger.

Waters' first records were cut during the war years for blues archivist Alan Lomax – a man responsible for rediscovering many of the great blues artists of the '20s and '30s who, at that time, had been almost entirely

unknown to white audiences. Lomax had been scouring the state with his Library Of Congress team looking for the legendary Robert Johnson. Before discovering that Johnson had died three years earlier, Lomax was told that there was a local man who played like him, and directed towards the Stovall Plantation where Waters was employed. Over the space of two years Waters cut 13 sides for Lomax, mostly accompanying himself. Songs like 'You Got To Take Sick And Die Some Of These Days' and 'I Be's Trouble', revealed a raw, as yet undeveloped talent, both in his powerful, even menacing, vocals and the intensity of his slide-playing.

124

Milestones

1915 Born 4 April McKinley Morganfield in Rolling Fork, Mississippi.

1941 Records Library Of Congress recordings for blues folklorist Alan Lomax.

1943 Moves to Chicago, where he gets his first electric guitar.

1950 Begins long association with the newly formed Chess label.

1960 Electric Chicago blues reaches a new audience as he performs at the Newport Jazz Festival.

1983 Dies April 30, in Chicago.

MUDDY WATERS – A TRULY ELECTRIC PERFORMER

Taken under the wing of blues ambassador Big Bill Broonzy, in 1943 Waters moved to Chicago, where he got his first electric guitar. In 1948 he cut some unsuccessful records for the Aristocrat label, which was run by, among others, the brothers Leonard and Phil Chess. Two years later when they formed their own Chess label, Waters was one of their first signings. His debut recording for Chess was made with harmonica soloist Little

Walter Jacobs. The combination of heavily amplified harmonica and guitar, and Waters' close-miked deep bass growl made 'Louisiana Blues' a national R&B hit.

Like many greats in other areas of music (Duke Ellington and Miles Davis to name but two), Waters was notable for surrounding himself with up-and-coming young players eager to learn from the master – and many notable names from the next generation of the blues passed through his ranks. Continuing to work with Little Walter, Waters formed an expanded line-up which included second guitarist Jimmy Rogers, drummer Elga Edmonds and pianist Otis Spann. Muddy Waters' ensemble recordings made between 1952 and 1960 provided the single most succinct blueprint for the next phase of development in R&B as a musical form. A succession of timeless anthems such as 'I'm Your Hoochie Coochie Man' and 'Got My Mojo Working' can truly be said to have dragged the blues into the modern age.

Waters' influence cut further afield, though, as his classic Chess recordings were plundered by the second-generation rock 'n' rollers of the early '60s. Indeed, Waters' 'Rollin' Stone' even inspired the very existence of one young English group. But if there existed a great divide between the two, it was the difference between man and boy. Through the lips of Mick Jagger, 'I Just Wanna Make Love To You' sounded more like a teenage fantasy. When Waters first boomed out the same song a decade earlier it was nothing less than a declaration of intent. This was a 40-year-old man of the world who knew what he wanted. And he knew that no woman in her right mind would refuse him: Muddy Waters was the *real thing*.

Throughout the '60s and beyond, few would dispute that Waters was the greatest living bluesman. He continued to record fine

Classic Recordings

The Chess Box (compilation, 1950s)

Muddy Waters' recordings for the Chess label during the '50s defined the development of rock music during the next decade. This crucial period is documented over the course of three CDs.

Live At Newport (1961)

A seminal R&B album which became a blueprint for a new generation of young white musicians like the Rolling Stones, the Yardbirds and Fleetwood Mac in Britain, and the Paul Butterfield Blues Band in the US.

Down On Stovall's Plantation (compilation 1940s)

Collection of Waters' first recordings made for the Library Of Congress series shows burgeoning raw talent.

125

albums, often collaborating with the younger musicians such as Paul Butterfield, Mike Bloomfield, Johnny Winter and Buddy Guy (*see* pages 106–7). Waters remained an active performer until his death in 1983. A venerated figure in his later years, even when he was well into his sixties, he could still blow any performer off stage with the sheer force of his personality.

Any list of American cultural pioneers would include names like Woody Guthrie, Duke Ellington, George Gershwin and Bob Dylan: the name of Muddy Waters stands tall in such exalted company.

Guitars

Muddy Waters took a shine to solid-body electric guitars as soon as they became available, beginning with the Fender Telecaster. However, from the mid-'50s onwards he would invariably use a Gibson Les Paul Standard.

CHAPTER EIGHT

A–Z
OF
GUITARISTS

126

JOHN ABERCROMBIE
(1944–)

At home in every last corner of jazz, from free improvisation to bebop, John Abercrombie has long been established at the vanguard of the jazz guitar world.

After studying at the Berklee School of Music – college of choice for so many of the finest jazz musicians – Abercrombie first turned heads alongside the Brecker brothers in the fusion band Dreams before moving on to work with drummer Billy Cobham and the legendary Gil Evans. His early playing showed influences as diverse as Tal Farlow and Jimi Hendrix (see page 108) – the sheer speed of his soloing no doubt helped to make him an attraction to many rock crossover fans.

Moving away from jazz-rock in the late '70s, Abercrombie began a fertile relationship with the German ECM label. His work from this period onwards, notably with Ralph Towner and saxophonist Jan Garbarek, showed a gradual shift towards a more melodic style.

....

Arcade (1978)

Sargasso Sea (1977, with Ralph Towner)

Eventyr (1981, with Jan Garbarek)

DIONYSIO AGUADO
(1784-1849)

Alongside Fernando Sor and Mauro Giuliani, Dionysio Aguado was one the key guitarists of the nineteenth century (see pages 18–21). His playing and compositions helped bring about a renewed interest in the guitar.

During the previous two centuries, the guitar had largely been strummed and used to accompany a vocalist. The late eighteenth century saw a revival in Spain of the *punteado* style of playing – the technique of plucking the strings with the individual fingers – which enabled a wider repertoire to be played on the instrument.

A virtuoso, Aguado travelled widely outside his native Spain, performing with great success in the concert halls of Paris, London and Vienna.

Although they approached the guitar in very different ways, Fernando Sor and Aguado were close friends – Sor dedicated his duet *The Two Friends* to his fellow countryman. Although Aguado's compositions are still performed, they have never reached the same levels of popularity or acceptance as those of Sor.

JAN AKKERMAN
(1946–)

The early '70s threw up an unusual array of misfits in the world of music. The birth of "progressive" rock – thought by some to signal pop music's coming of age – began to attract certain young musicians who seemed to be as familiar with the traditions of classical music as with rock 'n' roll. Thus appeared the Dutch contribution to the genre – the band Focus.

For a few years in the mid-'70s, guitarist Jan Akkerman became the thinking young man's guitar hero, a reputation seemingly based on the guitar instrumental 'Sylvia', which gave Focus a brief glimmer of pop stardom in 1974.

A regular music press poll winner, Akkerman left Focus in 1976. However, his solo career fell foul of over-indulgent playing and the sudden unfashionability of prog-rock. Since then, he has doggedly followed his own path, producing an endless succession of hyper-clinical fusion albums, or, in more recent times, New Age soundscapes.

....

Focus III (1974, with Focus)

The Complete Guitarist (compilation, 1986)

DUANE ALLMAN
(1946–1971)

Even today, many still mourn the tragic passing of Duane Allman, a man whose death at the age of 24 in a motorcycle accident left the music world scratching its head, wondering what might have been.

Allman first made his mark in the late '60s as a session player on the Muscle Shoals scene. Here he worked with many of Atlantic's top stars like Clarence Carter, Wilson Pickett and Aretha Franklin. His reputation soared, some finding it hard to believe that his electrifying fusion of soul and blues could be the work of a young white musician.

With the formation of the Allman Brothers Band (with Greg Allman and Dickey Betts) in 1969, Duane Allman was at once elevated to rock's premier division. The three albums released while he was alive provided a showcase for some of the finest bottleneck slide guitar playing ever heard. Also remarkable was that two such outstanding guitarists could co-exist within one band, Betts' country leanings complementing Allman's fiery passion to the full. In spite of his band's rapidly growing reputation, Allman still found time to pursue a session career – it's strange to think he is probably best remembered for his solo on an Eric Clapton record (Derek and the Dominoes' 'Layla'), rather than for cutting some of the definitive solos of rock history.

....

The Allman Brothers Band (1969)

At The Fillmore East (1971, with Allman Brothers Band)

Layla And Other Assorted Love Songs (1971, with Derek and the Dominoes)

LAURINDO ALMEIDA
(1917–)

An extraordinary musician, Brazilian-born Laurindo Almeida has managed to traverse

DUANE ALLMAN: PERHAPS THE GREATEST ROCK GUITARIST TO DON A BOTTLENECK

the worlds of jazz and classical music comfortably without alienating either camp. However, his greatest legacy might well be as the man who introduced the bossa nova to America in 1962. Born in São Paulo, Almeida had already embarked on a classical career when he saw Django Reinhardt performing (*see* page 116). A pivotal moment in his life, it was enough to convince him to move to New York, where he quickly found work in Stan Kenton's orchestra. During the early '50s he produced some rather unpredictable jazz recordings for Capitol, as well as a number of highly rated classical albums. In 1962 he recorded his most influential work, the album *Viva Bossa Nova*. It not only introduced US audiences to the composer Antonio Carlos Jobim, but also to Almeida's most famous song, Jobim's 'The Girl From Ipanema'.

....

Viva Bossa Nova (1962)

KOKOMO ARNOLD
(1901–1968)

A blues enigma, Kokomo Arnold was one of the most unusual bottleneck players of the '30s.

Not a great deal is known about Arnold's life. He was born in Georgia and moved to Chicago in the late '20s, where he divided his time between performing and bootlegging. During the early '30s he cut numerous sides for local labels, including his most popular hit, 'Milk Cow Blues'. He later recorded and performed with pianist Peetie Wheatstraw. When Wheatstraw died in 1941 Arnold retired from music.

In 1959, after Elvis Presley successfully revived 'Milk Cow Blues', Arnold was tracked down, but apart from performing a handful of festival gigs it was clear he wasn't that interested in reviving his music career. This has undoubtedly contributed to his relative obscurity.

Although a small body of his recordings remain available, Arnold is an unjustly obscure figure in guitar history. Nonetheless, his harsh, percussive slide-playing, though somewhat eccentric, inspired musicians of the calibre of Elmore James.

....

Kokomo Arnold Volume I (1930–1935, compilation)

CHET ATKINS
– *see* Legends

GENE AUTRY
(1907–)

It was at the beginning of the '30s that the great American public first took the guitar to its heart. The advent of the "talkies" had made cinema far and away the most popular form of entertainment throughout America – the best-loved film genre was the Western, and one of the biggest stars was Gene Autry, the "Singing Cowboy". His films usually followed a simple formula – mysterious folk hero rides the prairies, helps out folk in distress, wins the heart of the girl, and disappears alone into the sunset singing and playing his guitar.

Autry was rarely photographed without a horse and a guitar. It was in this way that the instrument became associated with the glamour and romance of Hollywood and the freedom of the Big Country. Autry, and popular rivals like Roy Rogers, became the impetus for the sale of millions of cheap Spanish guitars sold in the Sears Roebuck catalogues.

A footnote in the guitar's history, Autry was nevertheless influential: without the likes of The Singing Cowboy, the guitar would not be the popular instrument it is today.

....

The Singing Cowboy ('30s compilation)

DEREK BAILEY
(1930–)

First impressions of British guitarist Derek Bailey can be daunting. His is a world in which conventional notions of melody, harmony, rhythm and form cannot easily be applied. For some, Bailey's is an inspirational, dramatic, anarchic and sometimes humorous form of self-expression. More conventional listeners find him harder on the ear.

After working with a variety of orchestras and dance bands throughout the '50s, in the early '60s Bailey began to take an increasing interest in purely improvised playing.

Beginning in small group settings, he has since more often played as a soloist or in duets, most notably with saxophonist Evan Parker.

A controversial figure, Bailey has been a major influence in the world of "free" music, not only as a player, but as one of the founders of the Incus label, which for almost 30 years has unleashed some of the most interesting and uncompromising music found anywhere in the world. He has also published a fascinating book on improvisation, its history and the various forms in which it can be found in traditional ethnic music forms: *Improvisation – Its Nature and Practice in Music* (1980).

....

The Topography Of The Lungs (1970, with Evan Parker)
View From Six Windows (1982)

DANNY BARKER
(1909–1994)

Over five decades, Danny Barker played with some of the greatest names from successive generations of jazz: Louis Armstrong, Cab Calloway, Dizzy Gillespie, even a young Wynton Marsalis in the '80s.

In his early days he was more usually found playing the banjo, but in 1939 he switched to guitar when he joined Cab Calloway's band. Throughout his career, which he pursued well into his late seventies, he always remained rooted in the traditional New Orleans style of playing – a rhythm man who rarely stood up to take a solo.

Barker's assured place in jazz history is more likely to result from his work away from the bandstand. In his later years he took on the role of jazz academic which saw him actively involved in the New Orleans jazz museum, as well as a popular voice on American TV and radio.

....

Danny Barker's Band (1986)
Cab Calloway: Best Of The Big Bands ('40s compilation)

128

GEORGE BARNES
(1921–1977)

A prodigious musician, by the time George Barnes won a Tommy Dorsey Amateur Swing competition at the age of 16 he had already been on the road for three years with his own quartet. Following a stint in the army, he recorded with a variety of TV and radio orchestras in Chicago and New York, finally graduating to work with Louis Armstrong and many of the finest jazz musicians of the period.

In the early '60s, at a time when many jazz players were turning to rhythm and blues in search of a quick buck, Barnes chose to stay true to his jazz roots, forming a celebrated partnership with veteran guitarist Carl Kress. Much of their repertoire – among Barnes' finest work – centred on reworking standards such as 'Someone To Watch Over Me'. After Kress's death in 1965, Barnes attempted a similar coupling, this time with a younger partner, Bucky Pizzarelli. Although their music was intermittently spectacular, it was nothing compared to their spectacularly violent break-up. In 1973 Barnes formed a new quartet with cornet player Ruby Braff. For two years they dazzled jazz club audiences.

An underrated guitarist, Barnes seemed a victim of an elitism that saw his tasteful and lyrical style as somehow lightweight.

....

Two Guitars (1962, with Carl Kress)
The Best I've Heard (1974, with Braff-Barnes Quartet)

SYD BARRETT
(1946–)

Syd Barrett is probably best remembered as the epitome of the tragic '60s acid casualty. Although his songs continue to influence the new generations that continually discover his work, few yet recognize his significance in the development of rock guitar.

Born in Cambridge, Barrett formed Pink Floyd while at art school in 1965. A taste for the LSD-drenched times led him down some unpredictable paths. On the one hand he was capable of penning instantly memorable slabs of English pop, such as 'See Emily Play'; but it is for extended work-outs such as 'Interstellar Overdrive' that Barrett's credentials as an influential guitarist can be argued. Using echo, fuzz and feedback, Barrett's famous mirrored Telecaster took the electric guitar into uncharted territory. His was an intuitive and untutored approach to the instrument, his lengthy, winding improvisations creating the floating spaced-out soundscapes which were so much a hallmark of early Pink Floyd live performances – and an alternative soundtrack to Swinging London.

Sadly, during the recording of their second album, Barrett's LSD-fuelled eccentricities escalated out of control. Although he was the band's singer, songwriter, guitarist and creative force, he was viewed as an increasing liability and was expelled from the band. Dave Gilmour took over from Barrett, and Floyd went on to became one of the most successful bands of the '70s. Barrett himself produced a pair of extraordinary acoustic albums, but it was clear that his health was in a serious state. He disappeared from the music world, his whereabouts remaining a mystery until the '80s, when it was revealed that he lived a relatively ordinary existence with his family in Cambridge. He evidently no longer has any interest or involvement in music.

....

The Piper At The Gates Of Dawn (1967, with Pink Floyd)
The Madcap Laughs (1970)

JEFF BECK
– *see* Legends

ADRIAN BELEW
(1951–)

Although his reputation may have resulted from his work with the likes of Frank Zappa and Talking Heads, Adrian Belew's first brush with the mainstream was as another of David Bowie's noteworthy sidemen. Belew graced the *Scary Monsters And Super Creeps* album with a series of jerky, off-kilter solos which made the set of songs sound more interesting and slightly strange.

His relationship with Bowie brought him into contact with Robert Fripp, who drafted him into the second coming of his classic progressive band King Crimson in 1981. In a virtuoso line-up that also included Bill Bruford on drums and Tony Levin on bass, Belew brought a David Byrne-influenced pop sensibility to the project, giving Crimson a new lease of life at a time when the "old school" dinosaurs had been rendered all but extinct by punk and the new wave. Contrasting with the more academic inclinations of Fripp, the new Crimson produced a complex and yet accessible sound which gave space to some extraordinary duelling by two consummate guitarists.

Left to his own devices, albums such as 1992's *Inner Revolution* showed that, unlike many of his session contemporaries, Belew is a more than capable songwriter (if less focused), possessed of a natural inclination to experiment with sound and unusual instrumentation .

....

Desire Of The Rhino King (compilation, 1987)
Discipline (1981, with King Crimson)

GEORGE BENSON
(1943–)

George Benson is largely known to mainstream audiences as the silky-smooth voice behind such million-selling soul hits as 'Give Me The Night'. A much smaller number are

129

**GEORGE BENSON: THE BIGGEST-SELLING
JAZZ GUITARIST BY SOME DISTANCE**

130

aware of his considerable contributions to jazz and his total mastery of the guitar.

Singing and playing the ukulele from an early age, Benson was a prodigious talent who cut his first record at the age of 11. While still in his teens he recorded sessions with the Hammond players Jimmy Smith and Brother Jack McDuff for top jazz labels Blue Note and Prestige. In 1965 he formed his own quartet and shortly afterwards recorded a series of highly rated (if not commercially successful) albums for Columbia.

The '70s saw Benson increasingly drawn to the jazz-crossover market. It was in 1976 that he hit paydirt with the easy-listening classic *Breezin'* – the biggest-selling jazz album of all time. Although the title track was a Top 10 hit in its own right – an unusual feat for an

instrumental – it was the follow-up, Leon Russell's 'This Masquerade', that introduced his voice to pop audiences. Displaying hints of both Stevie Wonder and Nat King Cole (another great musician whose vocal success overshadowed his influential playing), this set the pattern for future releases well into the '80s – Benson's playing took a back seat role.

Strongly influenced by Wes Montgomery and to a lesser extent by Tal Farlow, Benson remains among the greatest of jazz soloists: even his most commercial releases have often featured superbly executed instrumental flourishes, sometimes played in unison with scat-style vocals.

....

White Rabbit (1969)

Breezin' (1976)

CHUCK BERRY
(1926–)

There is a good case for citing Chuck Berry as one of the most influential guitarists of all time, but few could argue with the view that he is the most significant musician in the early development of rock 'n' roll.

Berry arrived on the music scene relatively late in life. Although he had taught himself a few chords at high school, he didn't take the guitar seriously until he was in his mid-twenties. While playing in his own trio, a meeting with Muddy Waters put Berry in contact with Leonard Chess, the owner of the famous Chicago-based blues label, Chess Records. Initially following a blues path, Chess was impressed with his own up-tempo material. Berry's first single at the end of

1955, 'Maybellene', was the first R&B record to make a really big impact on white audiences.

Over the next decade Berry wrote numerous rock 'n' roll classics, many of which feature some of the most immediately recognizable guitar riffs ever recorded. A style of playing that simultaneously mixed rhythm and lead elements was a major influence of the next generation of young guitarists, among them Keith Richards of the Rolling Stones.

Berry was also a pioneering lyricist. His songs were full-blooded mini-soaps at a time when pop lyrics at best skirted around "real" issues. In fact, Berry put the case for the American teenage lifestyle of the '50s better than just about anyone – mildly ironic in that he was already well into his thirties when he wrote such classics as 'Route 66' and 'Johnny B. Goode'.

In spite of his indisputable importance in the history and development of popular music, Berry seems to have been unimpressed with precious accolades. He has always seen himself more as an entertainer going about making his living, rather than one of the great "artists" of the post-war era.

....

Hail, Hail Rock And Roll (compilation 1955–1964)

NUNO BETTENCOURT
(1966–)

In 1991, with a No. 1 single, the ballad 'More Than Words', and a platinum-selling album, the Boston band Extreme seemed poised to take over from the waning Van Halen as America's premier mainstream metal band. But while singer Gary Cherone grabbed the limelight with his "rock god" posturing, it was guitarist Nuno Bettencourt who lured fans of high-speed rock agility. Displaying a bewildering panorama of influences, Portuguese-born Bettencourt thrilled with pyrotechnic multi-harmony work-outs, such as 'Flight Of The Wounded Bumble Bee'. In a clamour of praise, he took numerous music awards and even saw his name appearing on his own "signature" guitars.

Just as quickly, however, it all seemed to go wrong. Keen to show off other sides of their musical personality, Extreme began making albums that may have been musically more versatile, but disappointed their hardcore rock and metal fans. Sales diminished and, in a final irony, Cherone quit the band to join Van Halen.

Taking stock of his situation, Bettencourt – now calling himself simply "Nuno" – unveiled his first solo album in 1997. Three years in the making, *Schizophrenic* was an impressive affair that saw

CHUCK BERRY ALMOST SINGLE-HANDEDLY WROTE THE ROCK 'N' ROLL GUITAR BOOK

131

Bettencourt writing and playing pretty much everything (not to mention dragging-up rather convincingly for the cover). If anything, it revealed a deeper interest in maturing his skills as a sophisticated composer and arranger of the modern pop song than in showing off at the fretboard.

....

Pornografitti (1991, with Extreme)

Schizophrenic (1997)

DICKEY BETTS

(1943–)

The Allman Brothers band featured perhaps the finest twin-guitar line-up ever. While it was Duane Allman who took the limelight with his extraordinary slide-playing, the intricate country style of Betts provided the perfect counterbalance.

At the time of Duane Allman's sudden death in 1971, the Allmans, active for barely two years, were widely held as America's greatest live band – listen to *Live At Fillmore East* for the evidence. With their focal point gone, the remaining members took the bold decision to carry on as a unit, Les Dudek stepping in on second guitar. Under Betts' leadership the Allmans remained a popular and highly respected outfit. His natural country leanings saw them pioneering the southern boogie sound that bands like Little Feat and Lynyrd Skynyrd purveyed so successfully.

Ironically, the first album recorded after Duane Allman's death – *Brothers And Sisters* – features 'Jessica', which over the years has established itself as one of the best-known guitar instrumentals ever and remains the Allman Brothers Band's most widely-heard track, either pre- or post-Duane.

....

Live At Fillmore East (1971)

Brothers And Sisters (1973)

ELVIN BISHOP

(1942–)

Formed in the early '60s, the Paul Butterfield Blues Band in Chicago mirrored John Mayall's Bluesbreakers in London. Both pioneered "authentic" electric blues played by young middle-class white men for largely white audiences. Both also featured some of the finest guitarists of the period, Butterfield's band starring Elvin Bishop and Mike Bloomfield.

Bishop encountered Butterfield while at university in Chicago during the late '50s. Between 1963 and 1968 the twin guitars of Bishop and Bloomfield traded licks in one of the tightest, hardest-gigging outfits of the period. After leaving Butterfield, Bishop formed his own band, but struggled in his attempts to cross over into the pop scene until 1976, when he charted with 'Fooled Around And Fell In Love', the solo featuring some of the most deliciously controlled blues-playing ever to hit the Top 10.

Success was short-lived and subsequent years were beset by a variety of personal problems. He returned during the late '80s and his albums recorded for the Alligator label have shown a return to a more traditional blues base. He remains a notable figure on the world blues scene.

....

East West (1966, with the Paul Butterfield Blues Band)

Ace In The Hole (1992)

ERNESTO BITETTI

(1943–)

Argentinian-born classical guitarist Ernesto Bitetti has forged an international reputation for himself as one of the modern-day masters of the Spanish classical tradition. While some critics have viewed his style of playing as old-fashioned, he has nonetheless recorded works specially commissioned for him by Rodrigo and Castelnuovo-Tedesco, two of the most notable twentieth-century composers of music for the guitar. His recordings of Rodrigo's *Concierto de Aranjuez*, probably the best-known work in the classical guitar repertoire (*see* page 23), have been hailed by some as the definitive versions.

....

Concierto de Aranjuez (various dates)

RITCHIE BLACKMORE

(1945–)

It was Deep Purple's fifth album, *In Rock*, that elevated Ritchie Blackmore – Jimmy Page's only serious rival in the early '70s – to the top league of rock guitar heroes, and established heavy metal as *the* music for teenage boys the world over. The album *Live In Japan* probably captures the best and worst aspects of Deep Purple. They were loud, they were highly accomplished musicians prone to throwing in the odd pseudo-classical flourish, the songs were based around a succession of simple yet powerful riffs (and went on for too long), and the lyrics were usually secondary.

Deep Purple were almost as well known for their in-fighting as their music. In 1975 Blackmore left to form his own band, Ritchie Blackmore's Rainbow, and enjoyed much the same level of success well into the '80s, playing music that was pretty well indistinguishable from his predecessors.

Although it's easy to look back and smile at Deep Purple through Spinal Tap-tinted glasses, Blackmore was one of Britain's most influential musicians of the period. For many years guitar shops throughout Britain and America continued to resound to the noise of a thousand teenage wannabes fumbling around the fretboard with ageless riffs like 'Smoke On The Water' and 'Black Night'.

....

Deep Purple In Rock (1970)

**RITCHIE BLACKMORE – HERO TO MANY A
TEENAGE "AIR-GUITARIST" OF THE '70S**

BIG BILL BROONZY – THE FIRST
AMBASSADOR OF CHICAGO BLUES

BLIND BLAKE
(c1890–c1933)

Although he was one of the most popular "race" musicians of the '20s, little is known about the life of pre-blues pioneer Blind Blake. Yet the 80 or so recordings he made between 1926 and 1932 as a house musician for Paramount, and word-of-mouth testaments of those who saw or worked with him, reveal him to be one of the guitar's genuine innovators.

Blake is known to have performed with many well-known musicians, such as jazz clarinet star Johnny Dodds, and blues singers Ma Rainey and Irene Scruggs. However it is his solo recordings on which his reputation rests. His work, made available in the '70s by the specialist blues label Yazoo, reveals an extraordinary command of his instrument. It is on ragtime pieces like 'Police Dog Blues' and 'That Will Never Happen No More' that his unique and complex style can be best appreciated. With a right-hand technique extraordinary for its time, Blake played a syncopated barrel-roll between the thumb and fingers which echoed the sound of a slow piano blues. Indeed, he was also known to have been an excellent pianist.

Blake remains most appreciated by the folk and blues cognoscenti – and a number of his pieces have been successfully transcribed by Stefan Grossman. Although Blind Lemon Jefferson is the best-remembered guitarist of the period, Blind Blake was the instrument's first non-classical virtuoso.

Ragtime Guitar's Foremost Picker (compilation 1927–1931)

MIKE BLOOMFIELD
(1944–1981)

It was playing in the Paul Butterfield Blues Band that introduced audiences to the majestic playing of Mike Bloomfield. In his own way, rated as a US equivalent to Eric Clapton, Bloomfield helped to bring authentic Chicago blues to a mainstream white audience. The Butterfield band made its mark performing at the 1965 Newport Folk Festival, not only with their own dazzling performance, but as the backing band on Bob Dylan's notorious first "electric" show, which was received with such extraordinary hostility at the time. Bloomfield went on to play on Dylan's ground-breaking *Highway 61 Revisited*.

Taken under the wing of Dylan's manager Albert Grossman, Bloomfield boosted his reputation as an innovator further by forming the imposing Electric Flag with drummer Buddy Miles. It was a short-lived but influential project which was among the first to merge blues and rock in any meaningful way. Thereafter, each passing project saw him drift further away from fulfilling his early potential.

Bloomfield's last significant work was *Super Session*, recorded with Stephen Stills and Al Kooper in 1968, although his 1977 primer *If You Love These Blues Please Play Them*, introduced a new young audience to the work of some of the blues masters, whose styles Bloomfield faithfully replicated.

Highway 61 Revisited (1965, with Bob Dylan)
A Long Time Comin' (1966, with Electric Flag)

GLENN BRANCA
(1948–)

It is Glenn Branca's innovative approach to composition that is noteworthy in taking the guitar into new and exciting territories. His style takes an orchestral approach that crosses the idea of a classical symphony with something approaching New York indie thrash. In fact, Branca's early work featured Sonic Youth's Thurston Moore and Lee Renaldo and was released on US thrash labels.

Although Branca's "orchestras" are not

GLENN BRANCA – A NEW FORM OF CLASSICAL GUITAR?

restricted only to the guitar, they form the primary components. The most interesting aspect is that conventional tuning is abandoned. Each string of the guitar is tuned to the same note, although not all of the instruments are tuned to the same note. This creates a monumentally powerful impact, especially in an auditorium where the volume can be overwhelming.

The Ascension (1981)
Symphony No. 10 (1994)

JULIAN BREAM
– *see* **Legends**

BIG BILL BROONZY
(1893–1958)

By the time of his death in 1958, Big Bill Broonzy – one of the most recorded blues stars of the '30s – was a genuine legend. He travelled all over the world singing, playing and talking about the blues to keen young college audiences. Back home in Chicago he found the time to help nurture upcoming talents like Muddy Waters and J.B. Lenoir. Big Bill Broonzy was the first ambassador for the blues.

ROY BUCHANAN, ONE OF THE FINEST PLAYERS TO STRAP ON A TELECASTER

Born in Mississippi from slave parentage, Broonzy was taught to play and sing the blues by his uncle. His first recording was 'Big Bill's Blues', made in Chicago in 1927. Although he was a gifted vocalist, it is as a guitarist and songwriter that he became best known. A ragtime picker, Broonzy's right-hand technique was centred on the rhythmic droning and damping of the bass strings. His playing was also a good deal swifter than that of most of his peers, both in the speed that he executed solo runs, and also in the unusual tempos that he used when playing his songs.

Broonzy's career dipped during the late '30s, but it was his "rediscovery" by white audiences in the '50s that helped to put blues on the map. His undoubted talent for self-promotion has led some critics to view him as an overrated artist, but his role in the popularization of the blues tradition is beyond dispute.

....

The Young Bill Broonzy 1928–1935

JOE BROWN
(1941–)

During the '60s and '70s, whenever a British television producer needed a Cockney cheeky-chappie stereotype the first name on the list was invariably Joe Brown. This has completely undermined his former reputation as one of Britain's premier guitarists of the late '50s.

Trading licks with many of the greatest early rock 'n' roll visitors from the States – like Eddie Cochran and Cliff Gallup – Brown's mastery of rockabilly guitar was every bit in the same league. He also fronted his own band, the Bruvvers, and some of his best work can be heard as sideman to Billy Fury, where briefly it looked as if Britain had finally produced a credible rock 'n' roll alternative to the embarrassing lightweight imitations being peddled by Tin Pan Alley.

Sadly, like most other British rockers of the period, Brown allowed himself to be steered toward the world of family entertainment, where he has remained.

ROY BUCHANAN
(1939–1988)

In the '70s, Roy Buchanan was known as one of the finest players working between the fringes of blues and rock – a master craftsman more appreciated by his fellow players than the public at large. And he seemed happy with that, more concerned with the important business of making music than being famous. Yet a decade after his death – he hanged himself in a police cell – Roy Buchanan stands on the brink of being sadly forgotten.

Starting out as a sideman with rocker Dale Hawkins in the late '50s, Buchanan put in 10 years of relatively anonymous session work before beginning a solo career in 1972. His playing style was strongly centred on the blues tradition – Albert King being a particular favourite. However, his breakneck solo flourishes were more akin to jazz players in the Charlie Christian mould.

Buchanan's reputation was forged with albums like *That's What I'm Here For* and *A Street Called Straight*, on which his ever-present Telecaster invariably burned a hole through largely undistinguished material. And this seems to have been his problem – apart from the awesome guitar technique his music had little widespread appeal. His legacy is having influenced some of the finest guitar craftsmen, among them Jeff Beck (*see* page

96). This alone must make him worthy of the title "The Guitarist's Guitarist's Guitarist".

....

In The Beginning (1974)
When A Guitar Plays The Blues (1985)

PETER BUCK
(1956–)

During the middle of the '90s, R.E.M. managed to pull off a considerable feat, combining worldwide commercial success with widespread critical acclaim. Vocalist Michael Stipe may have provided the enigmatic focus with his charismatic presence and baffling lyrics, but at the heart of the R.E.M. sound lies the subtle guitar phrasing of Peter Buck.

California-born Buck worked in an independent record shop in Athens, Georgia, when he met local university student Michael Stipe. R.E.M. was their first serious band. College favourites from

LESS KNOWN TO THE PUBLIC, JAMES BURTON IS ADORED BY OTHER GUITARISTS

their first single in 1980, they reached increasingly large audiences with successive albums until a deal with Warner Brothers in 1988 sent them into the commercial stratosphere.

Displaying a wide range of influences, from country-rock and '60s psychedelia to punk, Buck has sculpted a uniquely modern American sound. An avid music collector, he always seems open to the possibility of new ideas, which is partly what makes R.E.M. the most unpredictable and interesting "megaband" since the Beatles.

....

Murmur (1983)
Automatic For The People (1992)

T-BONE BURNETT
(1945–)

T-Bone Burnett occupies a unique territory in the music world, somehow managing to straddle the boundaries of rockabilly, soul, folk and country. A list of musicians with whom he has collaborated – Ry Cooder, Pete Townshend, Richard Thompson, Mick Ronson, for example – stands as testimony to his eclecticism.

A self-contained artist, Burnett is not only a fine guitarist, but respected producer (Leo Kottke, Los Lobos) and also sometimes outstanding songwriter, even if his often witty and barbed tongue has a tendency to take on the more obvious targets (such as 'Madison Avenue' from his debut album *Truth Decay*). His 1992 album *The Criminal Under My Hat* showed him to be a master of seemingly every facet of rockabilly and blues guitar.

....

The Criminal Under My Hat (1992)

JAMES BURTON
(1939–)

One of the all-time greatest session players, James Burton is another name to conveniently file under the "guitarist's guitarist" category.

138

WELL-KNOWN SINGER BUT ALSO SKILFUL
PICKER GLEN CAMPBELL

The public at large may not have heard of him, but they will certainly have heard his work on million-selling hits of the '60s and '70s, with some of America's biggest stars.

Burton's first enterprise of any note was at 18 when he played sessions for Dale Hawkins. One of the songs recorded was the hit 'Suzie Q', with Burton's widely imitated staccato solo. After a stint working in the studio band on TV's *Shindig*, he began a long association with Ricky Nelson, which saw the teen idol's gradual transformation to respected country star. Most of Nelson's '60s recordings feature Burton's unique Telecaster picking, achieved with a combination of flat pick and finger pick.

Although Burton has graced recordings by Michael Nesmith, Emmylou Harris and Gram Parsons, his highest profile work came when he was invited to join Elvis Presley's "comeback" band in 1969, a role he happily maintained until Presley's death eight years later.

....

G.P. (1972, with Gram Parsons*)*

JERRY BYRD
(1920–)

One of a small group of steel guitar players who helped to define the Nashville Sound in the '40s, Byrd was first known for his measured playing with the Pleasant Valley Boys.

This led him to a job accompanying country star Red Foley on many of his biggest hits of the late '40s.

A brief post-war vogue for the steel guitar brought Byrd minor success as a solo artist, but it was in his work as a sideman that his most effective playing was heard.

....

Hawaiian Beach Party (1951)

RANDY CALIFORNIA
(1951–1996)

Spirit were one of the more genuinely unusual groups to emerge during the late '60s. The creative heart of the band was Randy

California, a teenage, classically trained, Hendrix acolyte. Spirit's jazz-tinged psychedelia – aided visually and musically by the bizarre Ed Cassidy, a shaven-headed middle-aged jazz drummer – gained an immediate cult following.

A band deemed a little too difficult to achieve mainstream success, Spirit's first four albums, released between 1968 and 1970, provided a heady mix of sharp playing and hallucinogenic atmosphere. Intriguing and inventive arrangements, clever wordplay and the use of unusual instrumentation all typified the Spirit sound, but towering above was California's dazzling and versatile guitar work.

New listeners should be aware that although Spirit made albums until the '90s, the line-up fluctuated: even California didn't play on some of the mid-'70s recordings.

....

The Twelve Dreams Of Dr Sardonicus (1970)
Captain Kopter and The Whirlybirds (1973)

GLEN CAMPBELL
(1936–)

Glen Campbell is one of the most successful country artists to have crossed over to the lucrative middle-of-the-road market. His 1967 signature song, 'Gentle On My Mind', was one of the biggest-selling country records of all time. However, prior to his enormous success, which even gave him his own network variety show during the '70s, Campbell had been one of the West Coast's finest session guitarists.

Acquiring a $5 Sears Roebuck guitar at the age of four, Campbell had mastered the instrument by the time he reached his teens. At the age of 14 he turned professional, eventually ending up in California, where he played sessions for everyone from Dean Martin to the Beach Boys – and when one of them, Brian Wilson, decided to stay put in the studio, it was Campbell who toured in his place.

Campbell's earliest solo successes were all on the US country charts, and reached few non-country fans, so he ran his session career as a parallel activity. But even on his biggest crossover hits, Campbell's clean, tasteful country picking can still be heard clearly.

....

The Very Best Of Glen Campbell (compilation 1968–1978)

LARRY CARLTON
(1948–)

A superstar of the Los Angeles session scene, Larry Carlton's pure, clinical tones have been heard backing up artists as diverse as B.B. King, Steely Dan, Bobby Bland and Joni Mitchell.

When he joined the Crusaders in 1974, Carlton, a session player from his teenage years, reached a wider audience, his controlled solos driving along some of the most exceptional examples of jazz-funk to be put on record. On top form the Crusaders were both very musical *and* very danceable. Carlton also issued a series of solo instrumental albums in the '80s, which, although technically near-perfect, sounded much less inspired.

A brilliant all-round musician, Carlton has one particularly rare skill – the economy and taste he brings to other people's recordings: the reason he has remained one of the most in-demand session players for the past 25 years.

....

Southern Comfort (1974, with the Crusaders)
Aja (1977, with Steely Dan)

MARTIN CARTHY
(1941–)

A pivotal figure of the English folk movement, Martin Carthy has over the past 30 years played with every major name associated with the scene, from the Watersons to Steeleye Span.

WEST-COAST SESSION KING
LARRY CARLTON

Like many British teenagers growing up during the '50s, Carthy found the impetus to learn guitar with skiffle and the music of Lonnie Donegan. When skiffle fell from fashion, many of the musicians who hadn't drifted towards R&B explored traditional folk forms. It was here that Carthy found his true direction. Developing a fingerpicking style which combined American folk idioms with the phrasing of indigenous Celtic music, he recorded a succession of albums, many with violinist Dave Swarbrick (Fairport Convention), and all of which successfully used the traditional English folk song as a point of development.

Carthy was an early member of the successful folk-rock group Steeleye Span, who took traditional songs and gave them rock arrangements. But Carthy never seemed entirely at ease playing electric guitar, and left the band before their most commercial period. He continued to work intermittently in the folk-rock sphere with the Albion Band.

Although Carthy's music is quintessent-

CHAPTER EIGHT

140

ERIC CLAPTON. HE TRADED THE LICKS FOR WORLDWIDE AOR SUCCESS

ially English, he is now among the most respected folk guitarists in the world.

....

Martin Carthy (1965)
Life And Limb (1990) (with Dave Swarbrick)

AL CASEY

(1915-)

Al Casey had barely finished high school when he began to find fame while working for Fats Waller. He was apparently given the job on the

condition that he finished high school with good grades.

Casey went on to spend nine years working with Fats Waller's Rhythm, his graceful acoustic guitar solos featuring on some of his employer's biggest hits. One of them, 'Buck Jumpin', is based on some intricate use of guitar harmonics, one of the most interesting early applications of the technique.

When Waller died in 1943, Casey turned to session work, where he carved out a reputa-

tion playing with young beboppers like Fats Navarro. In 1945 he won *Esquire* magazine's guitar players poll. Repeating the accolade a year later, he was one of the stars of Leonard Feather's famous All-American Award Winners concerts at New York's Metropolitan Opera House.

In the post-war years Casey fell victim to jazz's commercial downturn and was later forced to turn to R&B to make ends meet – working with King Curtis between 1957 and

1961 – but he found a second wind with eager new audiences on the European jazz circuit during the '70s.

....

A Legendary Performer (compilation 1932–1941, with Fats Waller*)*

PHILIP CATHERINE

(1942–)

Philip Catherine first came to public attention in 1976 when he replaced Jan Akkerman in the band Focus. And yet in a respectable career which has spanned almost 40 years, this stands out as an entirely uncharacteristic career choice.

Inspired by Django Reinhardt (*see* page 116), Catherine, who grew up in Brussels, turned professional at the age of 17 and throughout the '60s played with many of Europe's best-known jazz musicians. An interest in jazz-rock led him to work with violinist Jean Luc Ponty between 1970 and 1972, before moving to America to study at Boston's Berklee School of Music.

After his brief aberration with Focus, Catherine impressed audiences at the 1976 Berlin Jazz Festival playing an impromptu duet with Larry Coryell. This pairing was so successful that they collaborated on a trio of highly rated albums.

For the past 15 years, Catherine has divided his time between working with his own highly regarded trio and freelance work, including Chet Baker's delicate 1985 trio album, *Chet's Choice*.

....

Twin House (1977, with Larry Coryell)
Philip Catherine, Chet Baker and Jean-Louis Rassinfosse (1983)

CHARLIE CHRISTIAN
– *see* **Legends**

ERIC CLAPTON

(1945–)

1963 was the year that the British R&B scene really took off. The Rolling Stones had already carved out a reputation based on their Sunday night residency at Richmond's Crawdaddy Club. The Stones were followed by The Yardbirds, featuring 18-year-old Eric Clapton on lead guitar.

Clapton had grown up listening to Chicago bluesmen, in particular Big Bill Broonzy and Muddy Waters. To him The Yardbirds were an extension of this tradition, but when a pop song – Graham Gouldman's 'For Your Love' – was chosen for their debut single, he decided to leave the band.

Clapton next found himself working alongside British blues veteran John Mayall in the Bluesbreakers. With them he established himself as one of Britain's greatest home-grown talents. Essentially applying a refined technique to Muddy Waters' emotive playing style, Clapton's effortless performances earned him the ironic nickname "slowhand". Worldwide fame came in 1966 when he formed Cream – the first rock power trio. The idea of duplicating guitar riffs on the bass provided the template for most of the heavy rock bands that followed in their wake.

Thereafter, Clapton began to show errors of judgement that would continue to dog his career. The first was the formation of "supergroup" Blind Faith with Steve Winwood, which barely stumbled out of the starting gate. He next chose to step back, working as backing player for Delaney and Bonnie. In 1970 he put together his first band, Derek and the Dominoes. Although their only album produced the rock classic 'Layla', it was Duane Allman who took credit for the guitar heroics.

During the first half of the '70s, Clapton was inactive, fighting a battle against heroin addiction. Since then his solo career has increased momentum to the point where he is once again among the most successful guitarists in any genre. Despite the recent tendency towards adult-oriented rock, Clapton's instrumental greatness and the appeal of his voice continue to guarantee him popularity.

....

Five Live Yardbirds (1964, with The Yardbirds)
Bluesbreakers (1965, with John Mayall's Bluesbreakers)
Disraeli Gears (1967, with Cream)

KURT COBAIN – THE FIGUREHEAD OF GRUNGE

ROY CLARK
(1933–)

Best known as the host of country music's best-loved TV show, *Hee-Haw*, Roy Clark also enjoys a reputation as a fine instrumentalist. He rose to fame early in life when, at the age of 13, he won the *National Country Music Banjo Competition*. Repeating his victory the following year, he became a regular on numerous country TV shows – even enjoying a brief stint as Cousin Roy in the *Beverly Hillbillies*.

Among his session recordings, Clark's guitar work on Wanda Jackson hits such as 'Let's Have A Party' showed him to be a fine country picker. Like others in his field, success as a singer with crossover hits such as 'Yesterday When I Was Young' has tended to overshadow his instrumental prowess, but he remains one of country music's best-loved characters.

KURT COBAIN
(1967–1994)

Kurt Cobain's suicide in 1994 was met with a level of public hysteria not seen since John Lennon's murder in 1980. Through his music Cobain became a reluctant spokesperson for the disenchanted youth of "Generation X". Leader of the powerful three-piece Nirvana, his great legacy is the track 'Smells Like Teen Spirit', a song which will forever evoke the early '90s every bit as much as the Beatles' *Sgt. Pepper* album conjures up the spirit of 1967. The Seattle grunge movement, which was spearheaded by Nirvana, peaked with their multi-million-selling anthem.

Although a lot of grunge was deliberately crude and alienating, Nirvana stood out from the crowd because when it came down it, no matter how harsh the music sounded, the songs were always exceptionally good. Ample evidence of Cobain's songwriting skills can be heard on their MTV *Unplugged* session.

The existence of Nirvana played a crucial

role in returning the guitar to the forefront of rock music.

....

Nevermind (1992)

In Utero (1993)

EDDIE COCHRAN
(1938–1960)

Young, handsome, a brilliant songwriter, a great guitarist, a studio pioneer, Eddie Cochran was the first self-contained rock star.

Cochran had been a session player until his looks got a cameo role in the film *The Girl Can't Help It*. His electric performance of his own 'Twenty Flight Rock' quickly resulted in a record deal with Liberty. A succession of influential hits followed – 'Summertime Blues', 'Somethin' Else' and 'C'mon Everybody'. He recorded avidly over the three years that led up to his premature death in a car crash in 1960.

Unlike almost any other pop star of the era, Cochran retained full artistic control of his career. In the studio he often overdubbed himself playing and singing all the parts himself – the drum sounds occasionally coming from beating out rhythms on cardboard boxes When he recorded with a backing band, he wrote and arranged the individual parts and insisted they were played as he intended.

Cochran's guitar style was a neat blend of country and blues. His sound was a result of experimenting with different pick-ups on his Gretsch Chet Atkins and mixing string gauges for different effects. He is widely viewed as rock's first *bona fide* guitar hero.

....

The Legendary Eddie Cochran (compilation, 1956–1959)

ALBERT COLLINS
(1932–1993)

Texas bluesman Albert Collins had a lucky start in life, being taught to play the guitar by

EDDIE COCHRAN – A BRIEF LIFE BUT A GUITAR LEGEND

his cousin... who just happened to be Lightnin' Hopkins. In 1958 his first recording – the blues instrumental 'Freeze' – was a modest success, and he continued in this vein until the late '60s. Encouraged by Canned Heat's Bob Hite, he then transferred to California, began a brief flirtation with the rock world and was championed by no lesser name than Jimi Hendrix. Sadly this failed to bring him the fame and fortune that many had predicted for him, and during much of the next decade he had to support himself by working in the building trade – in later years he fondly recalled helping to build Neil Diamond's California mansion!

An aspect of Collins' playing that gave additional originality to his sound was his use of altered tunings, usually an open minor chord, and the positioning of the capo high up the fingerboard. With its clipped staccato phrasing, the cold edge of Collins' Telecaster technique earned him the nickname "Iceman".

In true blues style, recognition came to Collins late in life. A deal with the Alligator

label, home to so many great modern-day bluesmen, resulted in some of the finest blues albums of the past 30 years –1978's *Ice Pickin'* featuring master cuts like 'Honey Hush' and the poignant 'When The Welfare Turns Its Back On You' is particularly recommended. By the time of his death in 1993 he was one of the biggest attractions on the world blues scene.

....

Truckin' With Albert Collins (1969)

Ice Pickin' (1978)

Don't Lose Your Cool (1983)

RY COODER
– see Legends

LARRY CORYELL
(1943–)

Larry Coryell is a largely self-taught guitarist. After dropping out of Washington University, where he was studying journalism, he gravitated to New York and life as a musician. In 1966 he formed Free Spirits, who were arguably the first ever jazz-rock group. A year later Coryell joined vibes player Gary Burton's quartet. Aided by Coryell's extensive use of feedback, the quartet surprisingly found itself popular with a non-jazz hippie audience, and towards the end of the decade were more often than not found playing on the same bills as psychedelic rock bands.

In 1973 Coryell formed Eleventh House, a powerful jazz-rock combo with whom he toured with great success throughout Europe, America and Japan. When he dissolved the band in 1975 he concentrated largely on the acoustic guitar, performing with John McLaughlin and Paco De Lucia as well as attempting an album of solo classical recordings.

Coryell is one of a rare breed of guitarists who, in a continuing search for a true musical

143

identity, have shown themselves to be masters of a bewildering variety of musical styles.

....

Introducing The Eleventh House (1974)
Standing Ovation (1978)
A Genuine Tong Funeral (1967, with Gary Burton)

ELIZABETH COTTEN
(1893–1987)

By the time Elizabeth "Libba" Cotten was regularly performing in front of audiences she was almost 70 years old, having spent her entire working life as a domestic servant. During the '50s she was employed by a wealthy family in Washington DC whose children introduced her to the city's coffee house scene, where she captivated young audiences eager to experience authentic American folk music.

Cotten's repertoire comprised ragtime, hymns and long-forgotten traditional folk songs. Especially impressive was her ability to execute the most complex of guitar rags using three- or four-finger patterns. She also wrote her own material, her best-known song being 'Freight Train', which most American folk singers have performed at some point.

Cotten achieved her greatest recognition in 1985 when she was awarded a Grammy for her album *Elizabeth Cotten Live*. In it, despite being 92 years old, she showcased a remarkable talent whose work documented a part of pre-blues American culture which was now all but lost.

....

Freight Train And Other Carolina Folk Songs (compilation, 1964–1967)
Elizabeth Cotten Live (1985)

JEFF COTTON
(1943–)

Little fact is known about Jeff Cotton – or Antennae Jimmy Semens, as he is usually known. In fact, his claim to fame is based largely on one album. But that album is arguably the greatest rock album ever made – *Trout Mask Replica* by Captain Beefheart and the Magic Band.

As legend has it, Beefheart (Don Van Vliet) gathered his band together at a hideaway in the Mojave Desert and ruthlessly rehearsed the album before it was recorded. According to his account, he wrote and directed every part himself – others consider this a fanciful notion.

Emerging in 1969 as if from another planet, *Trout Mask Replica* defies satisfactory definition – you simply have to hear it for yourself. It's a surreal world where Howlin' Wolf's 12-bar blues collides head-on with the worlds of the avant-garde European classical tradition and free jazz. The chaos is given form by the interplay between the two guitarists: the heavy riffing of Cotton playing counterpoint to the more nimble solo guitar of Bill Harkleroad (Zoot Horn Rollo).

Although the album failed to make an impact in the US, it surprisingly sneaked into the Top 30 in the UK, where Beefheart has always received greater recognition.

After leaving the Magic Band in 1972, Cotton disappeared to Hawaii, seemingly happy to leave the music world behind him.

....

Trout Mask Replica (1969)

ROBERT CRAY
(1953–)

The most commercially successful of the latest generation of blues musicians, Cray is unusual in that he came to the blues via the rock, soul and funk he listened to as a teenager. It was a chance meeting with Albert Collins' bass player that took Cray straight from playing in his school band to second guitar with arguably the greatest post-war blues musician.

In 1975 Cray left Collins to form his own band. A solid-gigging outfit, by the middle of the '80s they had recorded a series of Grammy-winning albums which transformed Cray into the biggest-selling blues artist of the period. He also began to attract attention in the rock world, his profile rising as a result of regular appearances with Eric Clapton.

The key to Cray's success has been in redefining the traditional blues of Collins and Muddy Waters (*see* page 124) and infusing it with a feel that comes close to the great house bands of '60s soul. While his period with Albert Collins clearly made an impact on him – Cray, too, has often used the open minor tuning – the influence of guitarists from other genres can also be heard, such as Steve Cropper or Jimi Hendrix (*see* pages 104 and 108).

....

Bad Influence (1983)
Don't Be Afraid Of The Dark (1989)

STEVE CROPPER
– *see* **Legends**

DICK DALE
(1937–)

In the early '60s, before the Beach Boys had gripped America, Dick Dale was the undisputed king of surf guitar. The technique and sound of the left-hander epitomized the surf instrumental. By alternating pick strokes at a lightning speed Dale was able to produce a unique staccato sound on his Stratocaster. When smothered in a heavy spring reverb its overall effect simulated the rhythm of riding the surf. His playing had many imitators – not least Carl Wilson of the Beach Boys.

In spite of his heroic status in California, Dale was overshadowed by the Wilson brothers as they became one of the few bands in America capable of rivalling the Beatles dur-

**ROBERT CRAY UPDATED THE CLASSICAL
ELECTRIC BLUES SOUND**

146

BO DIDDLEY – "500 PER CENT MORE MAN", AS HE CLAIMED

ing the '60s. By the time he retired from the music world in 1969, in favour of a life of farming and surfing, he was largely a forgotten figure.

Nonetheless, independent reissues of Dale's records have enthralled successive generations and by the '80s he had become something of a cult figure for many young guitarists. He finally hit the big time in 1995 when Quentin Tarantino used his recording of 'Miserlou' as the main theme for the film *Pulp Fiction*. The track became one of the most heavily played instrumentals of the '90s and Dale was lured out of retirement, whereupon he showed the world that at 60 his left hand was still firing as fast as ever.

....

The Best Of Dick Dale and the Deltones (compilation, 1961–1964)

REVEREND GARY DAVIS
(1896–1972)

One of the great "rediscovered" artists from the '30s, Reverend Gary Davis was not a church minister in any regular sense. Almost blind from birth, Davis was taught to play the guitar by Blind Willie Walker. From the age of 16 he adopted a hobo lifestyle, travelling from town to town earning small change singing and playing on street corners. It was here that he met Blind Boy Fuller and taught him to play the guitar. Davis recorded some of his earliest songs with Fuller.

After moving to New York City in 1940, the hard-drinking, cigar-toting Davis became an ordained Baptist minister. He continued to live as a street musician but combined his role with that of an itinerant preacher. He also taught sporadically at Brownie McGhee's Home of the Blues Music School.

It was in the '60s that Davis was rediscovered and he became an influential figure on the New York folk scene, not only for his own

recordings and performances, but through his first-hand accounts of mysterious names from the past whose work was, by then, long lost. Fine folk and blues guitarists such as Stefan Grossman and Dave Van Ronk benefited from his personal teaching.

....

The Complete Early Recordings (1933–1937)

PACO DE LUCIA
(1947–)

One of the foremost virtuoso guitarists of any genre, Paco de Lucia has done more than anyone to popularize flamenco, the music of the Andalucian region of southern Spain. He has given widely acclaimed solo performances on most of the notable concert platforms throughout Europe and America.

De Lucia was first noticed in the early '70s accompanying Camaron de la Isla, one of Spain's greatest singers. The duo recorded together extensively – the album *Arte Y Majestad* is a particularly vibrant offering. Although they are considered to be among the best flamenco performances ever captured, sadly little of this collaboration is widely obtainable outside Spanish-speaking countries.

De Lucia has also delved into the world of jazz, having recorded the successful *Passion, Grace And Fire* album with fellow guitarists John McLaughlin and Al DiMeola.

....

Fabulosa Guitarra (1989)

BO DIDDLEY
(1928–)

A stablemate of Chuck Berry at Chess Records, Bo Diddley's contribution to the guitar is based on a unique approach to rhythm.

Although he was a Chicago blues player, he rarely used the traditional 12-bar structure, his songs often appearing as a series of lengthy

verses punctuated by the odd break. Many of his best-known songs were played on a single chord. His formula was a simple one: his own chugging guitar melded with the bass, drums, piano and maracas to produce a unified rhythmic front that he called his "jungle" sounds.

Although Diddley never really hit the big time himself, his approach to rhythm seeped into the mainstream through the young white blues bands of the early '60s. The early Rolling Stones did note-for-note covers of some of his songs, and the trademark jerky rhythm can be heard on pop hits like 'Not Fade Away'. Later, Diddley's 'Cops And Robbers' provided inspiration for David Bowie's 'Jean Genie'.

....

Bo Diddley (1958)

The Chess Box (compilation, 1990)

AL DIMEOLA
(1954–)

DiMeola's background was relatively unusual for a jazz musician. He started out as a fledgling drummer until he caught sight of the Beatles at the age of nine. This compelled him to take up the guitar. By his mid-teens a fascination for country music led him to master the pedal steel guitar.

It was exposure to the Miles Davis group, featuring keyboard player Chick Corea, when DiMeola was a student at the Berklee School of Music in 1973, that finally fostered his interest in jazz. A year later, at the age of 20, he joined Corea's celebrated jazz-rock crossover project Return To Forever.

A virtuoso of both electric and acoustic guitars, DiMeola went on to perform as a part of a trio featuring John McLaughlin and Paco de Lucia as well as leading his own group the Al DiMeola project.

....

Cielo E Terra (1985)

Elegant Gypsy (1976, with Return To Forever)

148

LONNIE DONEGAN, KING OF SKIFFLE

SACHA DISTEL
(1933–)

It may surprise some to know that the handsome French easy listening singer who made housewives swoon throughout the '70s was once one of France's top jazz musicians.

Born in Paris, Distel's uncle was bandleader Ray Ventura, which ensured that he was brought up surrounded by musicians. Switching from piano to guitar at an early age, he was taught by the great bebop guitarist Jimmy Raney. The '50s saw him a regular on the Parisian Left Bank scene accompanying Juliette Greco in the caves of Saint-Germain-des-Prés with famed existentialists and poets at the tables. Distel regularly played with musicians of the calibre of Clifford Brown and Kenny Clarke. The year after the death of Django Reinhardt, he was voted France's top jazz guitarist.

In the late '50s Distel chose to follow the path of the *chansonnier*, his understated voice and good looks a virtual guarantee of success. So it was that the world gained another crooner and lost a potentially great jazz musician.

LONNIE DONEGAN
(1931–)

Along with Hank Marvin and Bert Weedon, Lonnie Donegan was one of the prime reasons that so many young British teenagers of the '50s felt compelled to take up the guitar. With an almost "proto-punk" attitude, Donegan's skiffle group format – cheap acoustic guitar, stand-up bass and washboard rhythm – taught the lesson that anyone could learn a few chords and within weeks be out there performing.

Initially a banjo player in the Chris Barber jazz band, Donegan's sparse covers of traditional American folk and blues songs, such as 'Rock Island Line' and 'Cumberland Gap', were instantly successful with the fledgling British rock 'n' roll audiences when they appeared in 1956. He continued having hits well into the middle of the '60s.

Among those who acknowledged Donegan's role in their own musical development were John Lennon, Jimmy Page (*see* page 114) and Brian May. This debt was acknowledged in 1978 when the album *Putting On The Style* came out, reworking some of his old hits, but this time featuring some of the finest musicians working at the time.

....

Putting On The Style (1978)

NICK DRAKE
(1948–1974)

In a tragically short lifetime, Nick Drake recorded three sublime albums for folk producer Joe Boyd. In spite of being well received by the music press, they were largely ignored by the public.

Although Drake's ever-increasing reputation is based on the haunting quality of his songs, it is the simple, sparse arrangements, allowing them the room to breathe, that create a brooding atmosphere of introspection. Much of this can be attributed to his subtle bluesy fingerpicking and string arrangements by his college friend Harry Robinson.

Drake's lack of recognition led to disillusionment which may have contributed to his depressive state. Ironically, as successive generations continue to discover his work, his albums have now outsold some of the biggest hits of the time.

The compilation box *Fruit Tree* contains almost all of Drake's known recordings, and is one of a very small number of anthology sets that can be recommended without any reservation.

....

Fruit Tree (4 CD boxed set, 1969–1973)

150

**RONNIE EARL – ONE OF MANY FINE PLAYERS
TO PASS THROUGH ROOMFUL OF BLUES**

RONNIE EARL
(1953–)

A late starter, Earl was 23 before he began playing the guitar. His progress was rapid in the extreme, and by 1980 he was deemed a worthy replacement for Duke Robillard in Roomful Of Blues, probably the most vibrant and exciting blues group of the past three decades.

Like so many bluesmen of Earl's generation, the dominant name associated with his playing is T-Bone Walker, although that's not to say his work is in any way derivative. He is a versatile player at home with any blues style you may care to name.

Continuing the Roomful Of Blues tradition as a training ground for new talent, Earl left the band in 1988 to be succeeded by Chris Vachon, another fine young talent. Earl has gone on to form his own band, the Broadcasters, and play with such classic blues luminaries as Eddie Vinson, Joe Turner, Snooks Eaglin and Joe Beard.

Grateful Heart (1996)

DUANE EDDY
(1938–)

With their hallmark twanging bass strings, Duane Eddy's worldwide hits like 'Peter Gunn' and 'Raunchy' made him the best-known guitarist of the late '50s.

In fact, much of Eddy's success can be attributed to producer Lee Hazlewood. To begin with he encouraged Eddy to write deliberately simple tunes which could be played on the bass strings of the guitar. The amplified sound (with electronic vibrato added) was fed through a unique reverb chamber which Hazlewood had crafted from a grain silo.

Another factor that contributed to the unique sound resulted from Eddy's tuning. The songs were written in the keys of E or A so they could be played on open strings, but these keys were difficult for the saxophone player, so Eddy detuned his Gretsch Chet Atkins by a semitone, producing a deeper sound.

Influenced by Les Paul and Chet Atkins (*see* page 94), Eddy revealed himself on B sides and later album cuts to be no mean picker himself, but it was his simple tunes that attracted many youngsters to the guitar in the '50s – kids who found that within a few days they could play just like the "Guitar Man".

....

Because They're Young (compilation, 1956–1964)

EDGE
(1961–)

The era that followed punk was a difficult one for guitarists. The solo had long been established as a player's main creative outlet, but now, for credible bands, that medium had been all but outlawed. Other approaches had to be sought. The task was to find ways of making the guitar sound interesting without having to resort to flashy self-indulgence. One player who succeeded in this aim was David Evans – better known as Edge – of Irish band U2.

From their debut album in 1981, *Boy*, U2 gradually built up a following to the point where by the early '90s they were one of the biggest-selling bands in the world. Although much of the attention has been on the charismatic and outspoken front man Bono, it has been the delicate guitar work of Edge that has created the essence of the U2 sound.

Combining an intelligent use of simple playing techniques, like arpeggios and harmonics, and electronic delay effects, Edge creates a unique soundscape that sits above the sparse bass and drum arrangements. As U2 continue to develop and grow in stature, and their live shows become increasingly hi-tech, Edge's guitar remains the

very epitome of understatement. And that is one of the keys to their continued success.

....

The Unforgettable Fire (1984, with U2)
The Joshua Tree (1987, with U2)

HERB ELLIS
(1921–)

Starting life with the Jimmy Dorsey band, Herb Ellis is best known for his work as the replacement for Barney Kessel in pianist Oscar

DUANE EDDY, '50S
"GUITAR MAN"

Peterson's trio, which also featured bassist Ray Brown. For a grouping of such technically gifted musicians, the results exhibited a surprising degree of empathy.

After leaving Peterson in 1958, Ellis went on to work with two notable but very different female vocalists: he played with Ella Fitzgerald on her series of Jazz At The Philharmonic concerts; and once again took over from Barney Kessel, this time as Julie London's accompanist.

A player firmly in the Charlie Christian mould, from the '60s onwards Ellis involved himself in session work on the West Coast. He would later step out with occasional small-group collaborations, most notably with Ray Brown, and later a seamless set of standards produced with Joe Pass.

....

Nothing But The Blues (1957)
My Fair Lady (1958, with the Oscar Peterson Trio)

BUDDY EMMONS
(1937–)

One of the undoubted giants of the pedal steel guitar – a notoriously difficult guitar to master – Buddy Emmons is probably the most heavily used session man alive. His playing has graced recordings by just about every notable country musician since the '60s. He is also one of the biggest names in the design and manufacture of the instrument, having first set up the Sho-Bud pedal steel company and later produced his own Emmons models.

....

Minor Aloud (1979, with Lenny Beau)

JOHN FAHEY
(1939–)

A singular musician, John Fahey is a guitarist like no other. He is a superlative solo performer and his steel-string instrumentals traverse the

151

JOHN FAHEY IS ONE OF THE MOST UNUSUAL GUITARISTS OF THE PAST 40 YEARS

boundaries of country, blues and folk. In spite of a succession of album and song titles that seem unhealthily obsessed with the darker side of life – such as the marvellously titled *Death Chants, Breakdowns and Military Waltzes* – his music is without exception passionate, exhilarating and uplifting.

Fahey built up a considerable following on the '60s folk circuit, and his unusually avant-garde approach to what has tended to be – almost by definition – a form aimed at preserv-ing tradition has attracted many admirers, and influenced a great many other guitarists, among them one of his few collaborators, Leo Kottke.

Through a remarkably consistent 40-year career, Fahey has pursued his path with single-minded zeal. Truly an uncompromising artist.

....

Dance Of Death And Other Plantation Favorites (1964)

Blind Joe Death (1967)

TAL FARLOW
(1921–)

A late bloomer, Talmage Farlow didn't take up the guitar until his early twenties. Starting out as an accompanist for a succession of female vocalists, he made his name in the much vaunted trio of vibes player Red Norvo, which also featured the legendary Charles Mingus on bass.

A gifted improviser, Farlow's trademark as a player was the ability to execute extraordi-

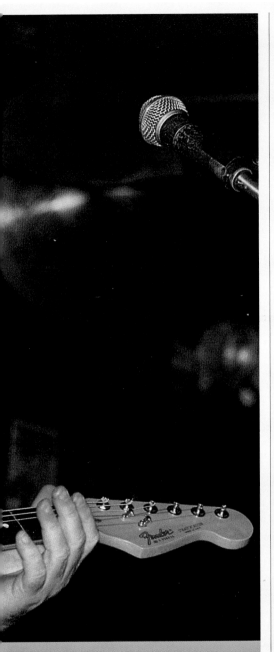

LESTER FLATT
(1914–1979)

Lester Flatt and his long-time partner, banjo player Earl Scruggs (*see* Chapter Six), became country legends while working with Bill Monroe – the man who invented bluegrass music. Flatt single-handedly defined an entire genre of country guitar during his time as one of Bill Monroe's Bluegrass Boys. It was his innovation that first saw chords linked together by bassline runs on the bottom two strings of the guitar.

In 1948, Flatt and Scruggs left Monroe to form their own Foggy Mountain Boys. They enjoyed enormous success right from the out-set, producing some of the classic country recordings of the period, such as 'Foggy Mountain Breakdown' and 'Flint Hill Special'. It was among other things Flatt's refusal to "go electric" that precipitated their split in 1969.

Scruggs formed the more lightweight Earl Scruggs Revue with his three sons, whereas Flatt continued to pursue his own traditional path until his death in 1979.

VIC FLICK
(1937–)

An unsung hero of the guitar if ever there was one. You may not know the name, but if you've seen one the early James Bond films, you know the sound. Vic Flick was the man who picked out that immortal riff on the bottom two strings of the guitar.

Flick got the job with the John Barry 7 (who played the Bond theme music) because he was one of a rare breed of English electric session players at the time who could sight-read. Throughout the '60s he was one of Britain's most in-demand session players, supporting a diverse range of artists, including Tom Jones,

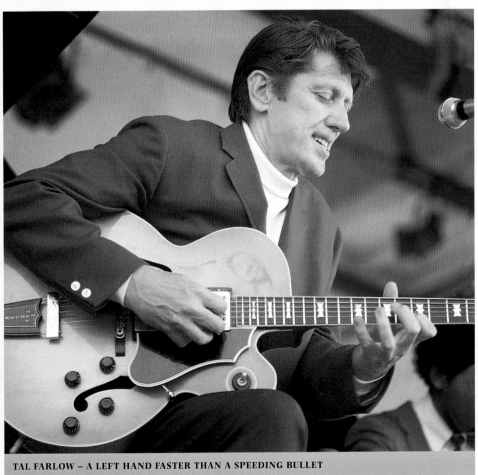

narily fast single-note runs and move between chord positions with great agility. But for all of that, some viewed his playing as a triumph of technique over musical content: in short, that it lacked heart and soul.

Farlow retired from full-time music in 1960 and worked variously as a sign-painter and teacher. However, he continued to perform and record periodically well into the '80s.

....

Tal (1956)

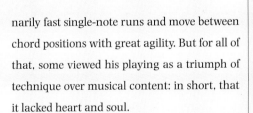

TAL FARLOW – A LEFT HAND FASTER THAN A SPEEDING BULLET

ROBBEN FORD HAS THE TECHNIQUE AND USES IT WITH TASTE

154

Nancy Sinatra, Burt Bacharach, Diana Ross, Cliff Richard, Herman's Hermits and Henry Mancini. He then moved to Los Angeles to work as a player and composer in the film industry.

A successful jobbing musician he may have been, but Flick will always be remembered for *that* riff which gave so many teenagers in the '60s their first taste of the guitar.

....

The Best of the John Barry 7 (compilation, 1961–1965)

ROBBEN FORD
(1951–)

Since the launch of his solo career in 1988, Robben Ford has proved himself to be a fine purveyor of sophisticated blues that never seem short of something eloquent to say.

After gigging around San Francisco with his two brothers during the early '70s, Ford gained some useful experience over several years playing sideman to blues singers Charlie Musselwhite and Jimmy Witherspoon. For his next move, he slid seamlessly into the jazz

world, working with Miles Davis and hornman David Sanborn.

Forming the trio Blue Line in 1992, he returned to a broadly traditional blues base. With a warmth of tone and sparkling technique that few could hope to match, their debut album *Robben Ford And Blue Line* showed him to be a worthy successor to the crown of the recently deceased blues king Stevie Ray Vaughan.

....

Talk To Your Daughter (1988)

ROBERT FRIPP
(1946–)

It's not unusual for experimental protagonists to find themselves sidelined, their impact on the mainstream restricted to the occasional subtle dose. Although Robert Fripp has had more mainstream successes than most in his field, they are in no way in line with the influence he has exerted on several generations of guitarists and experimental sound-makers.

King Crimson were one of the most interesting of the progressive rock bands. It was largely the carefully balanced playing of Robert Fripp that set them apart from others in the field. Quite simply, there always seemed to be a good reason for what Fripp was playing. In the early '70s he hooked up with Brian Eno, with whom he made the ground-breaking "Frippertronics" albums – a technique he developed that involved passing tape across the heads of two linked Revox tape recorders, enabling lengthy loops of sound to be layered into lush soundscapes over which Fripp could then play solo parts.

One of the few prog-rock musicians whose reputation increased throughout the new wave era, Fripp resuscitated King Crimson in 1980 in a line-up featuring Adrian Belew. The two guitarists interlocked brilliantly on their "debut" album *Discipline*.

In recent years Fripp has concentrated on his Guitar Craft schools, teaching an alternative philosophy of the instrument that includes altered standard tunings, and recording with Guitar Craft students or his wife – former new wave star Toyah Willcox.

In The Court Of The Crimson King (1969, with King Crimson)

No Pussyfooting (1973, with Brian Eno)

Discipline (1980, with King Crimson)

FRED FRITH
(1949–)

A completely "out there" guitarist, Fred Frith's music – band work or solos – has never fitted easily into convenient musical categories.

Frith's musical life started with Henry Cow, a band formed at Cambridge University in the late '60s. Nominally viewed as a progressive rock ensemble, Henry Cow's left-wing politics and anti-corporate stance always limited their commercial potential, but they developed a large and influential cult following throughout Europe and America.

For the past 25 years Frith has carved a niche for himself as one of the least compromising guitarists to be heard anywhere. He has at one time or another worked with most of the principal names in the field of "free" improvisation. Some of his work has been performed using "doctored" instruments. For example, on one project he fitted a pick-up to the nut of the guitar, allowing the vibration either side of the held note to be amplified.

Frith's most influential album is arguably *Guitar Solos*, recorded in 1974. The American *Guitar Player* magazine commented that it was "to mainstream guitar playing what quantum mechanics is to an auto mechanic." Not for the faint-hearted.

Guitar Solos (1974)

LOWELL FULSON
(1921–)

Born on an Indian reservation in southern Oklahoma, Lowell Fulson (or "Fulsom" as some of his records would have it) learned the guitar at the age of 12. Travelling around and playing in bars and gambling joints, he ended up in California where, after leaving the navy, he began a recording career which would establish him as one of the most significant West Coast bluesmen of the period.

A flexible musician, Fulson recorded extensively in a number of different styles all of which showed him to be equally at home with blues, country or R&B. He was also responsible for writing several R&B classics, including

155

ROBERT FRIPP, ONE OF THE INTELLECTUALS OF ROCK GUITAR

RORY GALLAGHER AND HIS FAMOUS BATTERED STRAT

'Everyday I Have The Blues', covered with great success by B.B. King.

In the '60s he transformed himself into a soul man, working in the noted Fame studios in Muscle Shoals. Here he produced some of his most commercially successful work.

In A Heavy Bag (1968)

RORY GALLAGHER
(1949–1995)

Irish-born Gallagher first experienced life on the road at the age of 15 playing in the Fontana Showband, a typical Irish dancehall cabaret band. When they broke up, Gallagher formed the blues trio Taste with the band's rhythm section. Taste built up a strong following on the European club circuit, and their three albums sold in healthy quantities.

In 1971, Gallagher, the indisputable creative force behind Taste, formed his own outfit to play under his own name. For the rest of the decade his ruthless gig schedules earned him a reputation as one of the hardest-working musicians around.

Gallagher was an expert down-the-line blues stylist whose playing was strongly influenced by the Three Kings – Albert, B.B. and Freddie. His reputation as an electrifying live performer meant that he maintained his core popularity irrespective of prevailing musical trends. Of the many albums he made during his career, the best are invariably the live recordings.

Live In Europe (1972)
Irish Tour (1974)

CLIFF GALLUP
(1935–1988)

The guitarist with Gene Vincent's Blue Caps, Gallup's most notable contribution to the canon of rock guitar was his influential picked

phrasing on the memorable 'Be-Bop-A-Lula' – where he seemed to be answering (or parodying) Vincent's mannered, "hiccupped" vocal sound.

Gallup is remembered for little else, other than being the subject of a heartfelt tribute from Jeff Beck recorded in 1992 (*see* page 96).

The Best of Gene Vincent (compilation, 1957–1961)

JERRY GARCIA
(1942–1995)

For 30 years until Garcia's death in 1995, his band the Grateful Dead were the ultimate live experience. Their early performances, some as the house band for Ken Kesey's Merry Pranksters, were reputed to have consisted of LSD-fuelled jam sessions that went on for five hours at a time. At the helm was the lead guitar of the smiling, bespectacled Jerry Garcia, always ready and prepared to play his bluesy

JERRY GARCIA, KING OF THE DEADHEADS

improvisations for as long as anyone cared to listen. At 23 minutes in length, the legendary track 'Dark Star' remains something of a benchmark in music of this genre.

The most celebrated of all the San Francisco groups, the Dead's free concerts and reputation for integrity helped them retain a hardcore of their following until the early '80s when, inexplicably, they found themselves with a growing audience of young "Deadheads". By the end of that decade the Grateful Dead were one of the biggest-earning rock bands in the world.

The Grateful Dead (1967)
Live Dead (1970)

DANNY GATTON
(1945–)

A favourite of many guitarists, Danny Gatton plays a blend of Chet Atkins-style country-picking, blues and jazz. A craftsman, to be sure

157

DAVE GILMOUR – A RARE FACILITY FOR SPACE

158

– his 1992 album *New York Stories* is nothing less than a country-blues masterclass – he particularly appeals to the listener eager to learn.

New York Stories (1992)

LOWELL GEORGE
(1945–1979)

Little Feat were rated as one of the finest bands to emerge in America during the '70s. They were formed, apparently on the advice of Frank Zappa, by former Mothers Of Invention member Lowell George. In a stark contrast to other "good time" Southern boogie bands, Little Feat's music, and in particular George's slide work, displayed a rare finesse – here was a man with a clear understanding of a wide variety of country and blues playing styles.

By the end of the '70s George was beset by drug problems and had all but burnt himself out after a succession of highly rated albums. Once a fine and prolific songwriter, he contributed only one composition to *Time Loves A Hero*, Little Feat's final (and most commercially successful) album. His definitive slide work can be heard on the New Orleans-flavoured *Dixie Chicken*, recorded in 1973.

Dixie Chicken (1973)
The Last Record Album (1973)

DAVE GILMOUR
(1944–)

There have been two very distinct Pink Floyds. The original acid version, largely the work of Syd Barrett, lasted for one album. Thereafter, the instantly recognizable guitar-playing of Barrett's successor, Dave Gilmour, largely characterized the Pink Floyd sound. During the '70s they became one of the most popular album bands in the world – their benchmark work, 1973's *Dark Side Of The Moon*, remained in the US charts for over a decade.

Always well measured and shunning histrionics, Gilmour's is one of the more intelligent examples of rock guitar. His playing in some ways predates the New Age guitarists of the past decade – gentle, roomy and with a slight hint of the blues. Yet for all that, it is somehow an unmistakably English sound.

....

Dark Side Of The Moon (1973, with Pink Floyd)
Wish You Were Here (1975, with Pink Floyd)
About Face (1978)

EGBERTO GISMONTI
(1947–)

Brazilian-born Egberto Gismonti's career has been an ongoing search for a new folk form. A highly trained classical musician – although curiously *not* on the guitar – Gismonti studied piano and composition for 15 years in Brazil before moving to Paris to extend his training further. Returning to Brazil in 1971, he felt a need to root his music in the traditions of his native country, rather than relying on the European classical model. He spent time living with Xingo Indian tribes in the Amazon, during which he decided to abandon classical piano in favour of the guitar.

Through his work on the ECM label Gismonti has been one of the pioneers of a new form of improvisation music which uses ethnic folk forms other than American examples. It's largely still categorized as "jazz", but that's a label that he strenuously denies.

Gismonti's style of playing is unique. He mostly uses custom-built acoustic guitars, usually featuring additional bass strings to give the instrument a range of notes closer to the piano. His technique also doesn't appear to have any direct precedents, perhaps because in spite of his classical piano training, he taught himself the guitar in isolation.

....

Danca Das Cabecas (1976)

THE COUNT'S RIGHT-HAND MAN, FREDDIE GREEN

159

MAURO GIULIANI
(1781–1829)

An important player and composer of the nineteenth century (*see* Chapter Two), little is known about the early life of Italian-born Mauro Giuliani.

It was when he moved to Vienna in 1806 – an important centre of music of this period – that he found fame. He is known to have played widely to large audiences throughout Germany, and given performances before Beethoven.

In 1819 he made his way to Rome, having been forced to flee Vienna under mysterious circumstances. His health failing, he spent his final years playing duets with his daughter Emilia, herself one the finest players of the period.

Giuliani was one of a select group of virtuoso musicians who helped spread the popularity of the guitar throughout Europe.

FREDDIE GREEN
(1911–1987)

Born in South Carolina, Freddie Green moved to New York as a teenager. Working as an upholsterer by day and in jazz clubs at night, he got his break in 1937 when he was spotted by impresario John Hammond, who recommended him to Count Basie. Looking for a replacement for Claude Williams, Basie was reluctant to audition the unknown Green, but agreed to hear him out in his dressing room that night. A day later he was in the band.

Green became the linchpin of almost every Basie band until the bandleader's death in 1984. Well known for precise timing, with drummer Jo Jones and bassist Walter Page, Green's four-to-the-floor chord work supplied the pulse behind one of the greatest big bands.

....

Basie Boogie (compilation, 1941–1967)

GRANT GREEN'S REPUTATION CONTINUES TO GROW

160

GRANT GREEN
(1931–1979)

Hailing from St Louis, Missouri, post-bopper Grant Green worked locally until the end of the '50s, when he began playing sessions in Chicago.

In the '60s Green recorded a series of underrated albums for the Blue Note label, the most notable being *Born To Be Blue* in 1962. During this period he played in the hallowed company of players of the calibre of Elvin Jones, Stanley Turrentine and McCoy Tyner. His playing is perhaps best appreciated in small group settings such as these, and Green seemed to be particularly effective when accompanying the Hammond players Larry Young and John Patten.

Unfortunately drug problems wrote off the latter part of the '60s, but in the period leading up to his death in 1979 Green, like many of his peers, worked on the fringes of jazz funk – a move which inevitably lost the interest of many jazz critics.

However, a healthy programme of reissues has helped to enhance his reputation as one of the finest jazz players of the '60s, and he is increasingly revered among the younger generation of jazz fans.

....

Born To Be Blue (1962)

PETER GREEN
(1946–)

The saga of Peter Greenbaum is one of the strangest in rock history. Another high-profile graduate of John Mayall's Bluesbreakers, he first appeared on the 1966 album *A Hard Road*, given the fearsome job of filling the slot vacated by Mayall's previous discovery, Eric Clapton. Green was easily up to it, impressing with a more measured, economical style.

Green left Mayall the following year to form Fleetwood Mac. Combining self-penned hits, such as the classic instrumental 'Albatross' and a smattering of covers like Willie John's 'Need Your Love So Bad', Fleetwood Mac became one of the biggest-selling British bands of the late '60s.

With a rare luxury of being loved by blues purists, music critics and the mainstream record buyer, Green seemed to have the world at his feet. But all was not well. In 1970, with the band at its peak, he quit and retired from the music world. Since then he is rumoured to have given away all of his guitars and to have variously been a tramp, gravedigger and hospital orderly. But such tales have boosted his reputation as one of rock's great enigmas and the late '90s have seen his most concerted period of activity since his heyday.

....

Fleetwood Mac (1968)

English Rose (1969, with Fleetwood Mac)

Then Play On (1970, with Fleetwood Mac)

STEFAN GROSSMAN
(1945–)

One of the great academics of American folk and blues guitar techniques, most of Stefan Grossman's recordings aim to reproduce traditional tunes with painstaking accuracy.

Perhaps his greatest service to guitar history is in his "rediscovery" of blues legends of the '20s and '30s, remarkable musicians whose recordings, techniques and stories would otherwise have been lost. Not only did Grossman relaunch the careers of Son House, Mississippi Fred MacDowell and Reverend Gary Davis, he also spent time with them learning their unique playing techniques and documenting their own first-hand accounts of an aspect of America's musical heritage that was largely unknown to white audiences.

Written in the '70s, Grossman's tutorial books on ragtime and blues guitar – to which Davis contributed significantly – are the definitive works on the subject.

....

Ragtime Cowboy Jew (1970)

PETER GREEN WITH HIS LES PAUL STANDARD

162

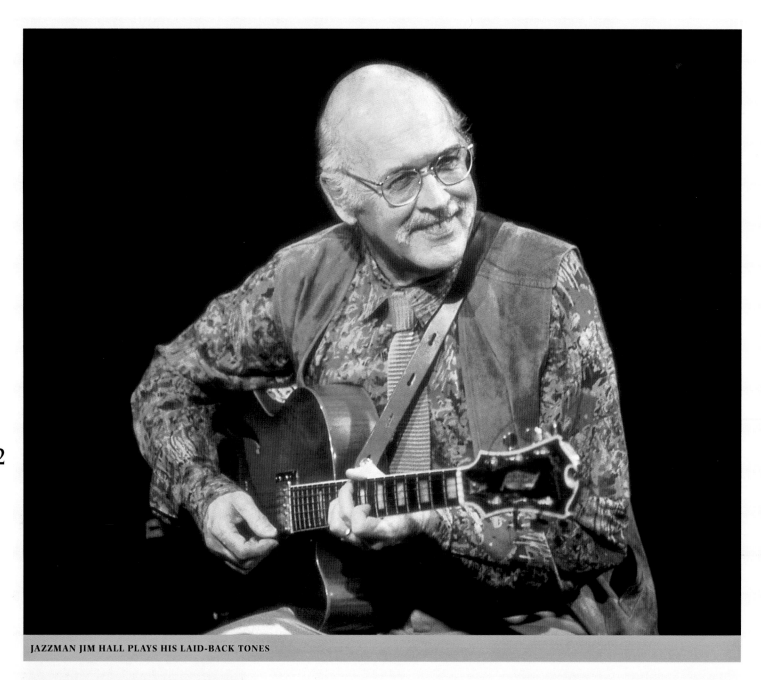

JAZZMAN JIM HALL PLAYS HIS LAID-BACK TONES

BUDDY GUY
– *see* Legends

JIM HALL
(1930–)

Hall found himself in good company from the start, working in thoughtful small-group surroundings, first with Chico Hamilton (1955–56), then Jimmy Giuffre (1956–59). He has played with just about every significant name in jazz, including Ella Fitzgerald, Chet Baker, Sonny Rollins and Bill Evans. His ability

to fit into any situation has made him one of the most versatile jazz musicians. Unusual for first-generation post-boppers, Hall's approach is far removed from players who sought to blind listeners with theory and technique. This, and his *very* mellow sound, has meant that his work is best appreciated after a period of acquaintance.

....

The Train And The River (1957, with Jimmy Giuffre)
Undercurrent (1959, with Bill Evans)

OLLIE HALSALL
(1949–1992)

Surely one of *the* unsung heroes of British rock music, on top form Ollie Halsall could generate the most extraordinary sounds from his guitar. Halsall's musical influences were the '50s pop records he had heard as a child, and numerous jazz saxophone and piano players. However, he always claimed never to have bothered listening to his own contemporaries.

Forming a long-standing partnership with singer Mike Patto, variously under the names

Timebox, Patto and Boxer, Halsall soon turned heads with a hammering technique that for its time was second to none. Quite simply, this enabled him to play blindingly fast. However this was not merely a trick that he mindlessly reeled out to impress: he was above all an intuitive master of melody.

Halsall was, by all accounts, an extremely self-effacing and modest musician, who was as happy to play to 20 people in a small club as in a massive stadium. This probably accounts for his appalling lack of recognition.

....

Roll 'Em, Smoke 'Em (1973, with Patto)
Below The Belt (1976, with Boxer)

BILL HARKLEROAD
(1950–)

Zoot Horn Rollo, as he was known by his employer Captain Beefheart, was one of the twin-guitar line-up that featured on 1969's ground-breaking *Trout Mask Replica* album. Sharing the honours with Jeff Cotton (Antennae Jimmy Semens), Harkleroad provided the wild soloing over Cotton's steam-driven riffs.

Staying with the Captain until 1973, Harkleroad then departed with other members of the Magic Band to form Mallard – whose comparative tameness some might think a reaction to the four years spent with Mr Van Vliet.

....

Trout Mask Replica (1969)
Lick My Decals Off, Baby (1970)
(both with Captain Beefheart)

GEORGE HARRISON
(1943–)

When discussing the development of the modern guitar, the name George Harrison is all too frequently overlooked. And yet his influ-

ence, even if you view him as "merely" the lead guitarist in the most popular group of all time, is extremely significant.

It is beyond doubt that a number of interesting developments in the use of the guitar were first popularized – sometimes even initiated – by the Beatles. 'I Feel Fine' features feedback, the first time such a sound had hit the pop charts. The driving guitar sound of 'Paperback Writer' led John Lennon to dub it "the first heavy metal record". There was the studio trickery heard on the pioneering psychedelic classic 'Tomorrow Never Knows', the fuzz box heard throughout 'Revolution' – and would the exotic sound of the sitar (and such widespread fascination with all things Indian,

THE MUCH UNDERRATED GEORGE HARRISON

for that matter) have been so characteristic of the era without Harrison's pioneering interest shown on album tracks like 'Within You Without You'?

But what of George Harrison's playing? Throughout most of the Beatles' career he showed extreme restraint as a lead player, offering crucial embellishing licks rather than taking a rip-roaring solo. However, their final recording, the *Abbey Road* album (recorded after *Let It Be*, but released before it), signalled Harrison's stepping out. For the first time, his own compositions could seriously be viewed as among the strongest on the record. What's more, a new self-assurance could be heard in his playing – aided, no doubt, by his close friendship with Eric Clapton – most notably on the beautifully executed solo on 'Something'.

....

The Beatles ("White Album") (1968)
Abbey Road (1969) (both with the Beatles)
All Things Must Pass (1970)

RICHIE HAVENS
(1941–)

Richie Havens is a good example of someone who makes excellent use of open tuning, which is where the strings of the guitar are tuned to the notes of a chord – in Havens' case, E major.

Havens' finest moment came as one of the lower-ranking figures to play at the Woodstock Festival in 1969 where he gave a hypnotic reading of his own song, 'Freedom'. It was one of the highlights of the concert and gave a much-needed boost to an extraordinary double-album set, *Richard P. Havens 1983*, released the previous year. Subsequent albums over the next 25 years have revealed less of the pioneering spirit exhibited here.

....

Richard P. Havens 1983 (1968)

163

JEFF HEALEY
(1968–)

In concert, Jeff Healey is an extraordinary sight. Blind from the age of one, he learned to play guitar two years later, gradually developing his own unique style of lap-top playing, using a regular solid-body Stratocaster. The hallmark of his playing is an unusually powerful yet controlled vibrato technique.

Although his recordings are technically faultless, he seems still to be settling into his own particular musical voice. Consequently his albums so far are of most interest to those who value guitar-playing for its own sake.

....

See The Light (1988)

MICHAEL HEDGES
(1956–1997)

164

One of the stars of the Windham Hill label – the home of so-called New Age music – Michael Hedges' music is considerably more demanding than one might guess from such a description. Indeed, his fingerpicking technique was among the most advanced that one could hear anywhere.

Working alone in his own studio, Hedges created soundscapes on a variety of instruments over which his highly accomplished acoustic guitar was then layered. Although a formal classical musical education enabled him to compose with some skill, his choice of cover versions from the world of pop and rock are perhaps his most interesting recordings, not least the Beatles' 'Tomorrow Never Knows' and Frank Zappa's 'Sofa'. His album *Oracle* won a Grammy award in 1998.

....

The Road To Return (1994)

Oracle (1996)

JIMI HENDRIX
– *see* Legends

STEVE HILLAGE
(1951–)

As a teenager, Hillage was first noticed playing with the band Egg – one of a number of late-'60s progressive bands specializing in a uniquely English form of baroque whimsy.

Leaving Egg as a three-piece, Hillage went off to university, whence he returned in 1973 to join Anglo-French avant-gardists Gong. Hillage's guitar style pulls in elements from all over the place – his fluid, jazz-tinged lines often doused in tape echo effects. Gong became absurdly famous in the UK when the Virgin label introduced their album *Camembert Electrique* for the price of a seven-inch single. With their (seemingly) never-ending improvisations and lyrics depicting flying teapots, Gong became the archetypal mid-'70s "druggie" band. By now Hillage had jumped ship to form his own band. Still retaining much of the mystical nonsense of Gong, he worked in a more structured manner, producing noteworthy hit albums like *Fish Rising* and *L*.

Hillage's popularity dwindled with the prevailing change of fashion in the late '70s, and he branched off into a successful sideline career as a producer. Then, in the early '90s, working with the likes of the Orb, he successfully managed to reinvent himself as a hip, 40-something dance producer. Under the moniker System 7 he has since produced some of the more interesting works of the ambient dance genre. Whilst the guitar still makes the odd appearance, Hillage seems to view it as just another possible tool for creating sound.

....

Fish Rising (1975)

System 7 (1992)

ALLAN HOLDSWORTH
(1946–)

A singular talent, Holdsworth has always moved in his own direction, with apparently little concern for the prevailing trends of the moment. One of the pioneers of jazz-rock, he first became prominent in the band Nucleus, moving on to stints in John Hiseman's Colosseum and the later fusion incarnation of Soft Machine.

From the end of the '70s, Holdsworth based himself in the US where he became well known on the jazz festival circuit fronting his own bands. During this time he was among the biggest-selling fusion artists in the world.

The fluid, lyrical tone of his music can be traced back to his early musical training when, at the age of 17, he first took up the saxophone and clarinet. His playing since has often seemed to reach for the expressiveness of these instruments. He was one of the few prominent players to persevere with the Synthaxe guitar – a complex hybrid of guitar and synthesizer.

....

Velvet Darkness (1979)

Road Games (1980)

EARL HOOKER
(1930–1971)

The cousin of the great John Lee Hooker, Earl never found anything like the same of success, and is now largely viewed as a minor-league figure. And yet his slide-playing had few peers when he emerged on the Chicago blues scene during the early '50s. For all his lack of commercial success he has been acknowledged as an influence on, among others, Jimi Hendrix and Bonnie Raitt.

For all of his fine playing, Hooker had two significant drawbacks that limited his potential success: his singing voice was not in the same league as his nifty fretwork, and he suffered from chronic poor health throughout his life.

Nonetheless, an endearing, sardonic wit permeated his work, as can be heard in the naming of one of his best tunes – 'Two Bugs

And A Roach' – a colloquial reference to the tuberculosis from which he suffered, and which would finally end his life in 1971.

Sweet Black Angel (1970)

There's A Fungus Amung Us (compilation, 1972)

JOHN LEE HOOKER
(1920–)

When John Lee Hooker's *The Healer* was released in 1989 few imagined that it would create much of an impression outside the blues scene. Fewer still would have predicted that a 69-year-old man with over 100 albums to his name would suddenly become the hippest thing around, and produce not only the biggest-selling album of his career, but the biggest-selling blues album of all time.

Born in the Mississippi Delta region, Hooker moved on to Detroit in his twenties. In 1948 he made his first recording, 'Boogie Chillen'. It was as if an alien had arrived from another planet, heard the blues and tried it out – it was that different. But this was no gimmick: 50 years later Hooker still sounds much the same.

The elements that make Hooker's sound so unique are difficult to pinpoint. The guitar and his deep groan of a voice are interwoven so tightly that it is pointless discussing one without the other. But the overriding effect of his style is one of structural freedom – Hooker has never felt the need to adhere to a simple 12-bar formula, moving from bar to bar as he feels fit, extending vocals as the mood takes him.

Throughout his long career, Hooker has seen his popularity wax and wane with some regularity, but he remains one of the most influential figures in modern music, not only for generations of blues musicians, but also among fledgling rock artists of the '60s.

The Ultimate Collection: 1948–1990

The Healer (1989)

JOHN LEE HOOKER, TOP OF THE BLUES PREMIER LEAGUE

166

LIGHTNIN' HOPKINS – HE SOMETIMES MADE UP SONGS AS HE WENT ALONG

SOL HOOPII

(1902–1953)

Solomon Ho'opi'i Ka'ai'ai was born in Honolulu, Hawaii. The youngest of 21 children, he began playing ukulele at the age of three, progressing through the guitar to lap steel. A teenage stowaway, Hoopii ended up working in San Francisco and Los Angeles.

His first recordings in 1927 featured improvisation over jazz and blues tunes. Seven years later, he switched to the Rickenbacker 'Frying Pan' electric lap steel, for he is remembered as an innovator. Expert in applying the instrument's unique sounds to Hawaiian favourites

and standards, his playing was widely heard in the '30s on soundtracks to such films as *Bird of Paradise* and *Waikiki Wedding*.

In 1938 Hoopii gave up music to join the crusade of evangelist Aimee Semple McPherson. He made few recordings until his death in 1953 at the age of 51.

....

Sol Hoopii (compilation, 1929–1937)

LIGHTNIN' HOPKINS

(1912–1982)

One of the masters of country blues, Sam "Lightnin'" Hopkins spent his Texan youth

hanging around street corners performing to anyone who cared to listen. His greatest influence at the time was Blind Lemon Jefferson with whom he played on innumerable occasions.

Hopkins' recording career began in the late '40s. His earliest hits were 'Short Haired Woman' and the R&B perennial 'Baby Please Don't Go', launching a career which has taken in over 20 different labels. He is widely thought to be the most recorded blues artist in history. The Hopkins sound was characterized by the use of single-string guitar lines that often echoed or counterpointed the vocal melody. At one of his first recording sessions an engineer impressed with Hopkins' fretboard dexterity christened him "Lightnin'". It was a name that stuck.

Hopkins' lyrics were among the most explicit forms of social commentary. In the best folk tradition, he simply relayed stories of what he saw around him, letting the facts speak for themselves. In the early days, he sang of the hard life of black plantation workers. Later he moved on to news events, natural disasters, war in Korea and Vietnam; even the space race was deemed fertile territory as can be heard in 'Happy John Glenn Blues'. He also showed that the epithet "Lightnin'" could equally be applied to his agile mind: he often made up songs on stage based on ideas suggested by his audience.

....

The Gold Star Sessions Volumes 1 and 2
(compilation, 1947–1950)
Anthology Of The Blues (1957–1962)

SON HOUSE
(1902–1988)

Like pioneers in many fields, Eddie James "Son" House was not the first to enjoy the the benefits of his efforts. He may have been one of the founding fathers of Delta blues, but it was protégés like Robert Johnson and Muddy Waters (*see* page 124) who went on to develop the form and (in Waters' case, at least) reap the rewards. In fact, until his "rediscovery" in 1964, Son House had only been able to work part-time as a musician.

Son House performed with an anguished intensity born of his own circumstances. On numbers like 'Mississippi County Farm Blues' he is not singing about the hardship of others, but of his own life. In short, Son House was the Real McCoy – an authentic blues voice.

House's guitar work was always sparse,

giving added impact to his impassioned voice. Unspectacular it may have been, but it provided a blueprint from which greater talents were able to work. During the last 20 years of his life he was afforded some due respect, but his place in the history of modern music remains severely overlooked.

....

Delta Blues: The Original Library Of Congress Sessions From Field Recordings 1941–1942 (compilation)

STEVE HOWE
(1947–)

The music of Yes, and progressive rock in general, was never for the faint-hearted. With its music-college noodling filling every possible hole in the stereo spectrum, it often seemed to be aimed at people who liked to be impressed by their music rather than feel any emotion for it. These types wouldn't even have been moved by Solomon Burke.

At their peak, Yes were among the most interesting and listenable of all these bands – and they were certainly the most successful. It was the playing of guitarist Steve Howe that stood out on 1971's *The Yes Album*, combining an intricacy necessary to do justice to such demanding music with a surprisingly raw energy that positively pumped life into the whole proceedings. This would gradually be replaced by the slick technoflash that reached an extreme on *Tales From Topographic Oceans* – an album that perhaps had more influence than any other on the reputation of the prog-rock genre. In 1981, with Yes a thing of the past, Steve Howe joined up with other like minds to form the supergroup Asia, which conquered America with disturbing ease.

Although Howe continues commercially successful associations with various combinations of his old cohorts, much of his finest playing and most satisfying material can be

found on his solo albums, where his work on the acoustic guitar especially shines.

....

The Yes Album (1971, with Yes)
Turbulence (1991)

MISSISSIPPI JOHN HURT
(1893–1966)

Among the most enigmatic of the "rediscovered" bluesmen of the '60s, Mississippi John Hurt differed from the likes of Big Bill Broonzy in that apart from having cut a few 78s in the late '20s, he had never really been known outside of his home in Carroll County, Mississippi. Hurt was traced down by blues revivalist Tom Hoskins in 1963, by which time he'd already retired from a life spent working the land and occasionally performing locally. At the age of 70 he was introduced to the New York coffee house circuit, where he bowled over young audiences with a tight blues-picking style displayed to great effect on a largely obscure set of ragtime tunes and blues ballads. His success peaked with a triumphant performance at the 1964 Newport Jazz Festival and an appearance on Johnny Carson's *Tonight* show. Two years later he died of a heart attack.

....

Today! (1964)

BUD ISAACS
(1922–)

When flamboyant singer Webb Pierce (he of the coin-studded car and guitar-shaped swimming pool) hit the country charts in 1954 with 'Slowly', few would have imagined that it signalled a quiet revolution in country music.

Relatively new instruments – which Pierce had already become well known for including in his groups – some pedal steel guitars had already been built with pedal changer mechanisms allowing a wider range of keys to be used. However, on 'Slowly', during the intro and solo section, the pedal was used for the first time as a way of bending notes. This one song heralded a new sound that within a few years would become close to being the defining characteristic of the pedal steel guitar.

....

The Best Of Webb Pierce (compilation, 1968)

ELMORE JAMES
(1918–1963)

When Elmore James died of a heart attack in 1963, he had cut over 50 new tracks in the previous three years. Some considered them to be his finest work – and he seemed on the verge of being discovered by a whole new generation of young white blues fans.

Born in Mississippi, James learned to play the guitar at the age of 12. In his teens he kept company with Robert Johnson, a big influence on his playing – his 'Dust My Broom' gave James his first hit in 1951. The howling slide riff he used on this track (which he re-recorded at regular intervals) became his own stock-in-trade sound. Over the next decade, James and his band, the Broomdusters, produced some of the most consistently powerful electric blues.

James was a significant influence on younger blues guitarists, such as Luther Allison and Johnny Winter. His characteristic wail can be heard in the playing of just about every notable slide guitarist who followed, from Roy Buchanan to Duane Allman. He was all but worshipped by young white blues purists of the early '60s (Brian Jones of the Rolling Stones renamed himself Elmo Lewis in his honour). But for James' untimely death he would surely have enjoyed the same success that other blues veterans found in the '60s.

....

The Complete Fire and Enjoy Sessions Volumes 1–4 (compilation, 1960–1962)
The Complete Elmore James Story (compilation, 1951-1962)

ELMORE JAMES DIED TOO SOON TO REAP THE REWARDS OF THE '60S BLUES BOOM

BERT JANSCH
(1943–)

As far as fingerpicking guitar is concerned, Scottish-born folk musician Bert Jansch has few peers. A veteran of the British club circuit, Jansch emerged with a stunning solo debut in 1965 that displayed a fearsome technical ability and a sympathy for his material that prevented it seeming like an academic exercise.

Jansch's most public achievement was the contemporary folk supergroup Pentangle, formed in 1967 from a pool of well-respected solo artists. Pentangle were largely responsible for the revival of traditional English and Celtic folk music during this period. Although their *Basket Of Light* album sold significantly, yielding a minor hit single, they never managed quite the same degree of commercial success as some that followed in their wake, such as Steeleye Span or Fairport Convention.

....

Jack Orion (1966)
The Pentangle (1968)

BLIND LEMON JEFFERSON
(1897–1929)

The first star of the blues, between 1925 and his death Blind Lemon Jefferson was the biggest-selling black artist. He was the first blues guitar player to sell records in any great quantity. And, with a tragic predictability given the time and place he lived, Jefferson saw almost no financial reward and was buried in a pauper's grave.

Born in Couchman, Texas, Jefferson was blind from birth. In his teen years he made his keep begging and performing on the streets of Dallas and Houston. He was later discovered playing at rent parties in Chicago, which led to him cutting the 78s for the Paramount label which brought him fame.

Jefferson's recordings are now readily available, some of his songs having been passed down to new generations. However, it is his guitar technique that astounds to this day. His peers found it impossible to copy and developed their own takes on the Jefferson style. These players – Leadbelly, Lightnin' Hopkins, Robert Johnson and T-Bone Walker – provided the blueprints from which most R&B and rock guitar styles have evolved. Whilst it's possible (if demanding) to learn one of Jefferson's pieces like 'Easy Rider Blues' or 'See That My Grave Is Kept Clean', one can never understand *why* he played what he did. And this is the mystery. Rather than accompanying his singing with any conventional structure, much of what he did seemed to be improvising around the theme. As such, analysis fails to come up with any useful conclusion – Jefferson was just doing what came naturally, and he probably didn't give it a great deal of thought himself.

In 1967, blues enthusiasts discovered his unmarked grave at the Negro Cemetery in Wortham, Texas and belatedly added their own fitting tribute – "One Of America's Outstanding Original Musicians".

....

King Of The Country Blues (compilation, 1926–1929)

LONNIE JOHNSON
(1889–1970)

As popular during the '20s as Blind Lemon Jefferson and Big Bill Broonzy, Lonnie Johnson was one of the pioneering figures that helped to establish a commercial market for blues recordings. Johnson has also been described as the first great guitarist of the century. Although that may be overstating the case, it would certainly be fair to call him the first great technician of the blues guitar.

Johnson was born in New Orleans, but little seems to be known about his early upbringing. He made his recording debut in 1925, by which time he was already well known as a master of the guitar (both six-string and twelve-string versions), banjo and violin. His skills as a soloist also grabbed the attention of jazz musicians, and by the end of the decade he had recorded on significant sessions with Louis Armstrong, Duke Ellington and King Oliver. But it was a series of duets he recorded with Eddie Lang, the greatest jazz player of the period, for which Johnson is best remembered. These feature some of the first great virtuoso jazz guitar recordings, and influenced most jazz musicians who followed.

Johnson recorded extensively throughout his life, drifting between the worlds of blues and jazz. Although after the war he was well adrift of the cutting edge of either scene, he remained an active and respected performer until his death in 1970.

....

Steppin' On The Blues (compilation, 1925–1932)

ROBERT JOHNSON
(1911–1938)

It seems strange that one of the pivotal figures of twentieth-century music should have cut only 29 tracks (and 12 alternative takes) in his short but troubled life. And yet this tiny but

LONNIE JOHNSON –THE FIRST POP STAR OF THE BLUES?

169

ageless body of work has continually affected successive generations of musicians, shaping the development of blues, and ultimately rock music that wouldn't emerge for another 25 years.

Robert Johnson was born in Hazlehurst, Mississippi. As a teenager he kept company with Son House, Charlie Patton and lesser-known blues pioneer Willie Brown, all fine but very distinct guitarists. Combining such influences, Johnson synthesized a Delta blues style that, through the likes of Muddy Waters and Elmore James, would later find its way into the blues mainstream.

Johnson's legendary status can be attributed to the mysteries surrounding what was clearly a troubled life, and the way in which he documented pain and anguish through his music. Songs like 'Crossroads Blues' and 'Hellhound On My Trail' tell stories of an ever-restless spirit moving endlessly towards an inevitable doom. Here was a man clearly not expecting St Peter to be waiting for him on the day of reckoning.

As bleak and poignant as these works are, their crude beauty has a unique ability to communicate to us across time. They stand alongside the greatest musical achievements of the twentieth century.

A hell-raising, hard-drinking womanizer, Johnson ended his life predictably violently – drinking poisoned whiskey given to him by a man who suspected him of having an affair with his wife. Yet his music has lived on, growing in stature over time. If any proof were needed of his now legendary status, when his complete works were issued on two CDs in the early '90s they went on to sell half a million copies – not bad for some scratchy old blues sides recorded 60 years earlier.

The Complete Recordings (compilation, 1936–1937)

BRIAN JONES
(1942–1969)

Lewis Brian Hopkin-Jones was an ultra-middle-class kid from Cheltenham – an ultra-middle-class town in the west of England. And yet somehow the blues of the Deep South, the deep groan of Muddy Waters (*see* page 124) and the howling bottleneck of Elmore James, reached out to him.

In '50s provincial England, R&B was almost unheard of outside of London, and it was there that Jones headed in his late teens. Calling himself Elmo Lewis, Jones hunted out like-minded souls, coming into contact with Mick Jagger and Keith Richards. He told them he was forming a group named after one of Muddy Waters' best-known songs – they would be called the Rollin' Stones.

Now viewed as a rock tradition that looks set to run on forever, it's easy to forget that for their first few albums, the Rolling Stones were

BRIAN JONES AND HIS VOX "TEARDROP" GUITAR

a blues cover band, and Jagger was nothing more than the guy who sang. As the song-writing partnership between Jagger and Richards grew, Jones took less of the limelight.

A naturally talented musician who could turn his hand to any instrument, Jones provided some rip-roaring solos for the early Stones. Later he was responsible for the some of the more interesting (and influential) tonal characteristics that ushered the Stones into the psychedelic era. Sadly, by 1969, drugs had taken a massive toll on his creativity and he was ejected from the band. He was found dead in his swimming pool that same year.

The Rolling Stones (1964)

RONNY JORDAN
(1961–)

During the late '80s dance producers started to discover the organic grooves of classic Blue Note jazz recordings from 30 years earlier. Understanding its dancefloor potential, some started to integrate short digital snippets into their own work. Thus was born a synergistic relationship that also saw newly emerging jazz artists making active use of the sounds of hip hop in their music. This may not have pleased some jazz purists (for whom it barely counted as "jazz") but it was a useful element in the gradual repopularization of the genre. Ronny Jordan is probably the most significant British jazz guitarist to have emerged through this type of process: a good example of how a new generation of gifted young black British musicians pass through other musical cultures – funk, reggae or dance – before arriving in jazz. Indeed this is all a part of the gradual breaking down of traditional musical boundaries, which has characterized much music of the '90s.

The Quiet Revolution (1993)

elements of modern classical, had little obvious commercial appeal. Of the bands that emerged, such as Tangerine Dream, Kraftwerk and Faust, Can were probably the most fascinating – not least because two of its members – Irmin Schmidt and Holger Czukay – had studied under noted avant-garde composer Karlheinz Stockhausen.

Although they could hardly be described as a "guitar band", Michael Karoli's playing in Can showed an admirable understanding of space and dynamic restraint that fitted neatly and precisely into their long hypnotic improvisations.

Can have been a major influence on a lot of experimental music that has come since, perhaps the closest in spirit being Public Image Limited's *Metal Box* set.

....

Tago Mago (1971)
Ege Bamyesi (1972)

171

STANLEY JORDAN, THE MAN WITH TWO LEFT HANDS

STANLEY JORDAN
(1959–)

Stanley Jordan created something of a stir when he performed at the 1984 Kool Festival in New York with what seemed to be a revolutionary approach to playing the guitar. Positioning the instrument on his lap, as if it were a piano keyboard. he presses his fingers down on the fretboard rather than holding notes with his left hand and picking the strings with his right. This gives him the ability to play melodies by hammering on with his right hand, and chords and bass lines by hammering on with his left hand.

Awesomely spectacular though this technique is, it seems a little sad that Jordan – a Princeton music graduate – has so far tended largely to have been marketed as a gimmick. Indeed, his Blue Note debut, on which he played unaccompanied, proudly declared on the jacket that no overdubs had been used in making the record, as if that were particularly important to the quality of the music.

Jordan's music has not advanced as quickly as some might have hoped – his playing style a restrictive variation on jazz piano. He remains, however, in a league of his own, and his progress will continue to be viewed with great interest.

....

Magic Touch (1984)

MICHAEL KAROLI
(1948–)

The genre known as "Krautrock" was one of the oddest to find widespread popularity in the early '70s, not least because the music, which crossed "hippy" rock improvisation with

BARNEY KESSEL
(1923–)

Noted for the rich precision of his chord work, Barney Kessel is one of the finest exponents of solo and small group jazz.

Although for much of his long career he has played anonymous sessions for television and films, from the late '40s he became a well-known jazz player in his own right, having recorded with both Charlie Parker and Oscar Peterson, and featured in the Jazz at the Philharmonic tours.

Kessel is also well known for some notable non-jazz work, such as the fabulous 'Cry Me A River' sessions for Julie London, as well as dates with the Beach Boys and Phil Spector. This lack of perceived "jazz purity" has led him to be undervalued by some jazz critics.

....

Julie Is Her Name (1955, with Julie London)
Feeling Free (1969)

ALBERT KING
(1923–1992)

One of 13 children, Albert King (Albert Nelson) was born in Indianola, Mississippi – the same town that gave the world another King – B.B. (*see* page 110).

Influenced by Elmore James and T-Bone Walker, King played a rough, muscular blues with his guitar tuned to an open E minor chord. His earliest recordings, first in 1953 and then again in 1959, were not successful, but his reputation grew as he gigged around the blues clubs of Chicago and St Louis for the following five years.

It was in 1966, when King was signed to the Memphis R&B label, Stax, that he suddenly made a significant mark. Following his first hit, 'Laundromat Blues', King recorded a succession of magnificent sides, all featuring the magical sound of the Stax house band, Booker T and the MGs – on the surface an unusual alliance. These tracks were brought together for the album *Born Under A Bad Sign*. A combination of the unique Stax R&B sound and King's harsh, gritty Chicago blues was a revelation. It is widely considered to be one of the critical blues albums of the '60s, not only signposting a new phase of development, but influencing musicians like Hendrix (*see* page 108).

More willing to experiment with other forms than many contemporaries, the '70s saw King moving away towards soul and funk before he came home in the following decade.

....

Born Under A Bad Sign (1967)
Masterworks ('60s compilation)

BLUESMAN ALBERT KING FOUND HIS NICHE WITH THE SOUL-BASED STAX LABEL

B.B. KING
– *see* Legends

FREDDIE KING
(1934–1976)

One of the classic Chicago bluesmen of the '50s, Freddie King knew precisely where he fitted into the grand scheme of things: "I put my style right between T-Bone, Muddy Waters, Lightnin' Hopkins and B.B. King."

Playing around Chicago from the early '50s, he recorded widely while backing other artists, but it wasn't until 1960 that he was given the chance to record on his own. Signing to Cincinnati's King label, he recorded the instrumental 'Hideaway' which became an instant R&B Top 10 hit.

Although his career ebbed during the mid-'60s, King was particularly influential on the first generation of white bluesmen. Links to the likes of Eric Clapton and Jeff Beck (*see* page 96) helped bring him to the attention of a new young audience. Although towards the end of his life he occasionally eased uncomfortably away from blues, he remained a popular live attraction, playing regularly all over the world.

....

Freddie King Sings (1961)

Blues Guitar Hero: The Influential Early Sessions (compilation, 1993)

MARK KNOPFLER
(1949–)

Whatever one may think of the music of Dire Straits, there can no denying that Mark Knopfler is one of the finest and most influential guitarists to hit the mainstream over the past 20 years.

A former English teacher, Knopfler formed Dire Straits in 1975. Stalwarts on the London pub-rock circuit, their debut album passed with little fuss until around a year later when the track 'Sultans Of Swing' began to get air-

THE PASSIONATE INFLUENTIAL BLUES STAR, FREDDIE KING

play. A song about a bunch of bar musicians who play just for the fun, every line of every verse ended with a perfectly executed Stratocaster lick, building up to a thrilling climax with the famous picked arpeggios at the end of the song. Punk may have tried to outlaw such things, but it was clear that there was still a big market for a neatly executed guitar

solo. Subsequent Dire Straits albums have followed the same formula – memorable melodies, intelligent lyrics sung in Knopfler's Dylanesque groan, and fretwork on electric, acoustic and resonator guitars that redefines the term "subtle". Not surprisingly for such a fine player, Knopfler quickly found himself in the employ of others, providing sterling contri-

MARK KNOPFLER OF DIRE STRAITS PLAYS A NATIONAL RESONATOR STEEL GUITAR

174

butions to the likes of Bob Dylan, Steely Dan, Van Morrison and Tina Turner. He has also recorded duets with veteran country picker Chet Atkins (*see* page 94).

It's a testament to Knopfler's talent that his band were one of very few non-New Wavers to break through in the late '70s. That a major proportion of their popularity stemmed from word-of-mouth grass roots support rather than record label hype is even more remarkable.

Dire Straits (1978)

Brothers In Arms (1985)

PAUL KOSSOFF
(1950–1976)

Much lamented by rock fans, Paul Kossoff (the son of noted actor David), was fêted as one of the greatest rock guitarists of the early '70s. It was a combination of his subtle guitar work and the vocals of Paul Rodgers, one of *the* great white blues vocalists, that made the band Free such an immediate success when they formed in 1969.

It was an ability to play with depth and passion, without resorting to a mindless flurry of notes, that marked Kossoff out from the crowd. For most, his defining moment was the opening bars of the rock anthem 'All Right Now' – as immediately recognizable a riff as was ever heard.

In 1973, after three years of regularly reported personality clashes, Free called it a day. Rodgers and drummer Simon Kirke went off to form Bad Company, who enjoyed massive success, especially in the US. Meanwhile, Kossoff, his life already troubled by a severe drug addiction, formed the disappointing Back Street Crawler. He died in 1976 from heart failure during a flight between London and New York.

Fire And Water (1970, with Free)

LEO KOTTKE

(1949–)

For almost 30 years, Leo Kottke has followed an eccentric path of his own, much in the same way (if more commercially successfully) as his mentor, the great John Fahey. Like Fahey, Kottke has created a unique and very personal style of music that draws on a traditional American folk and blues base, and which can't be obviously likened to anything else.

Emerging in the late '60s, Kottke made an immediate impression with the album *Six And Twelve String Guitar* released by Fahey's Takoma label. An instrumental album of almost breathtaking virtuosity, it led to a contract with Capitol records in 1971. For Kottke this began a brief period as one of the most successful folk artists in the world, his albums selling in surprisingly large quantities for an instrumentalist.

Kottke's work has been characterized by a surreal sense of humour – again, the same kind that permeates Fahey's early album sleeves – and a seemingly almost wilful unpredictability. This has sometimes led him down unusual paths, nowhere more so than on the *Balance* album in 1979, on which he fronted his own country-rock band. Since the mid-'80s he has been linked to the Windham Hill label, even if in many ways his challenging music would seem to be the complete antithesis of New Age. His work is essential for students of fingerpicking and altered tunings.

Mudlark (1971)
Ice Water (1974)
My Father's Face (1989)

BIRELI LAGRENE

(1966–)

A frighteningly precocious talent, French-born Bireli Lagrene had evidently mastered

EDDIE LANG – THE MAN WHO MANY WOULD CLAIM INVENTED THE GUITAR SOLO

much of the Django Reinhardt songbook (*see* page 116) by the age of seven. Following such astonishing development, it came as little surprise that by the age of 16 he should record such a self-assured tribute to his overriding influence. *Roads To Django* saw the youngster recreate Reinhardt's most popular songs in their original settings.

Since then, Lagrene has developed into one of the most promising players in the jazz world, showing an intelligent understanding of a wide range of musical cultures.

Acoustic Moments (1991)
Standards (1992)

EDDIE LANG

(1902–1933)

A five-star jazz pioneer, Eddie Lang was the first player of the jazz age to create a distinctly solo voice for the guitar. Born Salvatore Massaro in New York, he studied the violin at the age of seven, before turning to the guitar and banjo in his teens. He played his first concert dates with his school friend, violinist Joe Venuti – an association that would famously continue throughout Lang's short life.

By the middle of the '20s Lang had already become well known for his unique single-string playing (previously the guitar had been exclusively a rhythm instrument). Between 1930 and 1932 he was a staff accompanist for Bing Crosby, but continued to work extensively in a chamber setting with Venuti. Although it is this work for which Lang is best remembered – it provided a blueprint for Django Reinhardt (*see* page 116) and Stéphane Grappelli across the Atlantic – some of his most incisive playing can be heard duetting with other guitarists, in particular his influential sessions with Lonnie Johnson, on which he called himself Blind Willie Dunn.

Jazz Guitar Virtuoso (compilation, 1926–1933)
Stringing The Blues (compilation, 1931, with Joe Venuti)

LEADBELLY

(1889–1949)

Huddie Ledbetter was the most famous of the Library Of Congress field recording artists discovered by Alan Lomax. A convict for most of his life, Leadbelly was serving time in Angola, Louisiana when Lomax discovered that here was not only a fine songwriter and performer, but a rich source of knowledge on a lost art form.

Under Lomax's guidance, Leadbelly became a much-loved figure in New York middle-class, left-wing political circles in the '40s, when he recorded many of his original songs for numerous small labels. His guitar work may not have been of the same stature as, say, Blind Lemon Jefferson's, but he stands out not only as an important figure in the history of guitar-based blues, but as one of a rare breed of early bluesmen to use a 12-string guitar.

A decade after Leadbelly's death, some of his best-known songs like 'Rock Island Line' and 'Goodnight Irene' became skiffle hits. Later still, 'Black Betty' became an unexpected '70s heavy rock anthem.

....

King Of The Twelve-String Guitar (compilation, 1935)

ALVIN LEE
(1944–)

If guitar greatness was all about playing as fast as possible, then Alvin Lee would surely be near the top of the list.

Lee's band, Ten Years After, were formed in 1966, when they gained a reputation for being one of the more authentic voices on the British blues scene. His finest moment came in 1969 when Ten Years After performed at the Woodstock festival. His astonishingly fast playing on the 13-minute 'I'm Going Home' proved to be one of the popular highlights of the subsequent film and soundtrack. Admittedly breathtaking, it won over many fans immediately.

Unfortunately, Ten Years After's albums were generally thought not quite so breathtaking, indicating that Lee was perhaps less inspired playing any other way. Eventually he became bored and retired from the cycle of endless touring and recording in the mid-'70s. He has made numerous solo albums, and is still revered by many rock guitar fans.

....

Woodstock: The Original Soundtrack (1969)

LIGHTNIN' SLIM
(1913–1974)

Born Otis Hicks, in St Louis, Slim spent his early life working on farmlands. It wasn't until he was well into his thirties that he learned how to play the guitar, working his own variations on the Lightnin' Hopkins repertoire. He made up for lost time and by the end of the '40s was playing the clubs around the Baton

176

ALVIN LEE, ONE OF THE STARS OF THE ORIGINAL WOODSTOCK FESTIVAL IN 1969

Rouge area. His first recordings were made in 1954 and were surprisingly popular. During the '60s his fame spread to Europe, where he toured on several occasions.

....

King Of The Swamp Blues (1958–64)
(compilation)

NILS LOFGREN
(1951–)

Latterly sidelined as lead guitarist in Bruce Springsteen's touring band, Nils Lofgren is also a highly respected solo artist, and was widely tipped for stardom in his own right in the '70s.

Born in Chicago, Lofgren formed his first band, Grin, whilst still in his teenage years. At their best, on 1972's *One Plus One*, Lofgren proved a fine songwriter and guitarist in the classic rock 'n' roll tradition of Chuck Berry and (Lofgren's teenage idol) Keith Richards. Although critically acclaimed, Grin failed to sell in significant numbers and disbanded.

Not surprisingly, a few years later Lofgren re-emerged with a cracking solo debut which showed that he had developed significantly both as a composer and musician. The follow-up, *Cry Tough*, although disappointing for some critics, was a commercial success, giving full reign to his burgeoning guitar-hero status. It highlighted a wide range of skills from Buchananesque licks to a skilful use of delicate fingered harmonics, which influenced many young players at the time.

At the start of the '80s Lofgren's solo career began to lose momentum and he accepted a job working with the all-conquering Springsteen band. As well as accompanying old friend Neil Young both on guitars and keyboards, Lofgren has maintained parallel careers ever since.

....

Nils Lofgren (1975)

Cry Tough (1976)

LARRY McCRAY, LATEST IN THE FINE TRADITION OF FLYING V BLUESMEN

LARRY McCRAY
(1960–)

One of the emerging stars of modern blues, McCray plays a hard, biting guitar in a tight, raw rocking band. Playing a Gibson Flying V, he betrays the influences of a pair of Kings – Albert and B.B. (*see* A–Z and page 110). However, on his own admission, Albert Collins was his greatest influence. Born in Stevens, Arkansas, McCray was the eighth of nine children growing up on a family farm. After moving north to Saginaw in Michigan with his sister (a professional musician), he was working in bands by the age of 15, playing blues, funk and soul covers. In the mid-'80s he formed his own band, which gradually acquired a live reputation. However, it wasn't until after the release of his debut album, *Ambition*, recorded for the British PointBlank label, that he was able to wave goodbye to his day job working on a car assembly line.

He has since recorded a further two albums and made useful contributions to recordings by James Cotton and Larry Garner. Major European tours supporting Gary Moore and George Thorogood have cemented a reputation as a bluesman more concerned with developing at his own pace than hitting an early peak.

....

Delta Hurricane (1993)

INFLUENTIAL 12-STRING PLAYER ROGER McGUINN OF THE BYRDS

ROGER McGUINN

(1942–)

Rarely has a pop band created such an innovative and characteristic sound as the Byrds during the second half of the '60s. They found immediate success with the release of an electric version of Bob Dylan's 'Hey Mr Tambourine Man' in 1965. The formula of sumptuous gentle folk harmonies and Roger McGuinn's jangling 12-string electric guitar was revolutionary and set a pattern that could be heard throughout one of the greatest bodies of work in rock history.

Although they may not have reached the same degree of commercial success as the Beatles or the Beach Boys, the Byrds remain in the same league as far as their influence has spread. At the time, the Beatles kept a very close eye on what they were doing – as can be heard on the *Rubber Soul* and *Revolver* albums.

Their integration of country music with rock helped to spawn one of the most popular genres of the '70s. And one of the most popular bands of the past decade, R.E.M., (along with many others) clearly owe a debt to McGuinn and the Byrds. Although low key by comparison, McGuinn maintained a well-

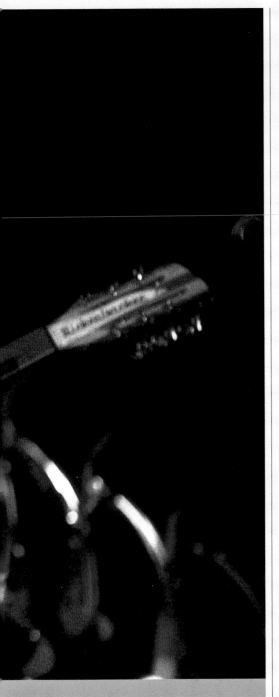

JOHN McLAUGHLIN
(1942–)

A much maligned musical form, jazz-rock fusion has too often been characterized by the pursuit of technical skill for its own sake. John McLaughlin is a shining exception to this excess.

McLaughlin began playing the guitar at the age of 11. His earliest interests were in traditional American bluesmen like Leadbelly and Big Bill Broonzy. In the early '60s he moved to London to be a part of the blues scene. Under the influence of eccentric band leader Graham Bond he began to develop an interest in Eastern philosophies, religions and cultures which would shape his direction in the future.

An increasing interest in free jazz led him to record his debut solo album in 1969. A ground-breaking piece of work, *Extrapolations*, with its high-technique jazz-style rock soloing, anticipated the whole fusion movement and created a sizeable buzz on the international jazz scene. This led to him being drafted into the Miles Davis band, with whom he recorded *In A Silent Way* and *Bitches Brew*, a double-album set that for many established fusion as the next leap forward in the development of jazz.

In 1971 McLaughlin formed his own band, the Mahavishnu Orchestra mixing jazz and rock electronics even further. Their albums achieved wide crossover success and also became mainstream chart hits, heavily influencing the jazz-rock bands that were about to emerge.

Much of McLaughlin's subsequent work has been on the acoustic guitar, often featuring Indian, classical and flamenco musicians. (In the mid-'70's, he abandoned electricity for a while and formed an all-acoustic trio, Shakti, with Indian musicians.) He remains widely respected by musicians of all genres, and is one of the most influential guitarists of the past 30 years, having anticipated not only fusion, but also much of the "ambient" jazz music produced in the past decade.

....

Extrapolations (1969)

Bitches Brew (1970, with Miles Davis)

The Inner Mounting Flame (1972, with the Mahavishnu Orchestra)

YNGWIE MALMSTEEN
(1963–)

Swedish-born Yngwie Malmsteen got his first guitar at the age five, but it was watching Jimi Hendrix (*see* page 108) on television in 1970 that made him determined to pursue a similar career. Relocating to America in his late teens, he joined the band Steeler who produced a crossover rock album inspired by classical composers like Bach, Vivaldi and Paganini. Malmsteen's solos were intricate and lengthy, and provided a glimpse of the approach that he would perfect over the coming years.

Malmsteen first reached metal audiences recording two albums with the rock band Alcatrazz, his high-speed fretwork ideally suited to such a style. Launching a solo career in the mid-'80s, he has concentrated his efforts on classical-tinged rock instrumentals, and his work stands apart from those of his peers by virtue of melodic superiority and a playing style that never seems to be (entirely) about technique for its own sake.

Malmsteen is widely respected in Britain and the United States for his formidable finesse, and although his sales may not match those of Vai or Satriani in the West, he is a genuine superstar in Japan and the Far East, his albums frequently topping the charts.

....

Rising Force (1984)

Inspiration (1996)

179

respected solo career from 1973 to 1977, when he took time out for the next 14 years. He returned with a triumphant album, *Back From Rio*, which also featured the talents of Elvis Costello and Tom Petty.

....

Mr Tambourine Man (1965, with the Byrds)

Turn! Turn! Turn! (1966, with the Byrds)

Back From Rio (1991)

MAGIC SAM
(1937–1969)

A highly rated figure among the Chicago blues community, Sam Maghett was a second-generation bluesman who, along with Buddy Guy (*see* page 106) and Otis Rush, set the agenda for the contemporary blues sound. He first made his mark at the age of 20 with a series of recordings for the Cobra label, but he truly hit his stride a decade later with a pair of classy and influential recordings for Delmark. His death from a heart attack at the age of 32 deprived the blues world of a guitarist whose potential was just beginning to flower.

....

West Side Soul (1967)

Black Magic (1968)

TAJ MAHAL
– *see under* Taj

HARVEY MANDEL
(1945–)

It's rather surprising that given the breadth of his work Harvey "The Snake" Mandel is not more widely recognized. He is probably best known to most rock fans for his slick work on the Rolling Stones' *Black And Blue* album after the departure of Mick Taylor – indeed he was touted as a likely successor until Ronnie Wood got the gig. However, a widely travelled sessioneer, Mandel has been a subtle influence on guitar-playing over the past 30 years.

Raised in Chicago, Mandel's break came as guitarist with Charlie Musselwhite. His reputation on the blues scene made him an obvious choice when the position of lead guitar in Canned Heat became vacant – he played on three of their albums and featured in their famed Woodstock appearance. Before being recruited by the Stones, he also spent a year in the hallowed position of lead guitarist with John Mayall's Bluesbreakers.

JOHNNY MARR – THE SOUND OF THE SMITHS

During the mid-'70s he produced a series of interesting instrumental albums that veered between rock and fusion, the most noteworthy being *Shangrenade*, on which he pioneered a two-handed finger-tapping system many years before Eddie Van Halen. Although much of the past two decades has seen him playing sessions, he resumed his solo recording career in the early '90s.

Shangrenade (1976)
Planetary Warrior (1997)

JOHNNY MARR
(1963–)

During most of the '80s, the word "rock" was a derogatory term in the independent music world. But whilst the pomp and solo excesses of the '70s had been expunged for much of its output, so too had the single most important virtue that made pop music so great – a good tune. It was the emergence of Manchester's the Smiths that turned around the "alternative" market, showing that it was possible to combine rich melodies, witty and intelligent lyrics, and, courtesy of Johnny Marr, some of the most sympathetic pop guitar heard in a decade or more.

Marr's luscious ringing details were perfectly suited to the Smiths' spartan sound, their recordings showing little reliance on studio overdubs. It was a contemporary hybrid of rhythm and lead guitar that Steve Cropper (*see* page 104) had perfected in the '60s. There was rarely soloing in the conventional sense, but the complex rhythm work and picked-out arpeggios were expertly played. It made Marr one of the few credible guitar stars of the '80s.

After the break-up of the Smiths, Marr became an in-demand hired hand working for established artists that might have worried former Smiths fans, such as Paul McCartney and Bryan Ferry. He has since combined this session career with the band Electronic, a periodically successful collaboration with Bernard Sumner of New Order.

The Queen Is Dead (1986, with the Smiths)
Electronic (1992)

JUAN MARTIN
(1943–)

London-based Juan Martín is one of the finest exponents of modern-day flamenco guitar. A native Andalucian, Martin grew up in Malaga before moving to Madrid where his extraordinary technical skills first gained widespread attention.

Although it is for his pure flamenco work that he is so rightly noted, he has crossed over into other areas of music with some success. During the mid-'80s he performed at Montreux with such jazz luminaries as Miles Davis and Herbie Hancock. His compositions are also noteworthy, drawing on traditional Spanish influences such as Falla and Tárrega. An increasing interest in the Moorish roots of flamenco led to the fascinating *Musica Alhambra*, a work which integrates arabic percussion and vocals with Martín's intense playing.

Martín's tutorial book, *El Arte Flamenco de la Guitarra*, is widely considered to be the definitive work on the subject.

The Andalucian Suites (1985)
Luna Negra (1993)

HANK B. MARVIN
(1941–)

Unashamedly populist, proffering a memorable melody rather than needless extemporization, Hank Marvin holds a peculiar place in the hearts of many British music fans. The Shadows are Britain's most popular instrumental group of all time. During the first half of the '60s they not only backed up pop idol Cliff Richard, but enjoyed over 20 Top 10 hits of their own. Their sound was unique – simple chords strummed out on acoustic guitars with a simple guitar melody embellished with tremolo arm, echo and reverb.

Marvin's playing is a direct equivalent to that of Duane Eddy in the US, and both of them were massively influential on the first generation of pop guitarists. Whilst a fine musician, on record Marvin has always restricted his playing to the formula he first used in the early '60s.

20 Golden Greats (compilation, with the Shadows, 1977)

J MASCIS
(1966–)

The so-called "grunge" sound that exploded commercially at the beginning of the '90s had been a while coming. The strands that brought it to that point could be traced to the thrashy guitar combos of the previous decade: the

181

HANK MARVIN – GIVE HIM A GOOD TUNE AND HE'S HAPPY

art-noise of Sonic Youth, and the attitude of bands like Dinosaur Jr, Hüsker Dü or the Replacements – all huge influences.

In many ways J Mascis *is* Dinosaur Jr. His strident rough-and-ready-guitar work and oddly plaintive vocals that recall Neil Young, created a marvellous amalgam of melody and noise, preceding the Nirvana sound by several years.

Dinosaur (1985)

Green (1991)

BRIAN MAY
(1947–)

Queen were unique . A mixture of Brian May's heavy Zeppelinesque riffs and the vaudeville and cod-operatic proclivities of singer Freddie Mercury may not have seemed like a winning formula, and yet from the mid-'70s Queen sold truckloads of records and were one of the biggest live draws the world over.

Like the other members of his band, May was unusually well educated for a pop star, having studied astronomy at London's Imperial College, and completed much of his PhD before music took control of his life. Whilst individually Queen were all highly accomplished musicians, it was May's guitar work that stood out. Always happy to make use of technology, the most dramatic device in May's armoury is the sound of his hallmark harmonized guitar "orchestras", built up one track at a time in the studio. This impressive effect can be heard on every one of a dozen or more Queen albums, but with greatest impact on *Sheer Heart Attack*'s 'Brighton Rock'. This sound is so strongly identifiable that any guitarist who plays harmonized solos is now likely to be compared to Brian May.

Sheer Heart Attack (1974)

A Night At The Opera (1975)

TAKING DELIGHT IN EXCESS, BRIAN MAY OF QUEEN

JOHN MAYALL
(1933–)

Although John Mayall is a fine blues guitarist in his own right, his real significance in guitar history is as a catalyst of the British blues scene. Indeed, Mayall could be said to have had a sizeable impact on rock music since the mid-'60s. From 1963, his band, the Bluesbreakers,

182

provided the launching ground for some of the finest guitarists in rock. Eric Clapton (1965), Peter Green (1966) and Mick Taylor (1967) were all teenage stars discovered by Mayall. Listening to Bluesbreakers albums from this period therefore provides a fascinating glimpse of some of the greatest young raw talents that were coming into bloom.

....

Bluesbreakers (1965, John Mayall with Eric Clapton)

BARRY MELTON
(1947–)

Of all the names that came out of San Francisco's Haight-Ashbury scene, Country Joe McDonald is probably best remembered for his anti-establishment, anti-Vietnam stands. Take, for instance, his famous "Fish" chant – "Give me an F! Give me a U! Give me a C! Give me a K!" – which shocked commentators at concerts and political rallies throughout the late '60s. His music career, however, was also noteworthy.

McDonald's musical sidekick throughout, initially as a fellow folkie and then in the band Country Joe and the Fish, was Barry Melton. With its strong blues leanings, Melton's playing drew from obvious influences, but was somehow uniquely identifiable.

Influential British DJ John Peel has described the band's debut album, *Electric Music For The Mind And Body*, as the most psychedelic record ever made. That ought to be recommendation enough for most. However, the more overtly political material, such as the famed anti-Vietnam anthem 'Feel Like I'm Fixing To Die' is best viewed as a piece of contemporary US social history.

During the '70s Melton took a step back from music, studied law and is now a success-ful lawyer. He continues to play in California with ex-members of other luminaries of the period such as The Grateful Dead, Jefferson Airplane and Big Brother and the Holding Company. The ultimate psychedelic guitarist, Barry Melton's place in musical history is well deserved.

....

Electric Music For The Mind And Body (1967, Country Joe and the Fish)

MEMPHIS MINNIE
(1897–1973)

Born in Algiers, Louisiana, Lizzie "Memphis Minnie" Douglas learned guitar and banjo as a child. She made her recording debut in 1929, jointly with her husband Joe McCoy. Calling themselves Kansas Joe and Memphis Minnie, they scored novelty blues hits for several years with a series of instrumental guitar duets featuring sassy, suggestive backchat. Separating from McCoy in 1935, she later took up with another guitarist, Little Son Joe, with whom she worked throughout the '40s. At the start of the following decade, the emergence of the likes of Muddy Waters (*see* page 124) rendered her kind of blues rather old-fashioned, and she retired to Memphis.

Minnie's rhythmic, country blues picking was influenced, liked many players of the time, by Big Bill Broonzy, who said of the first lady of blues guitar: "She could pick a guitar as good as any man... make a guitar cry, moan, talk and whistle the blues."

....

Hoodoo Lady (compilation, 1932–1938)

183

MEMPHIS MINNIE – THE FIRST LADY OF BLUES GUITAR

PAT METHENY
(1954–)

Of all the jazz guitarists to emerge since Wes Montgomery's death in 1968 (*see* page 112), Pat Metheny is one of a select group who can truly be said to have found his own unique voice.

Metheny's first instrument was the French horn, which he continued to play throughout his school life. However, from the age of 13 the guitar has been his overriding interest. The term prodigious doesn't really do justice to the progress Metheny made as a guitarist – by the end of his teens he had *taught* at both the Berklee School of Music and the University of Miami.

He burst onto the jazz scene at the age of 19 when he joined vibes star Gary Burton, but it was the formation of the Pat Metheny Group in 1977 which indicated that a major new talent was stepping out onto the scene. His albums for the German ECM label stand out as examples of the state-of-the-art jazz, featuring accessible compositions and a melodic style of soloing a million miles away from the speed-over-content merchants who too often find homes in the jazz world.

Metheny is now consistently among the biggest-selling jazz artists around, many of his albums having sold well in excess of 100,000 copies – a figure beyond the wildest dreams of most jazz musicians. That he has been able to do this without even the slightest hint of compromise is a remarkable feat.

....

Pat Metheny Group (1978)

Song X (1985, with Ornette Coleman)

MEMPHIS MINNIE
– *see under* Memphis

MISSISSIPPI JOHN HURT
– *see under* Hurt

SCOTTY MOORE DEFINED THE FUSION OF COUNTRY AND R&B GUITAR

WES MONTGOMERY
– *see* Legends

CARLOS MONTOYA
(1903–1993)

Living a self-imposed exile from his native Spain while it lay under the fascist rule of General Franco, Carlos Montoya used his US base to develop and popularize flamenco music throughout the West.

His greatest achievement was to elevate the role of flamenco guitar as a style in its own right by presenting the music without its traditional singers and dancers. In turn, this made it possible for flamenco to be presented in more auspicious surroundings: for example his *Suite Flamenco* which he recorded and performed with the St Louis Symphony Orchestra.

....

Suite Flamenco (1966)

guitar by crossing R&B with country picking.

Presley's Sun recordings represent a genuine turning-point in the history of popular music, and still sound as fresh and vibrant to this day. They remain an essential purchase for any true music fan.

....

The Sun Sessions (compilation, 1954, with Elvis Presley)

1956 (compilation, 1956, with Elvis Presley)

THURSTON MOORE
(1956–) and
LEE RENALDO
(1957–)

Such was their influence on bands of the early '90s that Sonic Youth have been referred to as the "godfathers of grunge". The twin guitarists, Thurston Moore and Lee Renaldo first worked with contemporary guitar composer Glenn Branca on the New York art house scene in the early '80s.

There is little differentiation to be made between the playing of either guitarist: both specialize in the use of prepared guitars (no doubt influenced in part by their association with Branca), "random" altered tunings, discord and feedback. They can therefore be considered as continuing a line of heritage that stretches back to the Velvet Underground, although Sonic Youth's music is on the whole less compromising or accessible.

....

Confusion Is Sex (1982)

Dirty (1992)

TOM MORELLO
(1964–)

Rage Against The Machine were one of the more interesting new bands to emerge during the first half of the '90s. Avowed socialists, their direct-action politics has brought them into conflict with several conservative US

185

SCOTTY MOORE
(1931–)

As guitarist with the "King" of rock 'n' roll, Elvis Presley, during his peak years, Scotty Moore can be said to have had a considerable impact on the development of the guitar as a "rock" instrument.

It was label owner Sam Phillips who brought Elvis Presley, Scotty Moore and bassist Bill Black together for the first time in 1954.

Although it was his RCA work (starting two years later) that made Presley the biggest music star the world has ever seen, the sessions that the band recorded for Phillips' Sun label have become part of music folklore. Classics like 'Mystery Train' and 'That's All Right, Mama' set a pattern for much of what directly followed. Although the sound is obviously dominated by Presley's extraordinary voice, Moore pretty well defined rockabilly

national institutions. They were banned from TV's *Saturday Night Live* for making a political gesture with the US flag, and once performed an all-feedback set, naked with taped-up mouths in protest against Tipper Gore's music censorship organization.

The RATM sound is a powerful hybrid of heavy rock and rap, which revolves around Tom Morello's radical guitar work. His credentials for working in such a politicized band are impeccable: his father was a member of the Mau Mau guerrilla army which freed Kenya from British colonial rule; his mother is a well-known anti-censorship organizer. Morello himself graduated in political science from Harvard University.

Morello's first band, the Los Angeles-based Lock Up, released a major-label album in the late '80s, but it was the birth of RATM in 1991 which brought him worldwide success. Although clearly a formidable technician, Morello's style is strongly influenced by the sampled sounds of rap and hip hop. Using a variety of custom-built guitars and effects, he has created his own hyper-modern rhythmic style, which gives the impression of triggered digital samples but in fact is performed live.

It all adds up to a cutting-edge guitar sound that makes the Vais and Satrianis of this world sound as if they come from a bygone age.

Rage Against The Machine (1992)

STERLING MORRISON
(1941–1996)

Nobody could seriously argue with the view that New York's Velvet Underground were among the most influential rock bands ever. Even though they struggled for recognition (not to mention record sales) between 1966 and 1972, their reputation over the intervening years has gradually grown to the point that their small body of work has gone on to

sell millions of copies and form the basis of entire careers for numerous independent bands.

Although attention on the Velvet Underground was initially focused on mentor Andy Warhol and other-worldly chanteuse Nico (and, following her departure, on Lou Reed's developing skills as a master songwriter), much of their influential sound can be attributed to the combined drone and feedback produced by the guitars of Reed and Sterling Morrison. This collage of noise is best appreciated on the blinding 17-minute 'Sister Ray'.

Following the band's demise in the early '70s, Lou Reed went on to a significant (if not always consistent) solo career. Nico, bassist/violinist John Cale and drummer Mo Tucker all continued to work with varying degrees of success on the fringes of the music world. Morrison, disillusioned, retired and eventually became an English professor.

In 1993, the original line-up reunited briefly. Selling out huge venues the world over, the final truth emerged: in spite of having sold pitiful amounts during their lifetime, the myths and legends of the Velvet Underground had gradually given birth to a massively popular cult. Sadly, however, although the tour brought sudden wealth to the lower-profile band members, Morrison didn't live long enough to reap the rewards, dying of cancer in 1996.

The Velvet Underground And Nico (1967)
White Light/White Heat (1968)
The Velvet Underground (1969)

LEO NOCONTELLI
(1946–)

Memphis may have had Booker T and the MGs with Steve Cropper (*see* page 104), but during the same period, New Orleans gave birth to its instrumental stars the Meters, with their very own master rhythm man, Leo Nocontelli.

Formed by producer Allen Toussaint, the

Meters became his own house band, backing singer Lee Dorsey on hits like 'Ride Your Pony' and 'Working In A Coal Mine'. In the late '60s they notched up a number of US hits of their own and in doing so helped to define the gritty funk sound that would be associated with New Orleans throughout the following decade.

Funky Miracle (compilation, 1964-1969)
Good Old Funky Music (1979)

JIMMY PAGE
– *see* Legends

GABBY PAHINUI
(1921–1980)

"Slack key" is the traditional guitar style used in Hawaiian music. It is so called because the strings of the guitar are "slacked" to provide a variety of open tunings. The most influential slack-key guitarist was Gabby Pahinui.

Beginning his recording career in 1947, Pahinui was the prime influence that kept slack-key guitar from dying out in the Hawaiian islands. He expanded the boundaries of slack-key guitar, creating a fully evolved style of solo playing which he used to interpret a wide variety of Hawaiian traditional and popular standards, and create a number of fine original guitar pieces.

Pahinui's work reached its peak in the '70s, when his band featured many of the greatest guitarists on the island, such as Leland Atta Isaacs, Sonny Chillingworth, and Pahinui's two sons Cyril and Bla. On many of the great recordings of this era, each of the guitarists would play in a different C tuning, creating a thick, textured sound.

Pahinui's work, and that of his son Cyril, who has given a new level of sophistication to slack-key guitar, may be difficult to find outside Hawaii, but is worth the effort to hear the finest examples of an undervalued musical culture.

Key Khoalu (1954)

Hawaiian Slack Key, Volumes 1, 2 and 3

(compilations, 1940s-1960s)

ANDY PARTRIDGE
(1953–)

Perhaps *the* quintessential English pop group, XTC have carved out a unique niche on the periphery of the music world in their 20-year career. Unlike guitarists of other bands who emerged at the end of the '70s, Andy Partridge's playing sounded as if he'd spent more time listening to Charlie Christian (*see* page 100) than Johnny Ramone. His spikey,

angular guitar jutted out of new wave classics such as their debut single 'Science Friction', creating a fast and furious sound that could appeal to punks and musos alike. Although as the principal songwriter and vocalist Partridge has always been perceived as the leader, crucial to the overall sound of XTC is auxiliary guitarist Dave Gregory and the melodic playing of Colin Moulding, surely one of pop's premier bassmen.

Over the years, XTC albums have shown a shift into a mellower pop tradition, a transition they have successfully made without ever becoming bland. Although they are now some distance away from the commercial main-

stream, their presence can still be felt in many of the mid-'90s "Brit-pop" bands.

White Music (1978)

Skylarking (1986)

JOE PASS
(1929–1994)

A prodigious talent, Joe Pass had already performed with a number of well-known artists on the New York jazz scene by the time he left high school. In spite of this, however, he spent most of his twenties in unspectacular surroundings, first playing in Las Vegas backing bands and then serving time for narcotics

187

JOE PASS – PERHAPS THE FINEST EXPONENT OF UNACCOMPANIED JAZZ GUITAR

188

PACO PENA: TAKING THE ART OF FLAMENCO INTO THE TWENTY-FIRST CENTURY

offences. On release from prison his career suddenly took off. He immediately secured a solo record deal and began playing actively on the West Coast scene. By 1963 he was named Best New Instrumentalist by *Downbeat* magazine.

In 1972 Pass was signed up by Norman Grantz, manager of pianist Oscar Peterson and owner of the Pablo label, with whom he stayed for the rest of his life. During the next 20 years he performed and recorded with just about every notable jazz legend, from Ella Fitzgerald, Duke Ellington and Count Basie to Dizzy Gillespie and Stéphane Grappelli.

Pass was less an innovator than a technical master who consolidated different jazz idioms to produce something new. Perhaps his greatest legacy is in his unaccompanied work in which his playing was able to encompass the role of the traditional jazz bass, and integrate lead lines within his considerable chord vocabulary. For this alone he is arguably the most influential jazz guitarist since Wes Montgomery (*see* page 112).

....

Intercontinental (1970)

Live at Montreux (1977)

LES PAUL
(1915–)

Lester William Polfus was one of the first popular guitarists of the post-war era. Having bought his first instrument from a Sears catalogue, he was already an accomplished country picker by the time he was 14, finding local fame under the name "Rhubarb Red". Moving to Chicago, and then to New York, where he accompanied Bing Crosby, "Red" adopted the immortal name Les Paul.

Paul also showed an interest in the fledgling technology of the day. In 1941 he pioneered one of the first solid-body electric guitars, known as "The Log". Paul tried to sell the idea to Gibson. Initially uninterested, in 1950

Gibson decided to involve Paul in the design of a new instrument as the Fender Broadcaster (later Telecaster) started to make its mark. The result was the Gibson Les Paul – one of the most famous guitars ever made.

Such a luminous career as an inventor has perhaps overshadowed Les Paul's skills as a musician. However, during this period he enjoyed numerous hits, many of which he recorded on home-built equipment, with his wife Mary Ford, including their own radio and television shows.

Echoes of Django Rheinhardt (*see* page 116) and Eddie Lang can be heard in Paul's jazz playing, and his fluid country soloing has many fans. He has remained an active musician and even now, in his eighties, he still plays weekly gigs at a small New York club. However, it is above all his Gibson signature model – now 45 years old and still in production– which will ensure that the name Les Paul remains immortal.

....

The Legend And The Legacy (compilation, 1950–1961)

PACO PEÑA
(1942–)

In recent years, flamenco, the traditional music of the Andalucian region of Spain, has enjoyed a boom period outside its native land. Much of this expansion is due to the work of Paco Peña, perhaps the finest flamenco guitarist to emerge over the past 25 years.

Born in Cordoba, Peña has worked professionally since the age of 12, first as an accompanist and then with a number of different dance troupes. Technically a highly accomplished musician, he elevated flamenco's reputation in his home country when in 1972 he became the first flamenco musician to give a recital at Cordoba's Conservatoria da Musica.

Although Peña's work has always

remained true to the rich traditions of flamenco, he is by no means a purist, taking what some would consider to be liberties in his approach. However, his own view of such criticism is forthright: "Flamenco is not a museum piece but a living, developing art form and as such it allows for the interpretation of the artists."

....

Fabulous Flamenco (compilation, 1987)

BONNIE RAITT
(1949–)

It's a sad and mystifying fact that the number of female players featured in any objective list of great guitarists can be counted on a single hand. One such woman is Bonnie Raitt, who in a 30-year career has established herself as one of the finest and most successful bottleneck blues players around.

Raitt first learned to play the guitar at the age of eight, cutting her teeth on traditional American folk songs. It was while working on the New York coffee-bar folk circuit in the late '60s that she was first introduced to the work of bluesmen such as Fred McDowell and Otis Rush, whose influences gradually found their way into her playing.

Between 1971 and 1986 Raitt recorded nine solo albums for Warner Brothers. Although none of them brought her as much success as later recordings, they illustrate a pattern of development which has seen a shift in emphasis from singer-songwriter to accomplished musician. It was signing to the Capitol label in 1989 that brought her the breakthrough album, the Don Was-produced *Nick Of Time* earning her four Grammy awards. The same year she duetted with John Lee Hooker on 'I'm In The Mood', an association that, given the blues legend's newly acquired status, did her no harm whatsoever.

....

Give It Up (1972)
Nick Of Time (1989)

JOHNNY RAMONE
(1948–)

The career of Johnny Ramone (born plain and simple John Cummings) lasted nearly 20 years. When his band, the Ramones, first got together his technique involved slashing away at an endless succession of power chords; nothing much ever changed. But as one of the band that kick-started punk, Johnny Ramone was also one of the prime musical influences of the late '70s. And he and his "bruddahs" (they were not related) recorded some of the most highly charged rock albums ever made.

Their debut set the pattern, as 14 high-speed, power-riff-driven vignettes shot by in barely 30 minutes. The beat was breathless, the lyrics about as contra-cultural as you could get. And it was magnificent.

Johnny Ramone's technique may not be the most sophisticated, but that was never the point: he was as influential as any musician whose playing all but defined a significant genre.

....

Ramones (1976)
Leave Home (1977)

LOU REED
(1942–)

Lou Reed's majestic reputation is based on impeccable credentials. A founder member and leading light of the Velvet Underground (*see also* Sterling Morrison), the ultimate cult band, he followed this with an unpredictable, attitude-filled 25-year solo career.

Reed is most widely admired as a songwriter, his lyrics especially displaying an unusual lucidity. However, he is also a significant and underrated guitarist, his feedback experiments in the Velvet Underground intro-ducing aspects of the avant-garde art world into the otherwise (relatively) mainstream rock and pop sounds of their debut album, *Andy Warhol Presents The Velvet Underground.* The sound created continues to influence new generations of musicians.

Albums late in Reed's career, such as *New York* and *Magic And Loss*, emphasize his position as one of a rare and elite group of rock performers whose advancing age provides no guarantee that they will mellow out, nor, for that matter, that their best work is behind them.

....

Andy Warhol Presents the Velvet Underground (1967, with the Velvet Underground)
New York (1989, solo)

HANS REICHEL
(1949–)

Improvising performer, composer, inventor, guitar designer, typographer – Hans Reichel occupies a unique position on the fringes of the guitar world. Indeed, his music is about as far from the mainstream as it is possible to get. Reichel taught himself violin from the age of seven, playing in school orchestras until, at the age of 15, he became interested in rock music and began to play guitar. His earliest influences were the Beatles, the Rolling Stones and later Frank Zappa, Cream and Jimi Hendrix (*see* page 108). However, it is perhaps (in a mutated form, at least) the early acoustic blues players who have inspired him the most.

In 1970 Reichel submitted a collage tape of his own guitar music to the jury of the German Jazz Festival in Frankfurt. This led to his appearance at a special concert for newcomers, and the release of his music on record. Although best known as a solo performer, Reichel has often appeared in duo and trio forms, often using his own invention, the daxophone.

Reichel has also designed and built his own guitars. Some have the pick-up positioned

LOU REED – UNPREDICTABLE BUT NEVER LESS THAN FASCINATING

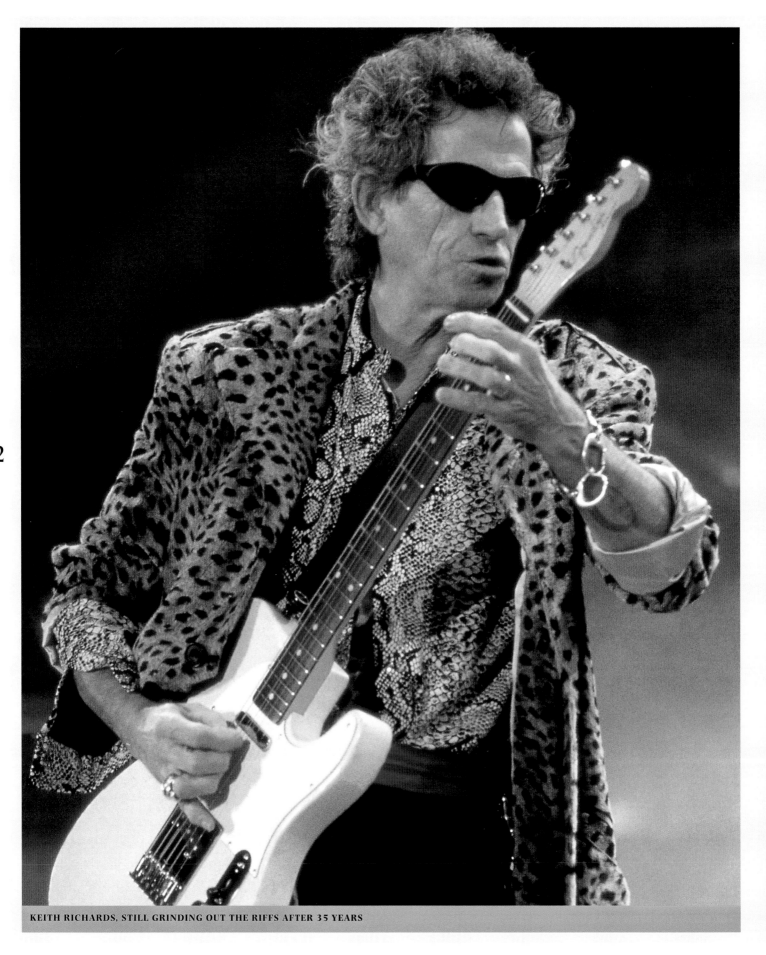

KEITH RICHARDS, STILL GRINDING OUT THE RIFFS AFTER 35 YEARS

behind the bridge so that the strings can be picked from the "wrong" side; others are semi-cutaway solid-body instruments with different kinds of pick-up or transducers attached in different positions. It is the use of such instruments that makes his music so unique, creating sounds that cannot be produced on conventional models.

....

Table Of The Elements: Beryllium (1993)
Shanghaied On Tor Road (1992, an opera for the daxophone)

DJANGO REINHARDT
– *see* **Legends**

LEE RENALDO
– *see* **Thurston Moore**

KEITH RICHARDS
(1943–)

In the realm of rock 'n' roll rhythm guitar, Keith Richards has few rivals. Taking his cue from Chuck Berry – his greatest idol – he has spent the last 35 years pumping out Telecaster riffs in the engine room of the mighty Rolling Stones. With a tenacious instinct for survival, even during his darkest periods in the '70s "Keef" managed not only to retain an almost child-like enthusiasm for rock 'n' roll, but sought to bring new influences, such as reggae and country, to his beloved band.

Although his lead work can be heard on rare occasions, Richards has always been more of a team player, viewing himself simply as a component of the rhythm section, allowing the likes of Brian Jones, Mick Taylor and Ronnie Wood to take the bows for their soloing. As he says, "The whole secret, if there is any secret behind the sound of the Rolling Stones, is the way we work two guitars together." In fact, few twin-guitar rock bands have ever come close to matching the interac-tion of the Stones at their best.

Although not a virtuoso guitarist in the conventional sense, many of the top session men who have worked with the Stones over the years have testified that Richards' rhythm work and natural sense of timing are second to none. More than that, however, he is one of the great riff composers, having written any number of simple, and yet immediately recog-nizable opening lines – just listen to tracks like '(I Can't Get No) Satisfaction', 'Brown Sugar' and 'Honky Tonk Woman' for the evidence.

....

Beggars Banquet (1968)
Let It Bleed (1969)
Exile On Main Street (1972)

LEE RITENOUR
(1952–)

Another West Coast session virtuoso to have embarked upon a respectable solo career, Lee Ritenour is a jazzer at heart, having taken his early cues from Wes Montgomery (*see* page 112) and Joe Pass. Although he has worked with some highly respected names, such as Herbie Hancock, Sergio Mendes and Gato Barbieri, his own albums are usually a merger of pop, jazz and tropical rhythms.

Ritenour's most accomplished and interest-ing recordings feature the acoustic guitar. Especially recommended are those on which he collaborates with ethnic musicians, such as *Festival*, which brings together some of Brazil's finest players.

....

Festival (1988)
Stolen Moments (1990)

ROBBIE ROBERTSON
(1943–)

The Band – led by guitarist and songwriter Robbie Robertson – hold a unique position in the history of American music. Starting out in the late '50s, backing rockabilly star Ronnie Hawkins, they emerged fully formed as Bob Dylan's backing group when he controver-sially "went electric". Laid up following a motorcycle accident, Dylan left the Band (as they were now called) to their own devices, giving them time to record their classic slab of exotic Americana, *Music From The Big Pink*. A classic album, this featured the Band fusing rock, country and folk styles to produce a music that was at once forward-looking and experimental, and by the same token a cele-bration of America and its history.

Since the Band's retirement in 1978, Robertson has enjoyed a highly respected (if slow-moving) solo career, the "purity" of his previous work tempered by sympathetic, but nonetheless hi-tech production values, and a shift in musical influence to a New Orleans sound.

....

Music From The Big Pink (1968)
The Band (1969) (both with the Band);
Storyville (1991)

DUKE ROBILLARD
(1948–)

A founder member of Roomful Of Blues, prob-ably the finest modern-day blues band, Duke Robillard has two distinct strings to his bow. Not only is he one of the consistently out-standing blues players of his generation, he is also a fine exponent of the lost art of swing jazz guitar.

Robillard's early influences as he grew up in Rhode Island included T-Bone Walker and B.B. King (*see* page 110). He formed Roomful Of Blues in 1967, being its dominant feature until he left in 1979 (although his replace-ment Ronnie Earl was a worthy successor).

His solo career has included work with the likes of Doctor John and Jimmie Vaughan, but some of his own solo albums have been more

194

DUKE ROBILLARD, THE SWINGING FOUNDER OF ROOMFUL OF BLUES

than noteworthy in their own right. 1995's *Duke's Blues*, for example, shows Robillard grappling with (and mastering) every conceivable style of blues guitar from T-Bone Walker to Guitar Slim.

You Got Me (1988)
Duke's Blues (1995)

JIMMIE RODGERS
(1897-1933)

One of the first American entertainers to be uniquely associated with the guitar, Jimmie Rodgers, and the "singing cowboys" like Roy Rogers and Gene Autry, were largely responsible for the popularity of the instrument in the early '30s.

Rodgers started worked on the railway at the age of 14, but when he was diagnosed as having tuberculosis he was forced to take up a less strenuous profession. Although he chose music, he would return to the railway at every opportunity his health would allow.

In 1927, he began appearing on North Carolina radio shows billed as the "singing brakeman", finding widespread popularity for his simple yodelling songs and picked guitar. Over the next six years his recordings made him one of America's most popular entertainers, although his illness prevented him from travelling widely. He finally succumbed to tubercular pneumonia in 1933.

A measure of his standing is that he was the first artist elected to the Country Music Hall of Fame in Nashville in 1961.

Early Years (compilation, 1927–1928)

NILE RODGERS
(1952–)

The disco boom of the '70s was often viewed with a barely veiled hatred by many musicians. And yet one such band managed to side-

195

NILE RODGERS –THE "DISCO SUCKS" CAMPAIGNERS CAN'T HAVE HEARD HIM

step the vilification, producing definitive works of the period, and became highly respected by their peers in the process. They were Chic.

Formed in 1975 by guitarist Nile Rodgers and bassist Bernard Edwards, Chic were in many ways successors to the great soul house bands of the previous decade. Their immediately recognizable sound revolved around a tight rhythm groove that combined Edwards' catchy and melodic bass lines with a spartan guitar sound worthy of Steve Cropper himself (*see* page 104).

Among their greatest hits were dancefloor classics like 'Le Freak' and 'Good Times', but their formula was also successfully applied to

recordings by Sister Sledge, Debbie Harry and, with spectacular commercial success, David Bowie. Chic's influence can still be heard today in the world of sampling and DJ remixes.

Les Plus Grands Succès de Chic (compilation, 1977–1981)
Real People (1980)

ZOOT HORN ROLLO
— *see* Bill Harkleroad

THE ROMERO FAMILY

An extraordinary phenomenon, Los Romeros represent the establishment of a new dynasty

in modern classical guitar.

At the head of the family is Celedonio Romero (born 1918). An outstanding classical musician in his own right, his three sons Celin (born 1936), Pepe (born 1944) and Angel (born 1946) can all be numbered among the finest classical guitarists working in the field.

All four musicians not only perform and record as artists in their own right, but also as an ensemble. To this end, perhaps their most noteworthy achievement was is commissioning Spain's greatest living composer, Rodrigo,

Andaluz (1967)
Concierto Andaluz (1967)

OTIS RUSH – A MAN WITH A VOICE TO MATCH HIS GUITAR-PLAYING

OTIS RUSH
(1934–)

Although Otis Rush was active and widely admired on the Chicago blues scene during its peak in the '50s, periods of reduced activity have conspired to give him an undeservedly lower profile than many lesser contemporaries.

Leaving his Mississippi home as a teenager, by 1956 Rush had already recording a number of classic singles, including 'I Can't Quit You Baby' and 'All Your Love' for the Cobra label. Both tracks feature a combination of powerful impassioned vocals matched by his trenchant guitar work.

Rush moved on to record for the Chess label, but apart from 1960's masterful "So Many Roads", the relationship failed to blossom as it had done for other noted bluesmen. Thereafter, although he continued to record and tour regularly, his career seemed perpetually dogged by a mixture of professional and personal problems. Relatively inactive during much of the '80s, Rush produced a fine "comeback" album *Ain't Enough Comin' In* in 1994.

As complex and mercurial a figure as Rush clearly is, when captured on form there are few guitarists who can match him for fire and passion – just ask Messrs Clapton, Beck and Santana, all of whom number among his fans.

....

Right Place, Wrong Time (1976)

SABICAS
(1912–1990)

Along with the great Carlos Montoya, Agustín Castellon Campos – otherwise known simply as Sabicas – was responsible not only for the birth of a new flamenco guitar tradition, but also for taking this indigenous music outside of his native Spain.

Having recorded over 50 albums in a career that spanned almost 60 years, Sabicas is widely recognized as having been the greatest exponent of flamenco in its purest form. Sadly, very few of his recordings are available outside of Spain and Latin-America.

FEW GUITARISTS HAVE SUCH A RECOGNIZABLE SOUND AS CARLOS SANTANA

CARLOS SANTANA
(1947–)

It was an appearance at the Woodstock festival in 1969 that introduced Mexican-born Carlos Santana to a wide audience. Merging blues-based rock with Latin American rhythms, Santana created a genuinely new sound. Similarly, as a guitarist, he is one of a rare breed whose tone – with its pure sustain and overdriven valves – is recognizable at once.

Enjoying immense popularity during the '70s, Santana even scored a Top 10 chart hit with the delicate instrumental 'Samba Pa Ti'. During the same period, work with John McLaughlin's Mahavishnu Orchestra saw him broadening his horizons to introduce some elements of jazz into his music.

....

Santana: Abraxus (1970)
Caravanserai (1972)

JOE SATRIANI
(1956–)

A pyrotechnician *par excellence*, Joe Satriani (raised in Long Island, New York) is a name perhaps too often mentioned in the same breath as his friend and former student Steve Vai. (Metallica's Kirk Hammett was another pupil.) For fans of high-speed, high-powered guitar trickery these two names are way out in front of most of the competition.

In many ways, Satriani's solo albums are even flashier workouts than Vai's. Make no mistake – they represent some of the most incredible guitar-playing ever heard on a recording, even if the basic material could be stronger. More listenable for many, however, are Satriani's appearances as a sideman with, among others, Alice Cooper and Greg Kihn.

....

Surfing With The Alien (1987)

197

BRINSLEY SCHWARTZ
(1947–)

A genuine English legend, Brinsley Schwartz was one of the key figures at the start of the London "pub-rock" scene in the early '70s.

Schwartz is a player seemingly able to turn his hand to any style of playing. His own band – also named Brinsley Schwartz – were tipped for greatness in the early '70s, but didn't seem matched to the hype that went before them. Despite recording a succession of fine good-time country-tinged rock albums, they somehow slipped through the net.

Schwartz and some of his former cohorts emerged later in the '70s as the Rumour. Best remembered for their work backing singer Graham Parker, they also recorded some highly underrated albums of their own.

....

Brinsley Schwartz (1970)
Frogs, Sprouts, Clogs And Krauts (1979, with the Rumour)

JOHN SCOFIELD, ONE OF THE TOP NAMES IN CONTEMPORARY JAZZ GUITAR

JOHN SCOFIELD
(1951–)

One of the finest jazz guitarists to emerge over the past 20 years, John Scofield is rare among his breed in that he has not lived his life in a jazz vacuum, happily admitting to have drawn inspiration not only from masters like Jim Hall and George Benson, but "shading", as he calls it, from R&B players (Otis Rush and B.B. King – see page 110) as well as mainstream rock and country.

Scofield's earliest break came as an accompanist to Chet Baker at New York's Carnegie Hall in 1973. Thereafter he quickly established himself on the East Coast "A" list, playing with the likes of Billy Cobham (replacing John Abercrombie in his band), Charles Mingus and Gary Burton. It was working with Miles Davis in the mid-'80s that cemented his reputation, not only as a player with a tasteful understanding of space, but as a composer of some note.

....

John Scofield Live (1977)
Grace Under Pressure (1992)

ANDRÉS SEGOVIA
– *see* **Legends**

ANTENNAE JIMMY SEMENS
– *see* **Jeff Cotton**

SONNY SHARROCK
(1940–1994)

Emerging in the '60s having spent a few months studying at Berklee, Sonny Sharrock staked his claim as the first free jazz guitarist.

During the mid-'60s Sharrock cut his teeth playing with Pharoah Sanders and Don Cherry, both musicians working on the fringes of pioneering jazz at that time. He became prominent from 1967 when he joined flautist Herbie Mann's group, with whom he often played an atonal role using feedback and other "noise" effects not usually found in a jazz setting. However, Sharrock's work could never be accused of being noise for its own sake, always retaining a rhythmic coherence.

Sharrock went on to play alongside Miles Davis and Wayne Shorter before forming a successful touring band with his wife Linda.

....

Memphis Underground (1968, with Herbie Mann)
Ask The Ages (1991)

HANK SNOW
(1914–)

A fine country picker, Canadian-born country star Hank Snow was obsessed as a teenager with early guitar star Jimmie Rodgers. During the '50s Snow became one of country's biggest stars, enjoying success with immortal hits like 'I'm Movin' On' and 'I've Been Everywhere'.

Snow's fascination with Jimmie Rodgers continued throughout his career – he recorded many tributes to the star picker, and even named his own son Jimmie Rodgers Snow. He also recorded an all-instrumental picking album with no lesser name than Chet Atkins. Snow was inducted into the Country Music Hall of Fame in 1979. Recent years have seen him devoting his energy to the Hank Snow Child Abuse Foundation.

....

I'm Movin' On And Other Great Country Hits (compilation, 1950–1957)

FERNANDO SOR
(1778–1839)

The pre-eminent guitarist during the first half of the nineteenth century, Fernando Sor and Dionysio Aguado were responsible for turning around the decline in the guitar's popularity and assisting its gradual spread outside its traditional home of Spain.

Born in Barcelona, Sor was taught the guitar by his father. Having studied the principles of harmony, counterpoint and composition at a monastery in Monserrat, Sor found celebrity at the age of 19 when he premiered his first opera *Telémaco en la Isla de Calipso*. Moving on to Madrid, he came under royal patronage, gradually introducing the guitar into the court of Charles IV. Later in his life, he is also known to have travelled widely throughout Europe, his recital tours taking in important musical cities such as Paris, Vienna and London.

Sor's greatest legacy is having created the first notable body of work composed for the guitar, much of which remains a part of the instrument's standard repertoire to this day. (See also page 18.)

POPS STAPLES
(1915–)

The grand old man of gospel R&B, Roebuck "Pops" Staples joined his first band in 1935. Working exclusively in the gospel field, he formed his own family group in 1951, with his son Pervis and daughters Mavis, Cleotha and Yvonne.

Although they recorded extensively beforehand, it wasn't until 1968, when they signed to the Stax label, that the Staple Singers established their reputation in the field of inspirational soul. Working with Steve Cropper they produced a run of classic hits like 'Respect Yourself' and 'If You're Ready (Come Go With Me)', creating an immediately recognizable sound that merged Pops' mellow gentle voice and clean R&B licks with the soulful tones of Mavis.

In 1992, Pops recorded a highly listenable solo guitar album which showcased an emotional quality that would embarrass many established guitar heroes. Considerably more active than most octogenarians need to be, Pops Staples remains one of the most loved and respected figures in the music world.

The Best Of The Staple Singers (compilation, 1965–1971)
Peace To The Neighborhood (1992)

MIKE STERN
(1954–)

Mike Stern, a student at Berklee School of Music was recommended to pop/jazz fusion band Blood, Sweat And Tears at the age of 23 by Pat Metheny, his teacher at the time. He quickly followed this with a stint in drummer Billy Cobham's band before, in 1981, fulfilling every young jazz player's dream – a job with Miles Davis.

The three years he spent with Davis represented an important period for Stern – as he said in the '90s: "I was absorbing a lot, learning a lot and even now I'm still working on the stuff Miles taught me then." Continuing his link-up with high-profile jazz stars, he went on to work and record with Jaco Pastorius (1984), David Sanborn (1985) and Michael Brecker (1986–88), before concentrating on his own career.

Given the company he has kept, it can be taken for granted that Stern is a master technician. His seven albums for the Atlantic label and numerous appearances at the world's major jazz festivals have singled him out as one of the most original and highly rated guitarists working in contemporary jazz.

Man With The Horn (1981, with Miles Davis)
Jigsaw (1989)

BIG JIM SULLIVAN
(1941–)

One of Britain's premier session guitarists since the late '50s, Big Jim Sullivan was one of a small and very select band of players who were recruited to back up visiting stars from the US and bolster the recordings of home-grown talent. An impressive list of clients includes Stevie Wonder, Eddie Cochran, the Kinks, the Walker Brothers and Frank Sinatra, to name but a few.

Nominally a member of Marty Wilde's backing group, the Wild Cats, Sullivan also recorded instrumentals as the Krew Cats. He has also produced a handful of solo albums, which particularly show off his great versatility as a player. Many a British 30-something will also fondly remember his air of bemused embarrassment that accompanied regular appearances teaching the mysteries of the guitar to the Bay City Rollers on their short-lived TV series, *Shangalang*.

Big Jim's Back (1974)

BIG JIM SULLIVAN PROVIDES SOME EXPERT PICKING FOR TOM JONES

199

ANDY SUMMERS
(1942–)

In an era when youth seemed to be all-important, it must have been a surprise to Andy Summers when his band, the Police, became pop megastars. Indeed, his youthful looks (and bleached hair) concealed the fact that by the time 'Message In A Bottle' topped the charts in 1979 he had already been a successful professional musician for the best part of 20 years.

Starting off his career in the early '60s, Summers joined up with Zoot Money's Big Roll Band, one of the pioneers of the London R&B scene. When Zoot went psychedelic in 1967 they became Dantalion's Chariot. Their single 'Listen To The Madman', with Summers' spaced-out guitar well to the fore, remains an obscure classic slab of acid rock.

A stint working with Eric Burdon and the Animals was followed by session work until Summers debuted with the Police in 1976. It was with them that Summers created a much-imitated sound, filling out the sparse reggae rhythms with his delicate, arpeggiated chords. His extensive use of reverb, echo and chorusing effects required a deft, minimalist touch that in the wrong hands could have destroyed the careful balance that characterized the Police at their best.

Since the demise of the Police, Summers has undertaken a low-key solo career, experimenting with ambient and new age sounds with varying degrees of success.

Regatta De Blanc (1979, with the Police)
Charming Snakes (1990)

TAJ MAHAL
(1942–)

A unique musician whose work defies easy categorization, Taj Mahal is a Delta-blues player whose music has integrated other ethnic styles, such as calypso, folk, rock and reggae.

Taj Mahal was born Henry St Clair Fredericks in New York. His father was a West Indian jazz musician and his mother a gospel singer from South Carolina. While at the University of Massachusetts he developed an interest in American ethnic music which coloured his development as a guitarist, and dictated his future musical direction. He is now considered to be an expert in the field. Following a short-lived alliance with Ry Cooder (the Rising Sons – *see* page 102), his solo career got underway with a series of albums that explored acoustic blues from every possible angle.

A considerably more influential figure than his album sales might suggest, Taj Mahal has the naturally inquisitive nature of a perennial researcher which ensures that he sees his musical development as a life-long journey.

Giant Steps/De Ole
Folks At Home
(1969)

ANDY SUMMERS OF POPULAR '80S BAND, THE POLICE – AN UNLIKELY POP STAR

FRANCISCO TARREGA
– *see* **Legends**

DICK TAYLOR
(1943–)

Throughout a long and impressive career, the Pretty Things were one of the finest, and perhaps most underrated, of Britain's rock bands. A member of the fledgling Rolling Stones, Taylor left the band to study at the Royal College of Art. Formed in 1963, the Pretty Things were immediately successful championing an abrasive no-holds-barred style of R&B, and a long-haired, unkempt appearance that made the Rolling Stones seem like Pat Boone.

With their popularity on the wane, the Pretty Things leapt headlong into the London underground scene, a period that was their most productive. In 1968, with singer Phil May, Taylor composed *SF Sorrow*, widely viewed as the first rock opera. However, despite critical acclaim it failed to sell as expected and, disillusioned, Taylor left the group. Since then, the Pretty Things have split up and reformed at regular intervals, sometimes staying together for long enough to record such fine albums as *Parachute* and *Silk Torpedo*.

....

The Pretty Things (1965)
SF Sorrow (1968)

MICK TAYLOR
(1948–)

Another in the great tradition of noteworthy graduates from the John Mayall school of bluesology, Mick Taylor's principal claim to fame is that he was lead guitarist in the Rolling Stones following the death of Brian Jones.

By the time Taylor joined the Stones in 1969, he was already a well-respected blues guitarist, having played on the Bluesbreakers' album *Crusade*. His first appearance with Jagger and Co. was before an audience of

MICK TAYLOR, THE STONES' LEAD GUITARIST WHO REPLACED BRIAN JONES

250,000 at a free concert in London's Hyde Park. Between then and 1975 Taylor gave an unexpected twist to the Stones' sound, his slick studied soloing an unlikely but effective complement to Keith Richards' rifferama.

Taylor left the Stones unexpectedly in 1975 and collaborated briefly with Cream's Jack Bruce. Although his solo career has not perhaps taken off in the way expected, his sporadic solo albums always highlight a thoughtful playing style which deserves to find the right home. He remains a fine sideman, having spent time during the '80s recording and touring with Bob Dylan and former employer John Mayall.

....

Exile On Main Street (1970, with the Rolling Stones)
Mick Taylor (1979)

RICHARD THOMPSON
(1949–)

Richard Thompson is a key figure in the crossover between British folk and rock. His distinguished 30-year career can be traced through three distinct phases: the pioneering folk-rock group Fairport Convention (1967–1971); his marriage to folk singer Linda Peters and subsequent career as Richard and Linda Thompson (1972–1982); his divorce and career as a solo artist (1983 to the present).

Thompson's considerable reputation rests both on the quality of his songwriting and on being one of the most tasteful, stylish electric guitar players Britain has ever produced. His fretwork is always, to say the very least, succinct, but covers a wide array of influences from the fluid lines of Charlie Christian to the fire and passion of Chicago bluesmen like B.B. King and Muddy Waters (*see* page 124).

Thompson's solo work, whilst championed by many music critics, has still failed to reach a large mainstream audience, although his name has been linked with some major artists, such as Crowded House, with whom he has played sessions. Ever forward-looking, Thompson has also recorded interesting works with "left-field" guitarists Fred Frith and Henry Kaiser.

....

Daring Adventures (1986)
Shoot Out The Lights (1982, Richard and Linda Thompson)

GEORGE THOROGOOD
(1952–)

Blues bombers from Delaware, George Thorogood and the Destroyers are the ultimate good-time bar band. They emerged in the mid-'70s, somehow poking their way through the haze of New Wave to show rock audiences that R&B was by no means dead.

Their debut album was recorded in 1977. Creating a minor buzz, Thorogood and the band achieved their dream audience opening for the Rolling Stones' world tour a year later. Although many bands would have used this as a stepping stone, the Destroyers found no urge to commercialize their sound, and just kept on doing what they did best – playing a raucous, powerful, rocking blues.

A mean Elmore James-style slide player, Thorogood continues with the Destroyers to be a popular attraction on the world blues circuit.

....

George Thorogood And The Destroyers (1977)
Bad To The Bone (1981)

JOHNNY THUNDERS
(1952–1991)

The New York Dolls have a special importance in rock history as the band that provided a blueprint for punk. It seems ironic, then, that in spite of this – and their radically anarchist aspirations – that singer David Johansson and guitarist Johnny Thunders (John Genzale Jr)

came across as being so strongly influenced by Jagger and Richards. In concert, Johansson could be seen pouting and stalking the stage, while much of Thunders' material – like that of Richards' – could be traced back to Chuck Berry.

The Dolls lived it like they played it and by 1974 seemed to have burnt themselves out, but Thunders emerged three years later as one of the heroes of the new wave scene. With an ever-changing line-up, his band, the Heartbreakers, ploughed a much tougher furrow than his New York contemporaries, which quickly established him as a cult figure in Europe. In spite of a somewhat punishing lifestyle, right up to the end of his life he could still draw a crowd. Indeed, it's perhaps on his numerous live albums that the true spirit of Johnny Thunders, the last of rock 'n' roll's True Believers, can be heard in its purest form. Thunders' drug-related demise in 1991 was tragically predictable. He never compromised, and there is surely an important place for him in the pantheon of rock legends.

....

So Alone (1978)
D.T.K. – Live At The Speakeasy (1982)

RALPH TOWNER
(1940–)

Ralph Towner is probably best known to jazz fans for his work on Weather Report's *I Sing The Body Electric* album. However, his work as a solo musician, and as leader of the group Oregon, has made him a significant figure in the development of the cross-cultural jazz of past 25 years.

A musician through and through, Towner started playing the piano at the age of three, trumpet at five and taking up the guitar in his teens. While studying composition at the University of Oregon, he supported himself playing piano in jazz clubs. He later studied

GEORGE THOROGOOD, A DOWN-THE-LINE GOOD-TIME R&B MAN

PETE TOWNSHEND WITH RIGHT HAND WINDMILLING OUT MORE POWER CHORDS

classical guitar at post-graduate level at the Vienna Academy of Music.

After working with Weather Report and Gary Burton in the early '70s, Burton formed the band Oregon, for which he also composed much of the music. Oregon specialized in a hybrid form of jazz that assimilated classical elements with folk and ethnic musics from around the world. Playing widely on the jazz festival circuit, Oregon can be said to have pioneered a new sound, which would certainly influence the ECM school of jazz, and later the Windham Hill New Age sound. Towner has since formed a useful working partnership with fellow guitarist John Abercrombie.

Music Of Another Present Era (1972, Oregon)
Five Years Later (1982, with John Abercrombie)

PETE TOWNSHEND
(1944–)

Pete Townshend can be viewed as one of rock's seminal figures on so many counts. A style icon in the mid-'60s as the Who became band of choice for the "mod" generation. A proto-punk songwriter of raucous "us-against-them" youth anthems like 'My Generation' and 'Won't Get Fooled Again'. A pioneer of story-telling power-pop, first in vignettes like the single 'Pictures Of Lily', and later in the concept albums *Tommy* and *Quadrophenia*. An influential guitarist who was one of the first to see the potential use of electronic effects and feedback, and who championed the lightning-fast strumming of the power chord over the solo every time. Not to mention the stage dramatics of smashed guitars and windmill arm movements.

Coming from a musical background – his father was a jazz musician – Townshend learnt the guitar and banjo in his early teens. A creative child, he was far more interested in self-

expression, sound and songwriting than learning music theory or intricate fingerwork on the guitar. While at art school he joined a band called the Detours, which later became the High Numbers and finally the Who.

Townshend stands out from other rock guitarist of the period for his unwillingness to play lengthy solos. This in turn allowed more space for bassist John Entwistle and drummer Keith Moon to make their own presence heard. It also enabled the Who to thrive throughout the new wave years – their early albums such as *The Who Sing My Generation* providing a neat template for some of the more musical bands of the time.

The Who Sell Out (1967)
The Who Live At Leeds (1970)

MERLE TRAVIS
(1917–1983)

Kentucky's Merle Travis has two considerable claims to fame in the annals of guitar folklore. As a player, his right-hand technique was so revolutionary that from the '40s country picking was often referred to as "Travis picking". He could also stake a claim as co-inventor of the solid-body electric guitar. During the '40s he got together with engineer Paul Bigsby to design the Bigsby Merle Travis guitar. Although there are several other claimants, in 1947 this became the first production solid body guitar, even if only a very small number were made. The design of the instrument was a clear influence on the revolutionary Fenders that would emerge a few years later.

Travis' musical career was varied and noteworth, though drugs and alcohol wrecked his life. Not only was his playing a major influence on Chet Atkins (*see* page 94) and most other country pickers of the era, he was also a successful solo performer and songwriter, composing a number of country standards, such

as 'Sixteen Tons' and 'Dark As A Dungeon'.

The Best Of Merle Travis (compilation, 1946–1968)

JAMES BLOOD ULMER
(1942–)

James Blood Ulmer is best known as an acolyte of saxophone player Ornette Coleman's harmolodic system, in which soloists perform "around" one another without the use of a regular harmonic structure.

Born in St Matthews, South Carolina, Ulmer started playing the guitar at the age of four. Although his early influences were R&B and the playing of Chuck Berry, during the '60s it was jazz musicians like John Coltrane, Miles Davis and Wes Montgomery (*see* page 112) who inspired his playing.

Moving to New York in 1971, Ulmer joined Ornette Coleman's group, having earlier been greatly influenced by his theories. In 1978, Coleman produced and played on Ulmer's solo recording debut, *Tales Of Captain Black*, a fiercely demanding but ultimately rewarding work which established him as a viable solo artist. Ulmer's follow-up, *Are You Glad To Be In America?* saw the inclusion of R&B and funk, and even included vocals on some tracks. However, the breadth of music contained within each album seemed too demanding for listeners as a whole.

In the late '80s, Ulmer developed new ensembles to concentrate individually on different musical styles: the James Blood Ulmer Blues Group play R&B; Music Revelation Ensemble focus on his jazz material; the Odyssey Band explore harmolodics; the Intercity String Quartet is a forum for his written compositions.

Tales Of Captain Black (1979)
Odyssey (1983)

205

206

JIMMY VAUGHAN'S THUNDERBIRDS WERE ONE OF THE BEST '80S BLUES OUTFITS

ADRIAN UTLEY

(1958–)

The trip hop sound of samplers Portishead is not the most obvious setting for a guitarist to thrive, let alone find international success. And yet that's just what happened when former jazz player Adrian Utley started working with young DJ Geoff Barrow in 1991. As he says: "I came in to play twangy guitar, and I ended up co-producing and co-writing the album." The resulting *Dummy* is one of the classics of the '90s, characterized by the combination of organic samples taken from vinyl, the incredible voice of Beth Gibbons, and Utley's perfectly measured guitar work.

As a teenager, Utley had been inspired to play guitar by Marc Bolan, Jimi Hendrix and Jimmy Page (*see* page 114). However, his interests shifted towards jazz, and in particular guitarists Wes Montgomery (*see* page 112) and Grant Green. After a lengthy spell playing in cabaret bands, Utley soon became a fixture on British jazz circuit, playing with Big John Patton and the Jazz Messengers, before eventually spending 18 months with the Tommy Chase Quartet.

After a brief spell as rhythm guitarist in the

STEVE VAI
– see Legends

GEORGE VAN EPS
(1913–)

Widely held in the jazz world to be the master of chordal jazz, George Van Eps played in bands led by Ray Noble, Freddy Martin and Smith Bellew, but he is best remembered as the guitarist with Benny Goodman during the early '30s – the period that saw Goodman assume the title "King of Swing".

A creative mind, during the '40s Van Eps designed a seven-string guitar with an additional lower string tuned to the note B. The new design, built by Epiphone, allowed him to play bass lines underneath his subtle chord arrangements by reworking his fingering. During the '60s Gretsch made a production version of the instrument available briefly, although it failed to catch on. Twenty years later Ibanez reworked the idea on Steve Vai's Universe guitar.

Stacy And Sutton (1953, Jess Stacey and Ralph Sutton)

EDDIE VAN HALEN
(1957–)

Throughout most of the '90s the likes of Joe Satriani and Steve Vai (*see* page 122) have taken the plaudits for their awesome displays of sheer technique. However, a decade earlier it was a young Eddie Van Halen who helped drag rock music out of the realms of the Spinal Tap parody and made the high-performance guitar solo respectable once again.

Born in the Dutch town of Nijmegen in 1957, Van Halen moved to California with his family in the middle of the '60s. Initially starting life as a drummer, Eddie and his brother Alex formed the band the Broken Combs in 1973 while they were still at school. Changing their name to Van Halen, they found fame with their 1978 debut album, *Van Halen*. It became something of a rock classic, selling well over two million copies and giving heart to a generation of young musicians who felt marginalized by the "anti-muso" stance of the new wave.

Perhaps more than any other single track, it was Van Halen's finger-tapping extravaganza on Michael Jackson's million-selling 1983 hit 'Beat It' that had analysts of the guitar solo scratching their heads. Since then, finger-tapping (or fret-tapping as it is also known) has become a standard part of the modern guitarist's armoury.

Van Halen (1978)
1984 (1984)

JIMMIE VAUGHAN
(1951–)

Along with George Thorogood's Destroyers and Roomful Of Blues, the Fabulous Thunderbirds are one of only a handful of white blues bands capable of playing an authentic-sounding Chicago blues.

The Thunderbirds were the brainchild of Jimmie Vaughan (elder brother of the celebrated Stevie Ray – *see* next entry), whose raw and "dirty" guitar sound echoes his heroes T-Bone Walker and Muddy Waters (*see* page 124). Their recordings are remarkable in that they go some way towards capturing the spectacular rousing effect of their live concerts. Jimmie Vaughan retired from his band in 1991 to be replaced, temporarily, by Duke Robillard, one of the founders of Roomful Of Blues. In 1990 he recorded the outstanding *Family Style* album with his brother Stevie Ray, capturing two very fine musicians playing at their peak.

T-Bird Rhythm (1982)
Tuff Enough (1986)

Jeff Beck band (*see* page 96), Utley turned his attention to production, his eclectic musical tastes and knowledge providing an ideal source for obscure loops and grooves. His influence can be heard throughout *Dummy* and its 1997 follow-up *Portishead*.

Dummy (1994)
Portishead (1997, Portishead)

208

STEVIE RAY VAUGHAN COULD HAVE TAKEN BLUES GUITAR INTO THE NEXT CENTURY

STEVIE RAY VAUGHAN
(1954–1990)

When Stevie Ray Vaughan lost his life in a helicopter crash in 1990, the music world, and
blues in particular, was stripped of one of its
star guitarists. It left a hole that no one has yet
come near to filling.

Born in Dallas, Stevie Ray Vaughan was
taught to play guitar by his elder brother
Jimmie (*see* preceding entry). His earliest playing influences were Otis Rush, Howlin' Wolf,
Albert King and Jimi Hendrix (*see* page 108).
In his late teens Stevie Ray followed his brother
to Austin where in 1978 he formed the band

Double Trouble. Although his talent was
quickly recognized on the blues scene, his big
break came in 1982 when he created a sensation at the Montreux Jazz Festival. This
resulted in numerous session offers, most
notably David Bowie's *Let's Dance* album.
When Vaughan made his first solo album that
year he immediately found a rock crossover
audience for his playing. Recorded by veteran
producer John Hammond, *Texas Flood* was a
big seller and Grammy award-winner.

On later albums Vaughan followed a rock-
ier path. 1985's *Soul To Soul* featured the crucial addition of a keyboard player, and a title

track indicating that Jimi Hendrix may have
been a bigger influence than some might have
thought (or hoped). His career during the second half of the '80s was interrupted sporadically by drug problems and a resultant lapse in
the quality of his work. However, his final two
studio albums – *In Step* and *Family Style*
(recorded with his brother Jimmie) – saw him
fully restored and in peak form.

Vaughan's recordings are now viewed as
templates for aspiring blues players. In 1992
Fender paid the ultimate posthumous complement – the introduction of a signature model
Stratocaster. But perhaps a greater measure of

the respect for him held by his fellow musicians can be seen in the names who happily agreed to be a part of a 1996 tribute album in his honour, including Eric Clapton, B.B. King (*see* page 110), Robert Cray and Bonnie Raitt.

....

Texas Flood (1983)

Soul To Soul (1985)

TOM VERLAINE

(1949–)

That the term new wave had rather different meanings depending on which side of the Atlantic you stood, can be seen vividly by the emergent names on each scene. In the UK it was the Clash and the Sex Pistols – in New York it was Talking Heads, the Ramones, Blondie and Television. But while Television had an undeniably rough edge, their music didn't sit happily in the punk era.

Fronted by guitarist Tom Verlaine, Television grew out of New York band the Neons. The release of their debut album *Marquee Moon* created a sensation. Bucking the trend for short sharp shocks, the first single lifted from the album – the title track – clocked in at over seven minutes and featured some intricate twin-guitar interaction between Verlaine and colleague Richard Lloyd. The sound was unique, almost as if someone had crossed the Stooges with the Allman Brothers. Standing the test of time, *Marquee Moon* consistently appears in greatest album polls. The 1978 follow-up, *Adventure*, was felt by some to suffer from over-production, and although highly rated was less successful. Television broke up the following year.

Throughout the '80s Verlaine continued to release outstanding solo albums, but to a relatively small audience. It seems strange that in spite of his brilliance as a guitarist, songwriter and vocalist (not to mention at least half a dozen superb albums), Tom Verlaine seems to have been marginalized as a cult figure who enjoyed a moment's clarity and genius more than 20 years ago.

....

Marquee Moon (1977, Television)

Tom Verlaine (1979)

HENRY VESTINE
– *see* Al "Blind Owl" WILSON

T-BONE WALKER

(1910–1975)

Not only was T-Bone Walker one of the father-figures of electric blues, he was also one of the first masters of the electric guitar, ranking alongside

Charlie Christian (*see* page 100) in his forward thinking and influence on other players.

Born Aaron Thibeaux Walker in Linden, Texas, "T-Bone" was inspired to learn the guitar at the age of 13 by the playing of Scrapper Blackwell and Leroy Carr. Later he fell under the spell of Blind Lemon Jefferson, who he often led around the streets of Dallas performing for small change. Walker's first recordings were made in 1929, although they were not successful and he didn't enter a studio again

KING OF TEXAS BLUES, T-BONE WALKER

for another decade. By the time he recorded his first hit 'T-Bone Blues', he had started using an amplified guitar. However, it was the track 'Mean Old World', recorded three years later, that some view as the first modern blues record. After an interruption by the war years, Walker, along with Muddy Waters (*see* page 124), more or less redesigned the blues as a form, making him a seminal influence on R&B and later rock.

Like Christian in the jazz idiom, Walker was largely responsible for the development of the single-note blues guitar solo, his playing giving others a glimpse of the creativity and expression the instrument made possible. Almost by definition this makes him a pivotal figure in guitar history, even if from the '50s onwards his popularity as an artist was nothing like as great as Waters, B.B. King (*see* page 110) or Howlin' Wolf.

The Complete 1940–1954 Recordings (compilation)

MUDDY WATERS
– *see* Legends

JOHNNY "GUITAR" WATSON
(1935–1996)
Johnny "Guitar" Watson enjoyed a varied career which passed from T-Bone-influenced electric blues to disco funk.

Born in Houston, Texas, Watson cut his first sides at the age of 17. Unlike most bluesmen, he showed an unusual interest in technology, his 1954 single 'Space Guitar' being one of the first to experiment with echo and reverb sounds.

Although widely rated as a player, he enjoyed only fleeting success as a blues artist and scored only minor hits such as 1955's 'Those Lonely Lonely Nights'. After playing as a sideman for many years, he teamed up in 1966 with ex-rock 'n' roller Larry Williams to record three respected (though poor-selling) soul-influenced albums.

Transcending fashion and showing an unusual degree of versatility, Watson re-invented himself in 1976 as a disco star. Whether or not it was a commercial decision, Watson produced some of the most finely crafted jazz-funk of the period, with hits like 'I Need It' and 'A Real Mother For Ya', even though his guitar work took a back seat throughout this particular ride.

During the '80s, Watson returned to his blues roots, although still finding time to work with Frank Zappa (on whom Watson was an acknowledged influence). Johnny "Guitar" Watson died on stage of a heart attack while playing in a Tokyo blues club.

Ain't That A Bitch (1976)
Hot Just Like TNT (compilation, 1966–1970)

BERT WEEDON
(1920–)
Bert Weedon was one of Britain's top session guitarists throughout the '40s and '50s, playing with a wide variety of stars from Mantovani's orchestra to Frank Sinatra, Nat King Cole and Judy Garland. Towards the end of the rock 'n' roll era Weedon enjoyed instrumental hits of his own – most notably 'Guitar Boogie Shuffle' – carving out a reputation as Britain's most popular guitarist.

However, Weedon's most influential contribution to guitar history has undoubtedly been his tutorial book *Play In A Day*, which taught the basics to numerous teenagers, some of whom now number Britain's greatest players. One of the biggest-selling guitar tutors of all time, the book remains in print, and is a classic of its type.

Although Weedon's music and playing style was extremely "straight" ("We are nor-mal and we dig Bert Weedon," quipped the Bonzo Dog Band in 1968), the esteem in which he was held was never in doubt. Indeed, his 1976 album, *22 Guitar Golden Greats*, sold well over a million copies in Britain alone.

22 Guitar Golden Greats (1976)

BUKKA WHITE
(1906–1977)
Born in Mississippi, Booker T "Bukka" Washington White led a varied youth, working on farms, living the life of a hobo, playing on street corners and juke joints, and even enjoying a brief career in pro-baseball. He recorded a number of sides between 1937 and 1940, during which time he was imprisoned for assault. His blues were resolutely autobiographical and given added power by an abrasive, percussive style of bottleneck playing. Shortly afterwards he retired from music, settling in Memphis with his second cousin B.B. King (*see* page 110).

In 1963 Bukka White was rediscovered by John Fahey, who recorded a fine album by White for his own Takoma label and introduced him to the festival and college circuit.

Sky Songs (1962)
The Complete Bukka White (compilation)

JOHN WILLIAMS
(1941–)
Along with Julian Bream (*see* page 98), Australian-born John Williams is one of the most significant classical guitarists to have emerged since the benchmarks were set by Andres Segovia (*see* page 118) during the first half of the twentieth century.

Having moved to London in the early '50s, Williams was taught the guitar by his father, who himself founded London's Spanish Guitar Centre, the first body to provide classical

BUKKA WHITE – ONE OF THE GREATEST BLUES REDISCOVERIES OF THE '60S

JOHNNY WINTER RE-EMERGED IN THE '80S ON THE ALLIGATOR LABEL

tuition in Britain. His general musical education at the Royal College of Music meant that its lack of a guitar faculty forced him to study the instrument overseas. He thus attended Segovia's famed master classes at the Academia Musicale Chigiana in Siena, Italy.

Williams made his London concert debut in 1958, soon afterwards playing in the US and Japan. In 1960 he was offered the first guitar professorship at the Royal College of Music. During the early '60s Williams forged a useful relationship with composer Stephen Dodgson, who has been responsible for some of the most demanding and interesting classical works in recent times. As a solo performer, Williams reputation was established worldwide. Especially rated are his performances with fellow guitarist Bream, and together they have produced some of the finest duets ever recorded.

In the late '70s Williams formed the classical-rock band Sky. Whilst extremely successful commercially, this alienated some diehard classical fans, without attracting the interest of as many rock fans as might have been expected.

John Williams Plays Spanish Music (1970)
Music Of Barrios (1988)

AL "BLIND OWL" WILSON
(1943–1970) and
HENRY VESTINE
(1944–)

The combination of these guitarists playing together largely defined the sound of Canned Heat, one of the most popular blues bands to cross over into the pop mainstream.

Wilson formed Canned Heat with vocalist Bob "The Bear" Hite in 1966. Both avid blues collectors and renowned experts on the form, they made their name during the latter half of the '60s with a succession of original blues

hits and triumphant appearances at the Monterey and Woodstock festivals. Less of a purist band than their British counterparts (such as Peter Green's Fleetwood Mac), they nonetheless scored heavily in the authenticity stakes when they recorded an album with one of their idols, John Lee Hooker (*Hooker 'n' Heat* – 1970).

The Canned Heat sound was best characterized by Vestine's razor-sharp solos and Wilson's bottleneck playing. In Hite and Wilson they also had two highly individual vocalists – Hite's deep growl contrasting with Wilson's unmistakably plaintive high-pitched sound, which can be heard on the band's biggest hit, his own composition, 'On The Road Again'. Wilson took an overdose in 1970, but the band kept going until Hite's death in 1981.

Living The Blues (1969)
Future Blues (1970)

JOHNNY WINTER
(1944–)

By the age of 14, Johnny Winter was already performing in the clubs of his native Beaumont, Texas. A stint in Chicago saw him making little headway and he returned home to continue honing his craft in clubland. It was a showcase gig in New York in 1968 that secured him a major-label record deal and launched him as one of the most successful blues-rock crossover players of the late '60s. His 1969 debut was highly rated and a commercial success, showcasing a playing style that eschewed the excesses of the period with solos that seemed neat and carefully crafted without losing a sense of spontaneity.

In his 1970 album *Johnny Winter And* he veered successfully into heavy rock territory, a move that reached a natural conclusion with the metal *Saints And Sinners* in 1974. During this time he was well known to rock audiences

the world over. His work had begun to show inconsistencies, but during the '80s he made a successful return to the blues with the *Guitar Slinger* album on Chicago's Alligator label. *Let Me In* (1991) and *Jack Daniels Kind Of Day* (1992), recorded for the PointBlank label, continued to restore his reputation as one of a handful of white musicians who can be said to have mastered the blues.

Johnny Winter (1969)
Johnny Winter And (1970)

HOWLIN' WOLF
(1910–1976)

Chester Burnett (as Howlin' Wolf was originally known) was a farmhand before joining the US Army. On his discharge in 1948 he formed the House Rockers, one of the first electric R&B groups. In 1951 he made his first recordings for Sam Phillips' Sun label, before settling for Chess – the only real home for a bluesman of Wolf's stature.

It was in the early '60s, at a time when most of his blues contemporaries (and many from a younger generation) had long since run out of steam, that Wolf enjoyed his most fertile run of hits. This giant of a man ("Big Foot Chester", as some called him), now in his fifties, unleashed a broadside of matchless singles that turned him into a legend.

It's difficult to overestimate the effect that hits like 'Wang Dang', 'Little Red Rooster', 'Down In The Bottom' and 'Killing Floor' had on the early '60s blues boom. Many became standard covers among the young white R&B musicians who were just getting bands together, not least of which were the Rolling Stones, the Yardbirds and, later on, Led Zeppelin's Jimmy Page (*see* page 114).

Wolf continued recording and performing until his death from cancer in 1976, somehow never mellowing or losing the sheer power of

213

HOWLIN' WOLF – A BIG MAN WITH A BIG SOUND

ing the ranks of rock's vocal elite, began to develop a parallel pop career that would soon overshadow his band. 1971 was a peak year for the duo. Not only did the Faces issue *A Nod's As Good As A Wink*, but Stewart recorded his solo masterpiece *Every Picture Tells A Story*. Both albums highlighted Wood's distillation of the classic Chuck Berry riff, and a lively raw blues bottleneck style.

When Mick Taylor left the Rolling Stones in 1975, various heavyweight sessioneers were mooted as a replacement (among them, fret-tapping pioneer Harvey Mandel). But it was clear that Wood was the man for the job. Dovetailing immediately with Keith Richards, Wood was also said to have enhanced the chemistry of the band during the '80s.

A familiar presence in all-star line-ups, Wood has also recorded a handful of solo albums, all of which feature a fine blend of good-time bluesy rock 'n' roll.

A Nod's As Good As A Wink (1971)
Every Picture Tells A Story (1971, Rod Stewart)

LINK WRAY
(1930–)
Link Wray's claim to fame revolves around one guitar instrumental, 'Rumble', released in 1958. Featuring a heavy duty riff immersed in echo and distortion, it was a simulation of a gang fight, and is now viewed as a seminal slab of proto-heavy metal guitar, hitting the US Top 20 well over 10 years before the term was applicable.

Born in Fort Bragg, North Carolina to part Native American parents, Wray learned to play the guitar using open tuning. His first experiences were working sessions for Doug and Vernon, Fats Domino and Ricky Nelson. After the success of 'Rumble', Wray recorded a number of unsuccessful follow-ups until he quit the music world in 1965.

his delivery. His later albums were peppered with star cameos from the likes of Eric Clapton, Steve Winwood and various Rolling Stones.

Howlin' Wolf (1958)
The Chess Box (1991 compilation of '50s and '60s)

RON WOOD
(1947–)
Ronnie Wood is one of rock's eternal sidemen, loved and respected by critics and rock fans alike. Although he has often shied away from the spotlight, his contributions to three gigantic rock careers – Jeff Beck (*see* page 96), Rod

Stewart and the Rolling Stones – should not go underestimated.

Wood started out in a London R&B/Motown covers band called the Birds. In 1968 he got his first break joining the Jeff Beck Group, variously as a guitarist and bassist, and playing on classic albums like *Truth* and *Beck-Ola*. When Beck disbanded the group a year later Wood and vocalist Rod Stewart formed the Faces along with renegades from the mod band the Small Faces. The Faces quickly forged a reputation as one of the most exhilarating live good-time rock 'n' roll bands, matched only by the Rolling Stones.

At the same time, Stewart, rapidly ascend-

RON WOOD – THE ROLLING STONES SEEMED MADE FOR HIM

NEIL YOUNG, THE "ABSTRACT EXPRESSIONIST" OF THE ELECTRIC GUITAR

He returned in the '70s with a string of albums that made almost no concession to the '60s having existed. A uniquely singular presence in the guitar world, he continues to maintain an interesting and successful career.

Good Rockin' Tonite (compilation, 1985)

Indian Child (1993)

NEIL YOUNG
(1945–)

In spite of an unending zeal for experimenta-

tion, whether as a pioneer of Californian folk-rock, a country balladeer, demon of feedback, or even electro-cowboy, Neil Young is rightly hallowed as one of the greatest North American songwriters. As a guitarist, he is also unique. Cleverly described by *Rolling Stone*

he formed folk-rock pioneers Buffalo Springfield with Stephen Stills. Leaving the group in 1968, Young set out on an immediately successful solo career. Although many of his best-known songs are low-key acoustic numbers (he toured extensively as an acoustic performer in the early '70s), it is when he plugs in that his work comes to life. His finest early moment was the 1969 album *Everyone Knows This Is Nowhere*, which saw him teamed up with the band Crazy Horse. In guitarist Danny Whitten, Young found the perfect foil for his own playing, most spectacularly on the track 'Southern Man' recorded a year later. Whitten's drug overdose shortly afterwards robbed the music world of an unusually empathetic musical relationship.

Picking out key albums from one of the most consistently excellent bodies of recorded work is not easy, although the magnificently raucous *Weld* (1991) stands out as a fine example of a magnificent talent that seems to grow greater with age.

....

After The Goldrush (1970)

Tonight's The Night (1975)

Rust Never Sleeps (1979)

Weld (1991)

FRANK ZAPPA
(1940–1993)

Uncompromising may be the best single word to describe the prodigious output of Frank Zappa.

Appearing on the San Francisco scene in the mid-'60s, he formed the Mothers of Invention, a satirical fusion of rock, pop, modern jazz, modern classical, doo-wop and just about any other kind of music imaginable. The targets included politicians, the mores of the middle classes, and even the hippy movement that (in part) had embraced the band. The Mothers peaked with 1967's *We're Only In It*

For The Money. Thereafter, Zappa followed his own path, often working in an area that could just about be described as jazz-rock, although sometimes adding elements of dubious humour. Throughout, however, his bands were run with an orchestral discipline calling on the talents of the likes of Lowell George and Steve Vai (*see* page 122).

Zappa not only invariably made high quality recordings of most of his live concerts, he also recorded guitar solos endlessly at home, some of which have been made available for public consumption. Although not exactly easy listening, they represent a fascinating glimpse into the creative process of one of the most creative musicians to have worked in the rock oeuvre.

....

We're Only In It For The Money (1967)

Shut Up 'n' Play Yer Guitar (1981)

217

FRANK ZAPPA, WHOSE CREATIVITY SEEMINGLY KNEW NO BOUNDS

as an "abstract expressionist" of the guitar, he breaks every rule in the book, his playing (at its best) a manifestation of absolute emotional energy. He's that good.

Born in Toronto, Canada, Young played on the San Francisco folk scene until 1966 when

INDEX

All page numbers in *italics* refer to pictures

219

221

222

PICTURE CREDITS

The publishers would like to thank the following sources for their kind permission to reproduce the pictures in this book:

AKG London/Erich Lessing
courtesy Arbiter, London
Steve Barber
Bridgeman Art Library, London/Bonhams,
  London, UK, Flamenco guitar made by Manuek
  Ramirez/Santos Hernandes, Madrid, c.1916,
  /Stapleton Collection, UK, Queen Elizabeth I lute
  by John Rose, 1580, from *Musical Instruments*
  by Alfred James Hipkins (1826–1903)
Christie's Images
Jean-loup Charmet/A. Bellet
Corbis UK/Davis Barber, Stephanie Maze,
  Bradley Smith,
Edinburgh University Collection of Historic
  Musical Instruments
ET Archive
Mary Evans Picture Library
Fotomas Index
Andrew Galindo
courtesy Gibson Guitars
Hulton-Getty
Lebrecht Collection/Jim Bennett, Betty Freeman,
  Nigel Luckhurst, Suzie Maeder, R. Musgrave
London Features International/Martin Esseveld,
  Jonathan Postal, D. Trebitz, S. Rapport
courtesy Marshall Amps
courtesy C.F. Martin & Co. Inc
Pictorial Press Ltd./Van Houten, Robert Lewis,
  Mayer, W. Rutten, Showtime, Wiltshire
Redferns/ Glenn A. Baker, Dick Barnatt, Chuck
  Boyd, Colin, Fin Costello, Geoff Dann, Ian
  Dickson, Brigitte Engl, William P. Gottkie, Mick
  Hutson, Max Jones Files, Bob King, Robert
  Knight, Leon Morris, Tim Motion, Michael Ochs
  Archive, Outline, Mike Prior, David Redfern,
  Simon Ritter, Ebet Roberts, G. Schlip, Barbara
  Steinwehe, David Vaugham
Retna/Gems, Gary Gershoff,
  G.Hankeroot/Sunshine, Nigel Hillier, Tony
  Mottram, Steve Pyke, Steve Rapport
courtesy Rickenbacker
Royal College of Music, London
S.I.N./Jana, Hayley Madden, Ian T. Tilton
courtesy Strings and Things Ltd.

Every effort has been made to acknowledge correctly and contact the source and/or copyright holder of each picture, and Carlton Books Limited apologises for any unintentional errors or omissions which will be corrected in future editions of this book.

223

ACKNOWLEDGEMENTS

Terry Burrows would like to thank:

Nick Kacal and Mike Flynn for their written contributions and advice; Suzie Duke and Lucian Randall for their editorial input; Jane Lambert for finding lots of nice pictures; Ace Records (Julia Honeywell), who have re-issued many of the classic recordings listed in the guitarists' A-Z (www.acerecords.co.uk); Mr Alta Vista; Jim Barber for his expertise on guitar hardware; Richard Chapman; Ralph Denyer; Los Bros Dillingham; Flamingo Records; Vic Flick; Robert Fripp; Fred Frith; Gibson (US); David Gross and Rene Deformeaux (Electric Snake productions); Joachim Rheinbold at JAR Music; Lovely Nay; Harvey Mandel; Helen Martín; Martin guitars; R. Stevie Moore; Not Lame Records; Dave Van Allen, proprietor of an excellent pedal-steel site; Viceroy Records; Andy Ward.

BIBLIOGRAPHY

Craig Anderton – *Home Recording For Musicians* (AMSCO, 1978)

Tony Bacon – *The Ultimate Guitar Book* (Dorling Kindersley, 1991)

Tony Bacon and Paul Day – *The Fender Book* (IMP, 1992)

Derek Bailey – *Improvisation* (Moorland, 1980)

Terry Burrows – *Play Rock Guitar* (Dorling Kindersley, 1995)

Terry Burrows – *Play Country Guitar* (Dorling Kindersley, 1995)

Richard Chapman – *The Complete Guitarist* (Dorling Kindersley 1993)

Ralph Denyer – *The Guitar Handbook* (Pan, 1992)

Leo Feigin – *Russian Jazz: New Identity* (Quartet, 1985)

Hugh Gregory – *1000 Great Guitarists* (IMP, 1992)

Mark Hanson – *The Alternate Tuning Guide For Guitar* (AMSCO, 1991)

Juan Martín – *El Arte De Flamenco De La Guitarra* (United Music, 1982)

Fred Miller – *Studio Recording For Musicians* (AMSCO, 1981)

Brian Priestly – *Mingus* (Paladin, 1982)

Don Randall – *The New Harvard Dictionary Of Music* (Harvard University Press, 1986)

Darryl Runswick – *Rock, Jazz and Pop Arranging* (Faber and Faber, 1992)

Erik Satie – *A Mammal's Notebook: Collected Writings...* (Atlas, 1996)

Gene Sculati and Davin Seay – *San Francisco Nights* (Sidgwick and Jackson, 1985)

Aaron Shearer – *Classic Guitar Technique* (Franco Colombo, 1963)

Nicolas Slonimsky – *Thesaurus of Scales and Melodic Patterns* (Scrivener's, 1947)

Happy Traum – *Flat-pick Country Guitar* (Oak, 1973)

Harvey Turnbull – *The Guitar* (Bold Strummer, 1991)

Mike Watkinson and Pete Anderson – *Syd Barrett: Crazy Diamond* (Omnibus, 1991)